Lost Christianity

Lost Christianity

A Journey of Rediscovery

JACOB NEEDLEMAN

JEREMY P. TARCHER/PENGUIN
a member of Penguin Group (USA) Inc.
New York

Most Tarcher/Penguin books are available at special quantity discounts for bulk purchase for sales promotions, premiums, fund-raising, and educational needs. Special books or book excerpts also can be created to fit specific needs. For details, write Penguin Group (USA) Inc. Special Markets, 375 Hudson Street, New York, NY 10014.

Jeremy P. Tarcher/Penguin
A member of
Penguin Group (USA) Inc.
375 Hudson Street
New York, NY 10014
www.penguin.com

I wish to express my gratitude to the Rockefeller Foundation for the award of a humanities fellowship during the period in which this book was written.

Grateful acknowledgment is made to the following publishers for permission to quote their published works:

Oxford University Press for HERMETICA, translated by Walter Scott, copyright © 1924 by Walter Scott.

Faber and Faber Limited for WRITINGS FROM THE PHILOKALIA ON PRAYER OF THE HEART, translated by E. Kadloubovsky and G. E. H. Palmer, published in 1951, by permission of the publisher.

Simon & Schuster, Inc., for TURNING EAST, by Harvey Cox, copyright © 1977 by Harvey Cox. Reprinted by permission of The Sterling Lord Agency, Inc.

New Directions Publishing Corp. for ZEN AND THE BIRDS OF APPETITE, by Thomas Merton, copyright © 1968 by The Abbey of Gethsemani, Inc. Reprinted by permission of New Directions.

Harper & Row, Publishers, Inc., for THE NAG HAMMADI LIBRARY, James M. Robinson, General Editor, copyright © 1977 by Harper & Row, Inc., MEISTER ECKHART, A MODERN TRANSLATION, by Raymond Bernard Blakney, copyright © 1941 by Raymond Bernard Blakney.

Chetana Publications for I AM THAT, by Sri Nisargadatta Maharaj, translated by Maurice Frydman, copyright © 1973 by Chetana Publications.

E. P. Dutton Publishing Co., Inc., for THE LIFE OF MILAREPA, translated by Lobsang P. Lhalungpa, copyright © 1977 by Lobsang P. Lhalungpa.

First published in 1980 by Doubleday & Company

First Jeremy P. Tarcher/Penguin Edition 2003
Preface copyright © 2003 by Jacob Needleman
Copyright © 1980 by Jacob Needleman

Library of Congress Cataloging-in-Publication Data

Needleman, Jacob.
   Lost Christianity / Jacob Needleman.
      p.   cm.
   Originally published: Garden City, N.Y.: Doubleday, 1980. With new pref. and index.
   Includes index.
   ISBN 1-58542-253-3 (alk. paper)
      1. Christianity—Essence, genius, nature. 2. Christianity—20th century. 3. Christianity and other religions. 4. Spirituality. 5. Needleman, Jacob. I. Title.
   BR121.3 .N+   2003050123
   230—dc21

Printed in the United States of America
10 9 8 7 6 5

CONTENTS

Preface to the Tarcher/Penguin Edition   ix

Chapter One: Introduction   1
    The "Old Religions"   1
    What Are Christians Looking For?   2
    A "Christian Monk"   5
    Father Sylvan   7

PART ONE: THREE CHRISTIANS

Chapter Two: Metropolitan Anthony of Sourozh   15
    Credentials   15
    The Two Streams   17
    Questions Without Answers   19
    "Occult" Christianity   21
    The Emotion of a Christian   23
    A Demand   25
    Athens   28
    Vulnerability   30
    The Contact of Forces   33
    The Origin of Spiritual Exercises   35
    Seeing and Gnosis; "Faith vs. Reason" 37
    New Emotion, New Thought   41

Chapter Three: Father Vincent   44
    What Is a Priest?   44
    Spiritual Psychology   49
    Psychology and Scale   52
    The Theory and Practice of the Search 54
    A Game of Cards   55
    Seeing Father Vincent   58
    "Acornology"   59
    Freud and Human Possibility   60

The Natural Attraction to Truth   62

Conversation in Two Worlds   66

The Life and Search of Father Vincent   70

Chapter Four: From the Journal of Father Sylvan   79

PART TWO: THE LOST DOCTRINE OF THE SOUL

Chapter Five: Christianity and Eastern Meditation   107

Christianity and Buddhism   107

Thomas Merton   113

Intermediate Christianity   117

Chapter Six: St. Joseph's Abbey   124

The Primal Christian Act   124

Father Thomas Keating   126

Contemplation as Knowledge   126

The "Middle" and Its Neglect   127

Knowledge and Love   129

The Fragmentation of Contemplative Prayer   130

The Scale of History   131

The Centering Prayer   132

Apatheia, or Emotional Freedom   136

The Location of Freedom   139

What Does the Church Really Want?   140

Chapter Seven: A Search for Conscious Christianity   145

Jesuit Spirituality   145

Attention and Virtue   151

The Attention of the Heart   155

Attention as Prayer   162

Chapter Eight: The Soul: Intermediate Being   166

Six Points About the Soul   166

Gurdjieff   169

Search as the Transforming Force   171

The Appearance and Disappearance of the Soul   175

Chapter Nine: The Soul in the Two Histories   178

Two Histories; Two Doctrines   178

The Intermediate in Hinduism   179

Micro-monotheism   181

The Intermediate in Buddhism   183

The Language of the Second History   187

The Soul Is Not the "Inner Being"   190

The Origin of "Heresy"   193
Gnosis Is Not Gnosticism   195
    The doctrine of the alien God   196
    Cosmic dualism   200
    The two races of men   203
"Practical Instructions"   207
A Fateful Ambiguity   213

Conclusion: The Lost Religion of Love   214

Index   223

PREFACE TO THE TARCHER/PENGUIN EDITION

Do you wish to know God? Learn first to know yourself.
—ABBA EVAGRIUS, FOURTH CENTURY

Never in recent memory has the world been at once so deeply drawn toward religion and so troubled about it. As is now clear, all self-assured predictions that the march of modern science would marginalize religion have proved false. As far as Christianity, Judaism, and Islam are concerned, we are, on the contrary, in a period of religious expansion throughout the Americas, Africa, the Middle East, and Southeast Asia. At the same time, it is clear that with the very survival of our civilization hanging in the balance, the question relentlessly insists itself: Is religion a force for good or ill in the life of humanity? Does the actual influence of religion, in fact, sometimes intensify the very defilements of human nature—ignorance, fear, hatred—from which its doctrines and practices are intended to liberate us?

As once again we witness the horrific engines of war being fueled by religious zeal of one kind or another, and under one kind of name or another, the answer to this question seems obviously to be: Yes, sometimes; Yes, often! Have not the darkest crimes of world history—the insane barbarism of genocide, the bloody crusades, the murder of innocents, and the depredation of defenseless cultures—have not many, if not most, of these crimes been committed under the banner of religion or through a quasi-religious frenzy attaching itself to religious ideals? Put next to these endlessly recurrent horrors, the intimate comforts of personal religious faith and the day-to-day individual efforts to live religiously may seem to count for little in the balance scales of human life on earth. Little wonder, then, that so many of the best minds of the modern era entirely rejected religion as a foundation for both ethics and knowledge. Just as the scientific turn of mind seemed to have entirely eclipsed religion's claim to *knowledge*, so—it has seemed to many—the same modern turn of mind must inevitably displace religion's claim to *moral authority*. Just as religion can no longer show us what is *true* but must yield that task to methods of thought that are independent of religious doctrine, so neither can religion, it was claimed, show us what is *good*, but must now surrender that task as well to the secular mind of modernity.

But in fact, no such assumption of moral authority by secular humanism has taken hold or now seems in any way likely or justified. The modern era, the era of science, while witnessing the phenomenal acceleration of scientific discovery and its applications in technological innovation, has brought the world the inconceivable slaughter and chaos of modern war, along with the despair of ethical dilemmas arising from new technologies that all at once project humanity's essence-immorality onto the entire planet: global injustice, global heartlessness, and the global disintegration of the normal patterns of life that have guided mankind for millennia. Neither the secular philosophies of our epoch nor its theories of human nature—pragmatism, positivism, Marxism, liberalism, humanism, behaviorism, biological determinism, psychoanalysis—nor the traditional doctrines of the religions, in the way we have understood them, seem able to confront or explain the crimes of humanity in our era, nor offer wise and compassionate guidance through the labyrinth of paralyzingly new ethical problems.

What is needed is either a new understanding of God or a new understanding of Man: an understanding of God that does not insult the scientific mind while offering bread, not a stone, to the deepest hunger of the heart; or an understanding of Man that squarely faces the criminal weakness of our moral will while holding out to us the knowledge of how we can strive within ourselves to become the fully human being we are meant to be—both for ourselves and as instruments of a higher purpose.

But this is not an either/or. The premise—or, rather, the proposal—of this book is that at the heart of the Christian religion there exists, and has always existed, just such a vision of both God and Man. I call it "lost Christianity," not because it is a matter of doctrines and concepts that may have been lost or forgotten; nor even a matter of methods of spiritual practice that may need to be recovered from ancient sources. It is all that, to be sure, but what is lost in the whole of our modern life, including our understanding of religion, is something even more fundamental, *without which religious ideas and practices lose their meaning and all too easily become the instruments of ignorance, fear, and hatred.* What is lost is the experience of oneself, just oneself—myself, the personal being who is here, now, living, breathing, yearning for meaning, for goodness; just this person here, now, squarely confronting one's own existential weaknesses and pretensions while yet aware, however tentatively, of a higher current of life and identity calling to us from within ourselves. This presence to oneself is the missing element in the whole of the life of Man, the intermediate state of consciousness between what we are meant to be and what we actually are. It is, perhaps, the one bridge that can lead us from our inhuman past toward the human future.

In the writings and utterances of the great teachers of Christianity over the centuries, one may begin to discern, like a photographic image gradually developing before one's eyes, the outlines of this vision of what is called in this book "intermediate Christianity." But modern man can no longer perceive that vision or hear the language that has been associated with it. Words like "humility," "purity of heart," "contrition" are no longer understood to require the individual, existential struggle for what the early Fathers called "attention in oneself." On the contrary, it is assumed that such qualities of character can be ours in the distracted and dispersed state of being that is more and more characteristic of life in the contemporary world. The result is self-deception which masks, and perhaps even intensifies, our weaknesses and which inevitably leads to the disillusionment with religious ideals that has been one of the hallmarks of the modern, secular worldview. Of course, the modernist attempt to establish ethical life without religion itself ignores the same lost element in human life that has been forgotten in the conventional understanding of religion. The result is often a sad ineffectuality under the name of rousing moral formulae—or, ironically, the decay of what began in opposition to perceived religious tyranny into its own brand of quasi-religious dogmatism and violence—as witnessed, for example, in the fate of communist ideology.

Whether it is conventional religion or secular humanism, or any other modern program of morality and inner human betterment, the question remains: Can there be any hope of our becoming what we are meant to be without first becoming fully and deeply aware of what we in fact are, now, here, in just this moment of our lives? Whether religious or not, is there any hope for man who has lost the capacity, or forgotten the need, to know himself and to be alive and present in himself?

The great ideas and ideals of Christianity continue to offer hope and comfort to the world, as do the ideals of Judaism and Islam—and of all the world's great religions. And as do the ideals of humanistic morality, with its passionate commitment to justice and human rights. Yet we see, we see, we cannot help but see that now, as ever, something is missing, something has been forgotten about ourselves and in ourselves. Our children see it as clearly as we sometimes do; *more* clearly! The words of St. Paul never sounded more distinctly than they do now in the lengthening shadows of our civilization:

> *For the good that I would I do not; but the evil which I would not, that I do . . . who shall deliver me from the body of this death?*
> —ROMANS 7

Chapter One

Introduction

The "Old Religions"

The impulse to write this book first arose a number of years ago when I was interviewing Christian and Jewish clergymen about the challenge of the "new religions." At that time, the turning toward the teachings of the East had just begun and was still limited mainly to the young. There was obviously a religious awakening beginning in America, and just as obviously, it was leading many people not toward but away from the established spiritual institutions of the West. I wanted to know what Christians and Jews were thinking about this, and how they were going to respond.

Meeting with bishops, priests, ministers and rabbis across America and in Europe, I soon became aware that a great deal of soul-searching was going on, and not only in reaction to the unconventional religiosity of the young. I began to suspect that the new religions were not the only sign that a new life was being breathed into the dying spiritual practices of our culture. I wondered: was there perhaps a secret fermentation going on as well within the seeming confusion of the "old religions"?

Certainly, the hunger of those who wished to remain within the fold of Christianity was often as intense as, sometimes even more so than, the motivation of many people turning to the religions of the Orient. In fact, of all the experiences I had while researching the material for my book on the new religions, none has remained more firmly in my memory than my meeting with a certain bishop.

We had been talking for several hours about the attractions of the Eastern religions. Toward the end of the interview, coffee and sandwiches were brought in and I put away my notebook. Conversation became informal and unguarded. I mentioned to him that in my own academic work as a professor of philosophy and religion I had begun to perceive things in the Bible that I had never dreamed were there. I was beginning to understand that everything I had seen in the Eastern teachings was also contained in Judaism and Christianity, although the language of the Bible was practically impossible to penetrate, because it had become so encrusted with familiar associations.

At that, he quickly nodded in agreement, with a sort of knowingness that somehow made me uncomfortable. For the next few minutes I couldn't believe I was speaking with the same man. Gone was the relaxed, genial conversationalist. Even his voice suddenly lost its resonance. He spoke nervously of the efforts he was making to bring contemplative methods into the life of his diocese. He was working closely with several well-known humanistic psychologists and had himself studied Zen meditation with this aim in mind.

Everything he said seemed completely lacking in conviction. He was constantly scanning my face for some sign of approval, and this eventually made me so ill at ease that I blurted out in a half-joking way, "Well, I've always imagined that you leaders of the Church have a secret monastery someplace, where you go to refresh your inner lives under the direction of a wise spiritual guide."

I was quite startled by his reaction. He leaned toward me over the top of his huge desk and, without any pretense or sense of position, asked simply: "Where? Where is it?"

What Are Christians Looking For?

The face of the bishop in that moment and the sound of his question came back to me time and again during the writing of *The New Religions* and long after its publication. Whenever I was invited to speak at conferences of Christians or Jews, I saw that face and heard that voice. To me it had become the face of contemporary Western religion and the voice of its need.

When time permitted, I began seeking out meetings with established religious leaders of every denomination, particularly where I had heard that efforts were being made to recover or re-create the inner, spiritual content of the tradition. But, invariably, I came away with a sense of frustration over my inability to understand what was going on.

On the desk in front of me now there are several thick note-books detailing the interviews and conferences of the past seven years.

Here is a meeting with a group of Protestant ministers seeking "a return to primitive Christianity through charity and meditation."

Here are the notes I made when visiting the ecumenical community of Taizé, France, "a community not bound to any one confession," whose "first vocation" is "passion for the unity of the body of Christ."

And here is the program of an "East-West" conference I attended several years ago in New York, "bringing together the One Spirit uniting all the paths to God through the exchange of truth among Christians, Buddhists, Hindus and Moslems . . . breaking down the artificial barriers of culture, race and nations."

Here is my conversation with a Roman Catholic nun just returned from "a community of Christian hermits" in the Arizona desert working "to bring back to Christianity the spirit of contemplative consciousness which the Church has lost."

Here is a talk with a group of Jewish students practicing "Kabbalistic meditation" under the guidance of a well-known rabbi, and here, too, is the record of a discussion led by a leader in the Lubavicher Hasidic community of New York, which seeks to bring all Jews back into the traditional contemplative discipline of "meditation on the Torah and obedience to the commandments of the Creator."

However, the latest entry in these notebooks is dated over four years ago. Between then and now there is nothing.

Not that I was no longer meeting Western religious leaders who identified themselves with the spiritual revolution. On the contrary, such meetings were taking place more and more often, and usually without my initiating them.

It is only, as I now realize, that I had given up hope of understanding what Christians were looking for in their own religion.

At the same time, it became increasingly clear to me that were Christianity actually to recover its own esoteric tradition, it would be a development of immense significance. In using this term, "esoteric," I mean to say the Christianity that works, that actually produces real change in human nature, real transformation. This word is far better than the word "mysticism," which has come to be applied to only one kind of special experience. If there ever had been such a thing as a Christian (or Judaic) esoteric tradition, it would have included what we ordinarily understand by mysticism, but only as one aspect of a total way of living and struggling with oneself.

But was this what Christians were looking for? If so, and if it were to be found, it would be an event that would make the phenomenon of the "new religions" pale into insignificance by comparison. At least so it has always seemed to me.

In any case, I eventually came to the conclusion that there must be something very wrong in the way I was looking at the situation in contemporary Christianity and Judaism. Why did that bishop's question and his groping efforts touch me so deeply —more so than the searching of so many people who were turning to the East? Why did I become so impatient when listening to that rabbi lecturing on the meaning of the Kabbalah and urging his young audience to meditate every day on the mystical Name of God?

Why was I so troubled by the nun I met who spent hours each morning reading the sermons of the great Meister Eckhart and who told me she was experiencing all of the things he had written about? Why my gnawing irritation at an organization of Protestant ministers who were collectively practicing Tibetan prostrations in order to bring back the "sacralization of the human body," which, they claimed, was the original teaching of Christ? Why my sense of frustration after a long conversation with a Jesuit living in the Far East who, after many years of association with Taoists and Ch'an Buddhists, tells me that "we can use Buddhism to approach God, but only Christianity can take us inside God"?

Who was I to judge all this?—I who had only learned about Christianity through books and who only learned about Judaism by running away from it early in my life? People I knew would ask me: "Why are you so interested in Christianity? You're not a Christian, are you?"

A "Christian Monk"

It was with a genuine sense of relief that I finally abandoned any plans of writing about the problems facing contemporary Christianity. The more I thought about it, the more I realized how subjective my own opinions were and how mixed with the contents of all the books I had read over a career of fifteen years teaching courses in the history of Christian thought. It is true that I had many strong feelings about the message of Christianity and, through my studies and meetings with people, I had come to several ideas that struck me as important for my own understanding of the Church's present situation. But all that only increased my sense of being an outsider with respect to the personal efforts of present-day Christians to rediscover the essence of the teaching.

My decision, and the reasons for it, were strengthened by a chance meeting in December of 1975 with a man who spoke about Christianity in a way I had never encountered before either in my academic work or in the numerous interviews I had conducted. This meeting took place while I was attending a conference in the Far East. Seated in the audience, toward the rear, was an interesting-looking older man, a Westerner, who from time to time put some pointed questions to the members of the panel. After the three-day conference, I happened to find myself standing next to him in line as I was waiting to board the plane from Bangkok to Hong Kong.

He spoke English with a strong accent that I was never able to identify.

As we approached the ticket counter, we heard an announcement that the flight would be delayed for about an hour, and so the two of us repaired to the airport dining room for a cup of coffee. There we passed the time pleasantly chatting. As we were about to return to the boarding area, an announcement informed us that, due to engine problems, our flight would be delayed another hour. We both knew what this meant: two, three, possibly four hours or more. We ordered more coffee and a meal and then began talking seriously.

I was surprised to learn that this man was a "Christian monk." I use the quotation marks not because I doubted him but only because that was absolutely all I learned about his identity. There never seemed to be an appropriate moment when I could even ask his name, and when I tried to discover which order he belonged to, I was told only that it was situated "in the Middle East" and was "quite old." Yet, strangely enough, I never had the impression of his being secretive, withholding anything from me. On the contrary, by the time our conversation had ended—after about three hours—I felt inundated, full to overflowing, with more ideas and information about the Christian tradition than I could possibly manage. I mean to say that not only was the amount of material he gave me overwhelming, but, much more significant, the nature of his thinking was quite extraordinary—so much so that during the conversation and long afterward I found myself revising almost everything I had ever thought about Christianity.

"Revising" is not really the right word. It would be more accurate to say that from this remarkable "Christian monk" I heard things stated fully that up to that point I had only dimly imagined as pertaining to the Christian teaching. Much of what he said—about the nature of Christian spiritual practice, interpretation of Scripture, views on morality, mysticism, metaphysics, the soul, the place of the Church, and so forth—was, to say the least, extremely unorthodox. At more than one place I had the impulse to demand "proofs." But he had activated something in me that was stronger than the scholar/professor in my nature. And I feared that were I to turn the conversation into an argument, he would feel less free to speak his mind.

But, over and above all these considerations, there was something about the man himself that compelled me to listen, rather than argue. It was a quality that I am beginning to recognize as *presence.* I will say no more about this quality here; except that, among other things, it gave what he said the ring of authority.

By the time we boarded the plane, I was craving to be alone with my notebook in order to write down some of the things he said. He traveled with me as far as Tokyo and we parted with a warm embrace. It was only when the plane was back in the air that I kicked myself for not having tried to find out how to get in touch with him again. Later I kicked myself even harder for not having gotten off the plane with him.

Off and on, during the remainder of my flight back to America, I tried to record the conversation. But although I filled many pages in my notebook, I had the impression that I was distorting most of his ideas even as I was writing them down. I saw that he had spoken to a "place" in myself and that I was no longer in that "place." My power of memory, which I usually regarded as a fairly well-developed instrument, was now pathetically inadequate.

But what I did retain was something extremely important to me. Through meeting this unforgettable man, I realized with certainty that there are worlds upon worlds of Christianity that neither I nor anyone else I had met knew anything about. In saying this, I am not referring to all the intricacies of Christian theology through the ages or to the million aspects of the history of Christendom among the nations of the world. Nor am I referring to the kaleidoscope of ritual forms that make up the practices of the various denominations within the tradition.

I understand that all of the above are important and very much need to be pondered. But what I am speaking of is something quite different. It has to do with a fragment of our conversation that does stand out very clearly in my mind as I am now writing.

It was well after we had finished our meal. Breaking one of the many long silences, I said to him, "What I need to understand is, what is the *heart* of Christianity? There must be such a heart, an inner core. But I don't know through what avenues in myself I can begin to sense this inner nature of the teaching. I don't know what sorts of perceptions or impressions will give rise to the intuition of what Christianity *is*. I want to know, what is the *being* of Christianity?"

To this he answered, "Also *my* question, that."

Father Sylvan

Returning to America, I no longer had any temptation to write about Christianity. If, before, I had felt like an outsider in terms of my own personal background, I now realized that all my conceptions about a possible "hidden tradition" of Christianity probably contained as much fantasy as reality. I mean to say that through meeting this man I was more than ever convinced that such a tradition exists, but, at the same time, I was equally convinced that access to this tradition was far more difficult than I had imagined, even in terms of glimpsing its theoretical outlines —not to mention its practical methods and disciplines. I saw how naïve it had been to think that a "lost Christianity" would become visible to me in the same way that the Asian religions were making themselves known in the modern world.

One morning, nearly a year later, I arrived at my office at the university to find waiting for me a large, battered package with Egyptian stamps on it. There was no return address. The outer wrapping had been torn and the whole thing secured with wire by the Postal Service. Pieces of string still hung loosely around the middle. I could see that it was a manuscript that had been damaged in transit, and my only thought was a hope that the poor author had not sent me his only copy. I set the package aside and did not open it until returning home, late that night.

When I did open it I could not at first make head or tail of it. There was well over a thousand pages of handwritten manuscript, some of it water-soaked and torn. The script was very hard to decipher, and at first glance I was not even sure it was in the English language. The top sheet, which seemed to be some sort of covering letter, had been so water-soaked that it was little more than a blur. Again I set it aside and, after taking care of some other work, I went to bed.

The following morning, before leaving for the university, I looked it over again. I was thunderstruck when I suddenly realized what it was. The script now seemed much more legible, for some reason, and even the covering letter could be made out, despite the smeared ink. It was only a few lines:

Dear Professor Needleman:
Father Sylvan, who died one month ago, left these papers to be disposed of by being forwarded to you. In Christ the Savior.

No signature.

I cannot describe the feelings that poured through me at that moment. In my chest there appeared a sensation of warmth which remained with me throughout the day.

During the afternoon, I could think of nothing but that manuscript at home on my desk. My students thought I was ill. When I returned home, I closeted myself in my study and began reading. I intended to spend the whole night and the whole next day, if necessary, reading. I canceled all my appointments and informed the household that I was not to be disturbed, for any reason.

Oddly enough, the most persistent feeling I had was a sense of gratitude that I now knew the man's name: Father Sylvan. I expected that in these papers I would find out all the other facts about him that I wanted to know: his background, what monastic order he belonged to, where it was situated, etc. But I must say now that no information of this sort was in the manuscript.

My intention to go through the whole manuscript at one sitting was quickly abandoned. After only an hour's reading I had to put it down. I could not come back to it until the following day, and again could only read a few pages before having to stop to digest the ideas it contained.

Reading in this way, it took me over two months to go through the entire manuscript. When I was finished, I was convinced that I had in my hands a document that could revolutionize the modern understanding of the Christian religion. On the other hand, I knew that many of the ideas would be completely unacceptable to most people—as indeed many were to me.

What to do? I selected what I considered to be the most striking and bold parts of the text, had them retyped on regular typewriter paper, and put the selections together in a paper folder. I then showed it to a colleague of mine, a biblical scholar with whom I had had some good conversations in the past. In order to account for the broken English grammar, I explained that the text was a literal translation of a treatise written by a Russian theologian that had been submitted to me for editing and publication in my Metaphysical Library series.

I was not at all surprised when, a week later, my colleague returned the manuscript to me with a disdainful laugh. "Frankly," he said, "I was only able to read half of this nonsense. There is not a single substantiated claim in the whole package. The man is obviously just riding his own horse, which is taking him right to never-never land."

Another colleague, also a New Testament scholar, reacted in a similar manner. To him, it was all just "warmed-over Gnosticism with a dash of pseudomystical allegorization." He added, "It's incredible that anyone calling himself a Christian theologian would so underplay the most distinctive feature of Christian theology: the historicity of Christ. In any case, the man is totally ignorant of the latest methods of biblical criticism."

I then made a new selection of material from the manuscript and had it typed up as before, after smoothing out the bad grammar. This time, I tried to make the selection as representative as possible—adding parts that were relatively straightforward and conventional (though there was nothing in the text that was entirely conventional) and including some of the lighter sections as well, in which Father Sylvan exhibited a somewhat pungent sense of humor. I also included sections that read like a travel journal (he had apparently investigated many cultures throughout the world, not as a missionary but as a participant).

Once again I showed it to friends and colleagues, telling them a similar fictitious story about the author.

Responses were much more positive, but equally discouraging to me. Everyone enjoyed what Father Sylvan said about life, and completely ignored what he said about Christianity. An old friend suggested that I had invented Father Sylvan.

Now I am here, wondering what to do, really. On one side are these hundreds of pages of writings that, in any case, touch *me* very deeply; and they are about Christianity—or are they? Are all the critics right? Could it be that the sort of fire these ideas generate in me has nothing to do really with Christianity, after all? And are Christians who are looking for the practical, mystical core of Western tradition actually looking for something that does not interest me?

I see that the question of a lost Christianity is a question about myself. It is an extraordinary notion. On the one hand there is what millions of people for hundreds of years have been saying about Christianity; on the other side is this sense of search that I personally feel with respect to what I understand of Western religious ideas, together—at the moment—with this peculiar manuscript that touches me so deeply.

It is no longer simply a question of whether this manuscript is accurate or not, right or not, authentic or not. It is not a question of my presuming to say something about a subject upon which I am not entitled to speak. It is myself that is in question, my own sense of what I am, what I need to know in order to begin living.

PART ONE
THREE CHRISTIANS

Chapter Two

Metropolitan Anthony of Sourozh

Credentials

London, 1977. I know this church, and not only because I have been here before, five years ago, to visit this man. It only just catches your attention; it is no soaring cathedral; it does not dominate the space around it; it does not stand etched against the sky with the assured simplicity of the Protestant meeting-house. If you are looking for it, it is easy to find—a sizable Russian Orthodox church in London's Knightsbridge section. If you are not looking for it, you will never notice it as you go by.

I "knew" it then, too, the first time. I explained it to myself that the Orthodox churches look and feel more like synagogues than Catholic or Protestant churches. This, of course, is true: the Levantine influence also predominates in the architecture of synagogues. But there was something else, even stronger now than before: a strange sense of intimacy. Perhaps it had to do with the nature of the questions I intended to ask Archbishop Anthony Bloom—or with the part of myself where these questions resided; I don't know.

I know that the synagogues of my childhood ceased having this sort of intimacy very early in my life. I am sure this has to do with the fact that, however a child does such things, I soon gave up hoping that the most inner part of myself would be addressed there.

Five years before, I had come to Ennismore Gardens on the first leg of a tour that would conclude with my visit to the Greek peninsula of Athos, the monastic center of Eastern Orthodox

Christendom. I have written elsewhere of my experiences during my short stay on Mount Athos.*

Like many Westerners, I had read *The Way of a Pilgrim*, that remarkable little autobiographical book describing the practice of "the prayer of the heart" in the Eastern Orthodox tradition. Here, I thought, may be the key to the practical *method* of Christianity, as distinguished from the rituals and doctrines that merely support belief in something that cannot be directly experienced.

It has taken the new religions to bring this idea of religious method back into the awareness of the West. Until recently, the whole idea of spiritual discipline was either incomprehensible or highly suspicious to modern people. Or else it was understood as such an ordinary thing as to be indistinguishable from familiar standards of ethical conduct.

No seeking Westerner can read *The Way of a Pilgrim* without having all his prejudices about spiritual discipline overturned. In that account, we are given a glimpse of the spiritual process, understood as the lawful development of forces within the *physical* body of man, rather than only in the intangible and vague realms of thought and emotion. Even the contemporary reader, if his mind is not jaded by hearing too much about Oriental *chakras*† and spiritual "energies," will be astonished to see the manner in which the body is involved and accepted in the traditional, Orthodox monastic discipline. Astonished, and perhaps touched by a certain new experience of hope. . . .

Anthony Bloom is Metropolitan of Western Europe, the Russian Orthodox equivalent of archbishop. A handsome, well-built man, somewhat shorter than average, he is now in his middle sixties. So much does his appearance give the impression of force and vitality that, no doubt because of my own prejudices about "clergy," I felt his black archbishop's garb, and even his rich, neatly trimmed black beard to be a sort of "disguise." Not that I felt he belonged to the world; far from it. But his gestures, his voice, his way of moving suggested anything but the conventional picture of "piety" or "spirituality" that we have in the

---

* Jacob Needleman and Dennis Lewis, eds., *Sacred Tradition and Present Need* (New York: Viking Press, 1975), pp. 1–19.

† In Hinduism, subtle centers of consciousness situated within the spinal system.

West. He struck me as being neither worldly nor "spiritual." But something else, of some realm more actual than either of these. What realm is that?

I sensed this particularly with respect to his eyes. There was a steadiness in his eyes that was really quite extraordinary. In fact, this was actually the first thing I noticed about him. I might add that I have great difficulty writing or speaking about "eyes" and "looks," not wanting to fall into sentimentality or imagination.

But, in the case of Anthony Bloom, something has to be said about "eyes." I have had occasion to meet a number of men and women considered to be exceptional. But often, I have found, what they are supposed to be is betrayed by their eyes. It is not only that certain kinds of movement of the eyes indicate someone stuck for that moment in the more superficial part of the mind; nor that the too constant, steady gaze may indicate a somewhat neurotic condition masquerading as sincerity or intensity. All that may be true; and a sensitive reader of faces may be able to tell far more from the eyes than most of us would care to admit.

I am not speaking about this sort of thing exactly. I am only speaking about the fact that in some people *something* is communicated through the eyes that authenticates them; while in others, something is communicated—or there is the lack of something communicated—that betrays them and contradicts what they are presenting of themselves.

A person may have all the "credentials" in the world, and something about him will prevent me from taking him really seriously. It is not what he says or what he does, it is what he *is*, and somehow this, in my experience, can come through the eyes.

The Two Streams

However that may be, I vividly recall my first meeting with Metropolitan Anthony. I had gone to the Cathedral of the Assumption of All Saints, in Ennismore Gardens, and took part as much as I was able in the Vespers service. Later that evening, I telephoned his home and was invited to come to his flat the following Saturday morning.

In the interim I went over my notes about his background. After working with the Resistance in Paris during World War II, he secretly lived a monastic life under the cover of his medical profession. In 1948 he was ordained to the priesthood and later became Metropolitan (or head) of the Russian Church in Western Europe, reporting each year to the Patriarch, in Moscow. When asked once by an interviewer about the difficulty of being at one and the same time politically alienated from and religiously committed to Russia, Metropolitan Anthony had an interesting reply. He is quoted as having said, "In the position of tension in which we are, between churchmanship and citizenship, our churchmanship is much freer than if we had a better harmony between Church and State."

Certainly, the history of the Christian Church cries out for an understanding of such questions. What student of civilization has not pondered the consequences for the world of the victory of Constantine in the year 312 and his ultimate assumption of complete power as emperor of the faltering Roman Empire? That Constantine who not only lifted the persecution of the followers of the Christian religion but actually proclaimed himself a Christian and made Christianity the "official religion" of the entire empire! It has always seemed to me that at just that moment the history of Christianity branched, and that from then on two streams of Christian destiny must be distinguished, however parallel they may seem to be during certain periods and however disparate these streams might seem in size or strength and however many other currents and eddies appear in each.

With Constantine, Christianity as a world religion takes form and decisively branches away from what might be called Christianity as an inner path. From that point on, there are two main histories of Christianity, a distinction, to my mind, far more fundamental than the various other aspects of Christian culture through the ages: the distinction between Eastern and Western Christianity, for example, or the history of Catholicism as opposed to Protestantism, or the history of Christian institutions such as the papacy, and the interaction between these institutions and the secular, political and economic forces of the Western world. Even the history of monasticism in its relationship to the Church does not necessarily coincide with these two histories I am speaking of, however much it may seem to during certain periods of time. This rather elusive idea of two histories is how I have come to regard the origins and development of Christianity, though of course I am far from being a trained scholar in this area.

However, it was not about the two histories in the broad sweep of time that I wanted to ask Metropolitan Anthony in that first meeting, but about these two streams as they exist within man. Was the appearance of the new religions and their popularity with the young a sign that the Western Church had neglected this distinction between fundamental impulses within man: the one that may lead to "happiness," and the other which has as its aim a state incomprehensible even to the most "religious" among us? Over the years, had elements within the Christian tradition that were once meant to guide the second impulse, the movement toward the incomprehensible, been aggrandized by the first?

Questions Without Answers

Saturday morning: balmy winds, gray skies, the fragrance of impending rain in the air. I ring the bell and am led up a long flight of stairs to where Metropolitan Anthony is waiting for me in his shirt sleeves. He ushers me into his kitchen and I am invited to sit down at an old, sturdy wooden table while he puts a pot of water on to boil.

I have already described his appearance: the compact body; graceful, energetic movements; his physical center of gravity surprising in "a man of the cloth"; his extraordinary eyes, firm, black, alive, that kept looking at me (though not too much) even when he was laughing; one knew from the eyes that he was behind what he was saying, and therefore, in an unexpected way, that he was also free to change, to let go of his views. There was tremendous commitment in those eyes, but not to words. The full, black beard; black cotton shirt with blousy sleeves; Orthodox crucifix (with the added transverse bar) hanging from a silver chain around his neck.

So much for his appearance. But this kitchen! I had to smile. I could have been in the kitchen of my Russian grandmother, who was also "Orthodox," but Orthodox Jewish. The same smell: the surviving essence of a thousand meals cooked always with garlic, onion, parsley, radish; I could detect the fish (maybe even which species); the boiled meat, the chunks of beetroot floating in the borscht.

The same peeling paint on the walls and table legs; the same cut-glass light fixture dangling by a slender, blackened chain. The same high ceilings and sense of space and light—bright, spare, and clean, however old and worn.

I felt immensely relaxed. Metropolitan Anthony poured the tea into my glass and placed before me a small bowl of individually wrapped candies. I took one.

I am sorry to have to say that what then followed is almost a complete blank in my memory. Perhaps it was because I was just at the beginning of my travels in search of the "lost Christianity." I had no way of knowing that one of the most important figures I would meet on this search would be among the first I encountered. I did not even make notes afterward. And it was only after my travels—actually, long after I returned home—that it began to dawn on me what Metropolitan Anthony was. Moreover, in all frankness, I must warn the reader that this sort of hindsight has been practically a constant in this search of mine. And so, most of the time I am offering here conversations reconstructed from memory sometimes very long after the event. But I must also add that this failure to recognize the level of Christianity in my presence was not only due to a lack of sensitivity. I believe it has something to do with the problem of Christianity itself in the contemporary world—Christianity's own inability to make itself known for what it really is.

I do remember very clearly the questions I asked him then, and which, five years later, I asked him again. These are questions that have guided my whole inquiry into the *lostness* of Christianity.

I asked:

"Metropolitan Anthony, what is the Christian mystery?

"Are there certain experiences which are necessary if Christian love and mystery is to penetrate into the whole of a man, rather than inflame a part of him with religious emotion? Can we rely on life to provide these experiences and on ourselves to receive them?

"Or does the mystery of Christianity always involve an *if*: 'If you will believe, . . . *if* you will surrender, . . .' and so forth.

"Is your message just for Christians or is it for anyone who is seeking?

"What is the real meaning of the universality or catholicity of the teaching of Jesus?

"If Christianity is for anyone, is it necessary to become a Christian, or could your ideas blend in with other teachings, or with no teaching at all?

"Is a church necessary?

"Is a spiritual father necessary?

"Some of the new Eastern religions in the West represent an adjustment to the West of ancient Asian forms. Could there be an adjustment of Orthodoxy? or must the forms remain fixed? How to touch the life that results in the creation of tradition, rather than dwell among the results alone?

"Is Christianity only for Christians?"

"Occult" Christianity

I wish now to explain why I had chosen to visit Metropolitan Anthony and why from him I had hoped to receive answers to just these questions. In his books, I had detected something remarkable amid all the religious literature that I was obliged to read both as part of my profession and as part of my own search for the lost Christianity.

The general theological literature never made an impression on me; it was too philosophical. I, as a professional philosopher, had long since been forced to accept that philosophical ideas by themselves change nothing in the life of an individual. Without the practical knowledge of how to bring great ideas into the heart and even into the tissues of the body, philosophy cannot take us very far. On the contrary, as Kierkegaard saw, it only supports the weakness in man that makes him believe he can make progress by his own efforts. Systems, explanations, clarifications, proofs—through these, modern man squanders his attention in the intellectual function while remaining cut off from the emotional and the instinctual sides of his nature, wherein reside the most powerful energies of our being, and without the corresponding development of which no authentic moral power is possible.

As for the flood of material dealing with "occult" Christianity,

I simply had been burned too many times. How many books had I started, how many people had I met offering the key to "esoteric" Christianity? Almost always, what I found in such cases was the juxtaposition of Christianity with another idea or system which was, if anything, farther from being understood than Christianity itself. One group tells us that Christianity is the ancient Egyptian wisdom. Very well, but who really grasps what that was? Another links Christ to Pythagoras. But when they try to explain how they understand Pythagoras, then the childishness of their claims becomes apparent. Or a biblical scholar, highly respected and with the best academic credentials, discovers a document from the early centuries of Christianity proving the existence of a "secret gospel." Intriguing. Investigation of evidence pertaining to this secret gospel indicates the existence of an "inner circle" of pupils to whom Jesus gave a teaching that was never known to the larger number of followers. Extremely interesting. Further investigation and theorizing suggests the existence of certain practical methods hitherto unassociated with Christianity; other evidence, gathered together, more than adequately justifies applying to Christ the name "Magician." Astonishing!

But wait. What does this scholar mean by the term "magician"? Does he mean a man of great knowledge and power, a being able to do what other men only dream of? a man with access to universal forces and purposes who knows both how to make use of the laws of nature and also to help human beings escape from their tyranny?

He means nothing of the kind. Jesus was a "magician" in that he practiced a "technique of self-hypnosis" that induced in him and his "inner circle" certain *illusory experiences*, such as ascending into the heavens. Moreover, "Jesus seems to have had a peculiar attraction for and power over schizophrenics. . . . The stories of his disciples' sudden, total abandonment of their ordinary lives to follow him . . . probably . . . indicate an instability in the disciples' characters. . . . Such group schizophrenia, . . ." *etc., etc.*‡

And so, for some time now I have never gone out of my way

‡ See Morton Smith, *The Secret Gospel* (New York: Harper & Row, 1973), esp. Ch. 12. See also his *Jesus the Magician* (New York: Harper & Row, 1978).

to look into "occult" Christianity. Not that I am uninterested in the relationship between the teachings of Christ and the teachings of the Egyptians or the pre-Socratic Greeks, or in similarities with other ancient spiritual systems. Far from it. Only, it is clear to me that if something essential in the Christian tradition has become invisible, it does not help to direct our attention to other traditions, whose core meaning is equally unknown to us. Some other kind of effort of understanding is required.

Nor were the writings of Anthony Bloom "devotional" in the familiar sense. Had they been so, I know that I would never have been drawn to see him. I seem to have been born with an allergy to devotional religious writing, especially of the modern Christian variety. I am told by discerning friends that such devotional literature is, like the *bhakti* yoga of India, an indication of the special nature of the Christian path—that it is a discipline directed primarily toward the emotional function in human nature.

The Emotion of a Christian

However, as my conversations with Metropolitan Anthony of Sourozh were to demonstrate, it is just this question of "the emotions of a Christian" that is the greatest mystery of all. Who dares to fall back on the emotional life? Is not *the emotion of a Christian* the "most lost" element of lost Christianity? This would not be an unfair summary of everything he was to tell me.

I will now blend together into one conversation the two meetings I had with Metropolitan Anthony, one meeting in which I remember only my questions and the second meeting—five years later—in which I also remember his answers.

We are now seated across from each other in his modest rooms behind the sanctuary of the cathedral. Late-afternoon light breaks in through the room's only window, throwing a soft and shifting play of shadows over Metropolitan Anthony's face. He is tired; from time to time he bows his head and coughs, in obvious pain. But there is something in his face now that I had not seen before; the same strength and steadiness, the same constant impulse to meet one directly, but now—hard to put into words—a quality of openness that one might wish to describe as "surrender," a surrender not to any individual—or to any particular force one could name. In fact, there was something *impersonal* about it. It was an extremely fleeting impression, not even noticed directly until later. I remember the sense, when seeing him, of something *new*. In myself, a fear, an alertness fell down by itself, without a struggle. As a result—with lawful precision—I moved toward the man from within myself; or, rather, there was in myself a movement toward the man. "I," whatever that is, went with that movement unquestioningly.

"Metropolitan Anthony," I began, "five years ago when I visited you I attended the services which you yourself conducted. And I remarked to you then how struck I was by the absence of emotion in your voice. Today, in the same way, where it was not you but the choir, I was struck by the same thing, the almost complete lack of emotion in the voices of the singers."

"Yes," he said, "that is quite true. It has taken years for that, but they are finally beginning to understand. . . ."

"What do you mean?" I asked. I knew what he meant, but I wanted to hear him speak about this—this most unexpected aspect of the Christianity I never knew, and perhaps very few modern people ever knew. I put my question further: "The average person hearing this service—and of course the average Westerner having to stand up for the several hours it took—might not be able to distinguish it from the mechanical routine that has become so predominant in the performance of the Christian liturgy in the West. He might come wanting to be lifted, inspired, moved to joy or sadness—and this the churches in the West are trying to produce, because many leaders of the Church are turning away from the mechanical, the routine—"

He gently waved aside what I was saying, and I stopped in mid-sentence. There was a pause, then he said: "No. Emotion must be destroyed."

He stopped, reflected, and started again, speaking in his husky Russian accent: "We have to get rid of emotions . . . in order to reach . . . feeling."

Again he paused, looking at me, weighing the effect his words were having. I said nothing. But inside I was alive with expectancy. I waited.

Very tentatively, I nodded my head.

He continued: "You ask about the liturgy in the West and in the East. It is precisely the same issue. The sermons, the Holy

Days—you don't know why one comes after the other, or why this one now and that one later. Even if you read everything about it, you still wouldn't know, believe me.

"And yet . . . there is a profound logic in them, in the sequence of the Holy Days. And this sequence leads people somewhere—without their knowing it intellectually. Actually, it is impossible for anyone to understand the sequence of rituals and Holy Days intellectually. It is not meant for that. It is meant for something else, something higher.

"For this you have to be in a state of prayer, otherwise it passes you by—"

"What is prayer?" I asked.

He did not seem to mind my interrupting with this question. Quite the contrary. "In the state of prayer one is *vulnerable.*" He emphasized the last word and then waited until he was sure I had not taken it in an ordinary way.

"In prayer one is vulnerable, not enthusiastic. And then these rituals have such force. They hit you like a locomotive. You must be not enthusiastic, nor rejecting—but only *open*. This is the whole aim of asceticism: to become open."

A Demand

Was it really so? And as if to illustrate the point, my attention wandered even while Metropolitan Anthony went on speaking. What a striking way to state the aim of asceticism, a concept that stymies all modern people even after they have shaken loose from the clichés of "self-torture." As though we have really been able to pass blanket judgments on the anchorites and monks of the earliest centuries of Christianity who went into the deserts to struggle— to struggle with what?

And in order to become— what?

"Open"? Then, in what sense is man "closed"? What has the Christianity of sin, guilt, penitence, etc. to do with "open" and "closed"? Was not asceticism finally rejected by modern people just because it seemed to close the individual, not open him, to life?

Certainly, renunciation, self-denial, in all the forms in which I had ever personally encountered it, repelled me and frightened me. In the same way, as a young man I had been repelled and frightened by a religious moralism that seemed to kill life in the name of the creator of life. That is why I turned not to pleasure or sensuous indulgence but to *science*, which seemed to me then to accept life in all its movement and forms.

It sounds strange, but it is true; at least it was so for me—the opposite of asceticism: science.

And I must say that, in essence, it has remained so for me. The impulse to understand, to learn the meaning of what is alive, whatever form it takes: surely this is what science once touched in us. Its power in the Western world does not originally come from the benefits of technology, but because it alone in the modern world once called forth and supported this impulse in man to understand the whole of life—this *new emotion*, which when it appears is so subtle and quiet that it may actually seem more like a thought than a feeling. "Dry souls are best," said Heraclitus, long before Socrates and Plato spoke of a power of universal intelligence in man that could become active only when the ordinary emotions are mastered. For the greatest of the ancient Greeks, the struggle—the real asceticism, we must say—is predicated on the enormous power within man of the *love of understanding*. Ultimately, this whole idea of the real asceticism became twisted into grotesque notions of self-flagellation, hatred of the body, rigid soul-body dualisms—a deep misunderstanding that has infected the entire world.

As my attention returned to Metropolitan Anthony, I caught the last words of a story he was telling me about King Sarouk of Persia. The king was observing the execution of criminals. His eye was caught by an intent old man among those watching the executions. "Who is that man?" the king asked. He learned that it was the father of a certain young man who was among the condemned. The old man waited and watched. Finally, the son was led up to the gallows and the rope was placed around his neck. The word was given and the trap door was sprung. The dead body of the son was cut down and taken away. Through it all, the father did not shed a tear. Seeing this, the king turned to his aide: "What a grief!" To the aide, who did not understand, he added, "One can cry tears over a cat."

Seeing that I had just come back from my own thoughts, Metropolitan Anthony waited for me to digest what he was saying. There was a long silence. I was at first uncomfortable and started to wish he would have some tea brought in, just to give me something to do with my hands. I searched around in my mind for something to say that would connect my own musings with the point he was making. No tea was brought in. No candy was offered. Nor was Metropolitan Anthony looking at me with any particular expectancy. And yet I felt a strong sense of a demand being made upon me.

Of course, I wanted very much to ask him more about openness, but I was afraid that if I did, he would not answer in a way that confirmed what the term suggested to me. I was afraid that he would not explain it as a holy state of consciousness that I, like any person, have tasted and that lies at the root of one's own given wish for life, a state that is our birthright and is instantly felt as such on the rare occasions when it is experienced. I was afraid he would take away the word "openness," which had such a sense of the transforming power of awareness; I was afraid that the word, were he to explain it further, would become "religicized" in the disappointing way so many real words had been in my own life—brought to some equation with an ordinary emotion, an emotion with which one was familiar and which in one's own conscience one knew to be egoistic—a powerful, sacred term brought into association with this ordinary emotion, but the whole association hypocritically pretending to be really "higher."

At the same time all this was spinning in my head, I began to sense something exceptional about the whole situation: no small talk. Very quickly, almost too quickly to perceive, there took place in me a recognition of being *respected*—quite unlike anything I had ever known under that name. And it was intimately bound up with the exceedingly difficult sense of demand that seemed to be placed upon me.

In short, there was for me as much egoistic fear as there was the wish to hear and understand. The two conflicting aspects of the situation, corresponding to two conflicting impulses in myself, no doubt prompted me to ask a question that was not on my "official" list: "Father Anthony, there is one question that I would like very much to ask you."

Metropolitan Anthony put his head down and coughed, grimacing from the discomfort. I waited. I did not feel embarrassed in the slightest. Ordinarily, I might have experienced a twinge of regret that I was taking someone's time, etc., especially someone who was so fine a person, etc., and so busy, etc. I was not even tempted to utter the polite "Perhaps . . . if you're not feeling well today. . . ." The question I wanted to ask was *my* question. Somehow, that gave me an unusual sensitivity. For example, I *knew* that even with all his discomfort, Metropolitan Anthony really wanted to speak longer to me.

"Ask," he said.

I pulled myself forward in my chair. "How does a Christian respond to the event of Good Friday?"

I went on to explain my question: "I ask this because it has been in my mind ever since my visit to Athos five years ago. Do you remember that when I first came to see you I was on my way there? [He nodded.] I wrote a description of my visit with Father Vasileios at the Stavronikita Monastery, which I believe I sent to you? [He nodded again.] But over the years something else from Athos has penetrated into me and has affected me even more than the meeting with Vasileios."

Athens

What I wished to relate to Metropolitan Anthony was a full account of the first hours of my visit on Athos, something which I had previously written about only in passing, simply because I didn't realize its importance.

I had spent a busy week in Athens before flying to Salonika, where one boards the bus to Ouranopolis to take the motorboat to Athos. In Athens there had been many people to see—including a number of old friends—and some representatives of the Orthodox Church to interview.

And, of course, there was the Parthenon. Although my reason for being in Greece was to investigate Christianity, and although my imminent visit to Athos filled me with anticipation, nevertheless at night I fell asleep thinking of the Parthenon. I was of course aware of the element of romance in this—all those years as a schoolboy looking at photographs of it had had their effect, as had all those years in college studying philosophy and the civilization of ancient Greece. I fantasized that I might commune with the spirits of Socrates and Plato, or perhaps sense in the proportions of the building the Pythagorean vision of the universe, a universe of mathematical law. It was, after all, to ancient

Greece that the modern world had turned for its ideals of knowledge and freedom of the mind. The entire development of modern scholarship and education (at all levels), as well as the canons of science, owed their origins to what was interpreted as the genius of Greece. And let no one underestimate the overwhelming influence on modern man's life of *scholarship* as we know it, in its broadest sense. All that we call knowledge, all our perceptions of reality, our sense of what the mind of man is and can do, the way we go about informing ourselves about anything at all, for whatever motive, is the fruit of the Greek civilization as we have perceived it over the past several centuries.

It was on the morning of my last day in Athens that I finally went to see the Parthenon. I awoke at sunrise, but as luck would have it the sky clouded over on my way to the Acropolis, and a light rain was falling by the time I arrived.

As I climbed up to the site of the Parthenon, I tried to keep my eyes averted until I was directly in front of it. A few partial glimpses were unavoidable, and they served to inform me of the state I was in: not a bad state, rather receptive and relatively free from the images I had been entertaining during the past week.

Nevertheless, I was completely unprepared for the impression that met me when I stood facing the Parthenon. This impression was so unexpected, so instantaneous (it could not have lasted more than a second) and at the same time so extraordinarily quiet and stable, that I almost did not recognize it as an experience. My attention was drawn by the thought that accompanied this experience: *Somebody has tampered with something*.

The whole impression of the Parthenon as a *copy* of something, an *imitation* (somewhat like a reproduction) was so unexpected that I cannot even say I was disappointed. But, even today, long after this experience, and not anywhere near the state of openness I was in at that moment, I cannot dispute the impression of the Parthenon as an attempt to reproduce something on a scale or for a purpose that does not correspond in any way with the original. Not life, but an explanation of life.

A copy or imitation of what? I do not know. One colleague who agrees with my perception of the Parthenon has suggested to me that the temples of Egypt might have been the inspiration for the Parthenon.

Another friend, who has never been to Greece, observed that my descriptions sounded like art whose center of gravity is too much in the head, too "invented," not necessarily an imitation of any particular original.

I returned to my hotel in Syntagma Square, packed my bags and wandered around the streets of Athens before taxiing to the airport. The sky had cleared and the August sun was blazing. The heat soon became oppressive; exhaust fumes from the cars and trucks jamming the tiny streets overwhelmed the aromas of food and spices. The blaring horns and the loud noise of motorcycles cut through the hubbub of human voices in the markets and the shops. My shirt was soaked with perspiration. Yet, for some reason, I felt quietly exhilarated, full of energy and contained. Was it because of the experience at the Parthenon? Perhaps so. One really understands very little about the sort of impressions that are liberating. Certain kinds of seeing bring joy, no matter what it is that is seen.

I was walking by an old Byzantine church that I had passed dozens of times in the past few days. Without thinking twice about it, I went in. It was empty, and I sat there for a while, resting, savoring the silence. The icons, the dark, intimate space, the huge face of Christ staring down at me—all this I "appreciated." But I was unmoved by it. . . .

Vulnerability

And now I am in front of a similar church in Karyes, the central village of the ancient monastic community of Mount Athos. The past forty-eight hours have been hell. The flight delayed from Athens to Salonika; hours spent waiting in a sweltering airport, a blinding headache my reward. Flying through a storm that tossed the plane around like a Ping-Pong ball. Late arrival at the Salonika hotel—no rooms left, my reservations forfeited. One in the morning. Taxiing to one hotel after another—finally, a miserable room in a fifth-class hotel. No sleep; noise, vermin, heat. Out at six in the morning to catch the bus to Ouranopolis. Bus breaks down en route; five-hour trip lasts eleven hours; arrive in Ouranopolis half dead from exhaustion and various digestive disturbances. Board a caïque early the following morning—four seasick hours over choppy waters, inhaling gasoline fumes, hanging over the rail while trying with some part of my brain to take in the stunning Aegean coastline. Stuffed into a decrepit bus with dozens of monks and tourists—literally forced to lie on my side on the floor of the bus, pressed against two other people. Long, tortuous climb up winding mountain roads and unable to move a muscle; certain the dangerously overcrowded bus will fall apart and spill everyone into the canyons.

Herded into the main administrative building of Karyes to be examined and questioned by the council of elders to see if I am fit to visit the monasteries. Long wait.

And now I am here in front of the Karyes cathedral. I enter. Intense silence. Darkness. Icons glowing on the walls as though by their own light. Yet somewhere I am smiling to myself at everything my body has been through, the aches and pains—the sense of adventure still buoying my spirits. My eyes move up to the ceiling: there again the stupendous face of Christ, like the central fact of the universe, looks down at me.

My thoughts are stopped. A certain sensation passes through my body, down my spine and into the pit of my stomach. From deeper down in my mind, something I have known about the Orthodox tradition rises to awareness: the whole of the universe rests on the sacrifice of God. But this Christ looks directly at *me*. The immensity of this sacrifice, which I do not understand or even wish to understand, is directed to me, personally. For the first time, I feel that something is required of me, a response to this sacrifice. I glimpse, for the first time, what it means that Christianity demands a response. I am obliged by the fact of Reality and the fact of my existence. I have felt this before about the whole of my existence and the existence of the world. But I have never felt it with respect to Christianity. Nor have I ever felt it so realistically as now, regarding this face. Existence here has a human face which I did not invent or imagine; it is an objective *I*, as much a part of Being as stars and trees. I am obliged, but what in myself can possibly answer this obligation? Nothing. And yet . . . it cannot be nothing, the sacrifice could not have been made or communicated like this if there were nothing that could come from man. . . .

I feel on the edge of a new understanding of the greatness of Christianity. But, even in this state, with these new thoughts, my mind wanders. I begin to worry about the next few hours.

Where will I go? What monastery will I visit? Will I like the food? Will I even be given food? Where will I sleep? What kind of toilets will they have?

I return to the face, but already everything is different.

And now I am out on the trails, having taken a good meal at one of the village restaurants. It is afternoon; sunlight alternates with swift-moving storm clouds. My body feels free and alive. All the aches and pains are still there, but they now amount to nothing. Why were they so troublesome before?

Hours later, with the sun nearing the horizon, I arrive at the Stavronikita Monastery, a huge, fortresslike structure. They refuse to take me in. I plead, I wait, I accept their hospitality of coffee and a piece of candy. My body is really tired—*I* am really tired—now. And I want very much to stay in this place; I have been told about it.

Then a "miracle": someone appears out of nowhere, translates for me, sets everything right. I am taken in. Invited for Vespers.

Vespers: standing in the dark crypt with some fifteen of the monks. The service proceeds: "Kyrie eleison, Kyrie eleison": "Lord have mercy," over and over again. Each time, the monks prostrate themselves, and I, too, fall on my knees on the stone floor, touch it with my head, stretch out my arms.

The service goes on and on. All the aches and pains return with doubled force, now joined by knees agonizing against the hard stone, and my back—never very good—tormenting and frightening me more and more with each prostration.

Cold, hungry, tired, my body aching, I go up and down, mechanically repeating *"Kyrie eleison, Kyrie eleison."* Twenty, thirty, fifty times. During the recitations, I try to collect myself and prepare for the next series of prostrations. I try to find a thought or a feeling to guide me so that I will not get lost in the physical discomfort. But, each time that I prostrate myself, every idea vanishes from my mind. Resentment takes over, and I simply stand there for a while as the prostrations go on. Soon I see myself joining in again—down and up, down and up, *Kyrie eleison, Kyrie eleison;* what do these words mean? I ask myself. Lord have mercy, Lord have mercy. My body is aching again, I begin to fear that I will actually do some damage cracking my knees against the hard, uneven stone floor. From somewhere, I try to compel myself into a "mystical" experience. But, each time, the sharp pain of my knees and back takes me away.

Then, for a few moments, something seems to separate myself within me. While all of me is going up and down, mumbling strange sounds, suffering the physical pain, a subtle warmth appears, together with an entirely free and separate awareness of the room: the candles, the icons. My eyes fall upon a particular icon of the Virgin. And what takes place then is in its way extraordinary, though I doubt if I can convey it in words. For a moment, *I am looking at the icon completely without associations*. It becomes concrete.

The Contact of Forces

All this is what lay behind my question to Metropolitan Anthony, but before I could begin to speak about it in detail he was already replying:

"You ask what in yourself can respond to the sacrifice of God? But this sacrifice, as you call it, is *love*. What is the proper response to love?"

At first, I thought Metropolitan Anthony was expecting me to answer. I had no answer.

"The proper response to love," he continued, "is to accept it. There is nothing to *do*. The response to a gift is . . . to accept it. Why would you wish to *do* anything?"

I found myself looking directly at him. I had absolutely no impulse to reply to what he had said. I noticed something taking place in my body, however. All by itself, my physical center of gravity began to shift to a locus in my abdomen and thighs. My back straightened, my shoulders became looser.

I broke the silence by repeating my question in another form, even though I knew the answer was already being given. I spoke about the different impressions I had in the Gothic cathedrals of Western Europe, the sense of being drawn upward within a vast cosmic scale filled with light. Through reading and personal experience, I had come to regard the Gothic cathedral—as have others—as one of the few surviving remnants of the Christian *gnosis*, an example of sacred art in the strict sense of the term, art that guides man toward knowledge of the real. From the quality of living light produced by the stained glass to the alchemical symbolism in the statuary, to the quiet, immense vertical spaces and the upward self-movement of the columns—which have been described as the spiritualization of stone—leading to the cross-vaulted forces of the ceiling: all of this transmitted to me the sense of a greatness and mystery. Who conceived and built these cathedrals?

I was completely unprepared for Metropolitan Anthony's response:

"I have always been revolted by Gothic," he said.

"And for a long time," he went on, "I did not understand why. But when I was living in Paris I came to understand it. All that aspiring, aspiring upward—yet not all the way.

"The Romanesque church is an utterly different idea. In Romanesque something has already come down to man: love."

"Are you speaking about a symbol," I asked, "or a fact?" Actually, I don't believe Metropolitan Anthony heard me—I must have spoken very indistinctly. Why I should have spoken with such hesitation on just this point I do not know. After all, it was the whole issue. One can go just so far with the great symbolic representations of the relationship between God and man. And I saw very clearly in the Vespers services at Athos—something I have seen under other extraordinary conditions—that the fact of a relationship between God and man, or between the higher and the lower, the actual contact of forces is much, much more rare and difficult than one imagines. Surely, the great symbols of this contact, if they are mistaken for the inner event itself, can actually take one farther away from the truth. How much of the degeneration of Christianity—and of all religion—is due to this? In ritual, is not the aim the actual contact of forces within the being of the individual?

But here I am anticipating what I later understood from the manuscript of Father Sylvan. I wish only that I had known about the teachings of Father Sylvan while I was speaking with Metropolitan Anthony. I would have wanted to question him further about this point: about how people's subjective emotional associations to Christian ritual and symbols gradually took the place of the struggle of forces that ritual is designed to make possible within the individual. And it is here, and only here, that the spiritual role of the human body can be understood. But of this later, in its place.

The Origin of Spiritual Exercises

Even without the language of Father Sylvan, however, I was groping toward this issue, and Metropolitan Anthony's reply, as will become apparent, threw open the door to the lost Christianity within ourselves.

Wanting to keep the conversation focused on this question of struggle and aspiration, I asked Metropolitan Anthony again about the various spiritual exercises described in the writings of the early Fathers. Surely there, if anywhere, was effort, aspiration. And method; exercises and method. Weren't Westerners now being attracted to Oriental religions because they could find in them the sort of methods for inner work that may have been predominant among the early Fathers?

And again, what of the body? Was there not—*is* there not—in Christianity the kind of guidance that one sees in Eastern systems that teach about the need for a certain posture, relaxation . . . ?

It was the same question I had put five years before to Father Vasileios, the abbot of Stravronikita Monastery. The answer I received then had left me profoundly dissatisfied. He had said: Yes, of course there were methods, but the main and the first thing was the need for *faith*. I was sure I had not made clear to Vasileios what this issue meant to Americans, who, like most Europeans as well, had long been part of a culture in which religion was only a matter of words, exhortations and philosophy, rather than a matter of practical guidance for experiencing directly the truth of the teachings. Methods, exercises, brought the possibility of experience, something that had been largely the province of that very suspect group called "mystics." Due to this historical fact, the sacred response of *faith*, which emanates from a higher level than the ego in man, became confused with the ordinary reaction of *belief*, only one of the numerous egoistic mechanisms within the mind that seem designed solely for the purpose of making people feel they are in the right and that everything is going to be all right. Was not the frustration of modern people, frustration amounting to desperation and even madness, due to hearing the Church say again and again, "Have faith," to people in need, people who saw that the effort to "have faith" fragmented their lives even more, adding the violence and self-deception of religious belief to all the other psychological maneuvers by which the mind, driven by fear, tries to inflict its products on the whole of the human organism—including the body, which not only cannot understand the language of the head but is not even, as it were, "interested"?

The new religions, in a word, produce *results*. But it was upon this whole question of results—actual experiences and changes— that Metropolitan Anthony cast a new light. I am convinced that at this juncture in the conversation we had reached the edge of one of the components of truth, which all too easily slip out of human awareness throughout the history of religion and throughout the life of every individual, and that this component is one of that limited number of factors which make all the difference in the life of man on earth and in the life of every authentic teaching.

He agreed with me that the new religions gave results, but the real problem, as I understood him, was in identifying the actual nature of these results and, most important, in forming a right attitude toward these results.

"The problem of these new religions," he said, "is just that they do give results. But not necessarily in a religious sense. People are going to these new religions for emotions, for experiences, not for reality. An experience always seems real, even if what you experience is illusory in nature.

"These results can do a great deal of good for people, of course, but not religiously, not in terms of truth. In that sense, all exercises are dangerous."

"Even Christian exercises?"

"Even Christian exercises."

"But what of all that one reads and hears about in the practices of the desert Fathers, for example?"

"Yes," he said—and paused. In that pause my mind went back to an unforgettable moment with Father Vasileios during our long night's conversation in the monastery turret of Stavronikita. He had startled both me and our interpreter by saying, "I could tell you of things a thousand times better than your Yoga." But he never said more, not even when pressed by the stunned interpreter.

I asked Metropolitan Anthony again about the work with the

body, about the methods, the exercises that I knew were in the Christian tradition—somewhere, in some time. Where did they come from? Where have they gone? The whole modern world is beginning to look for them as an indispensable element of what has been lost from the Christian path. In many places, contemplative practices are being reinstituted, spiritual retreats are attracting thousands upon thousands of people all over America. Are these methods written down somewhere? Is there a text that has not yet been rediscovered which speaks about them in a way that could guide this new search for the practical mysticism of the Christian path?

I waited for him to continue. He said something about the Athonite Christians having this work with the body, and then paused once again. And once again, I waited for him.

Finally, he raised his eyes toward me. "You have been to our service. If you stand in the service with your hands down to the side, with your head slightly down—not too much—your weight evenly balanced . . . if one does this, one begins to see changes taking place in the body. The breathing changes, certain muscles relax, others become firm—not tense. All this comes from the religious impulse, . . ."

Again a pause.

He continued, speaking softly and deliberately. *"The exercises you ask about originated in this way, from the Fathers observing what happened to them when they were in a state of prayer."*

Seeing and Gnosis; "Faith vs. Reason"

The notes I made just after leaving Metropolitan Anthony show this last statement circled and underlined. I had to write these notes rapidly, sitting in a noisy cafeteria on nearby Brompton Road, where I was due to meet with one of Metropolitan Anthony's pupils. Fortunately, she was late in arriving and I had time to reflect on the significance of what he had said.

My thoughts kept turning around the word "observing," "the Fathers observing what happened to them . . . in a state of prayer." This statement, if approached from a certain angle, completely undercut the distinction between "faith" and "reason" that has bedeviled people's understanding of Christianity over the centuries. The real division, the real choice, is not between "reason" and "faith." The important distinction is between consciousness of one's own states and the unconscious reactions of both thought *and* emotion. To choose between thought and emotion, "reason" and "faith," is to miss the point. Self-attention is the point; it is this that brings both real knowledge and real faith, which are in no way opposed to each other.

Here I felt, was the real approach to Christian *gnosis*, or salvational knowledge—knowledge that transforms the life and being of man. And I began to understand why this knowledge is spoken of so rarely or in such indirect ways in the known literature of the tradition. It has nothing to do with "knowing vs. believing."

In its most familiar form, the dichotomy between knowing and believing rests on an obvious element in everyone's experience. What the intellect knows may contradict what "the heart" believes. One may want to believe in immortality, for example, or in heaven and hell, or in the goodness of the world or in the existence of God. But, at the same time, such beliefs may be opposed to all one's logic, completely against the evidence at hand. Truth is independent of my wishes.

At the same time, Christianity recognizes that thinking, by itself, cannot bring about a change in human nature. Like every great religion, Christianity does not offer itself solely as an explanation of things but as a means of making things different, making man different. I may think great and true thoughts, I may have absolute integrity in my intellect, and yet at the same time I may not be able to live my life according to what I know is true or right. This, too, should be an obvious fact in everyone's experience. As long as my emotional life remains the way it is, all the right thinking in the world will not change my essential nature, my intimate self, my very being.

This latter point, however, is not at all obvious in our experience. Somehow, the intellectual grasping of a great idea is accompanied by the conviction, a sort of unconscious vow, that I will live according to this idea. It seems that no matter how often life proves us wrong about our powers in this regard, we continue to fall under the sway of this illusion. Thoughts, perhaps especially thoughts about the greatest truths, have this property of absorbing all our awareness, leaving us blind to the actual quality of the emotional and physical impulses that govern the whole of our everyday lives. In the language of Christianity, thought begets pride.

A similar teaching is to be found in all the religious traditions of the world. Proscriptions against making visual images of God or His messengers no doubt relate to this teaching. The severity of the punishments or consequences that the traditions say result from violating such rules can be best understood in modern language as an indication of the enormity of what man loses through failure to realize this seductive property of the thinking function. He loses everything; he loses the possibility of actually becoming what he seeks to become. When the traditions tell us that God is beyond the comprehension of the mind, they are not saying it is impossible to grasp the nature of God in the same way that it is difficult to grasp a complex scientific theory or to explain natural phenomena. On the contrary, the problem is that the mind, alone, can "comprehend" God, can form a thought of God. Only, such thoughts by themselves cannot change anything in ourselves. Something else is required, something far more difficult and elusive. Man must not place his hopes in the isolated intellect.

To put it another way, the hope of the mind, the wish for a relationship to Truth and Being, to God, does not lie in developing a part of the mind.

In the early centuries of our era, the teachings of Christianity encountered the tradition of Greek philosophy, which for the most part had long since become detached from the inner, moral discipline of the schools of Pythagoras, Socrates and Plato. For the ancient and medieval Christians, Greek philosophy was, generally speaking, the equivalent of what scientific thought is in the modern world: the intellectual explanation of reality. The greatest Christian theologians, such as John Scotus Erigena and Thomas Aquinas, never opposed the teachings of Plato to Christianity, but—especially in the case of Erigena—they recognized that a specific inner struggle was the foundation upon which metaphysical concepts could guide the transformation of human nature. Intellectual explanation as such could lead a man to begin the struggle but could never and must never take the place of the struggle within. These theologians offer a form of philosophy which we might call *contemplative metaphysics*, a form of inner empiricism in which the ideas about the invisible universe are studied and experienced in one's own inner world.

Our point here, however, concerns the wrong dichotomy between belief and reason that has gradually established itself in the Western approach to both the meaning of religion and, indeed, the meaning of life itself. The message of Tradition, in this respect, is that there is in man a force that draws him toward Truth. This force is neither the thinking function nor the emotional function as they are commonly understood. The word "faith" may be introduced here. But this word simply cannot be equated with "belief," in the sense of a conviction that is emotionally charged but opposed to intellectual explanations.

This internal force or impulse is "opposed" to *the whole of the ordinary mind,* including *both* reason and belief as they are conventionally defined. A far-reaching error thus seems to have crept into the understanding of Christianity when one part of the ordinary, or "fallen," mind, the thinking function, was distinguished from another part of the ordinary mind, the emotional function, and when this distinction was presented as exhaustive and central to the human condition. Man was asked to choose between belief and reason. But, from the present point of view, the enemy of faith is neither belief nor reason as such. The real enemy is man's tendency to give his trust to what is only a part of the mind or self, to take the part for the whole, to take a subsidiary element of human nature as the bringer of unity or wholeness of being.

The distinction between belief and reason has led, over the centuries, to historically momentous debates about the nature of religious authority and revelation. The Church in general required belief in ideas and propositions that the intellect could not assent to on the basis of ordinary experience and reflection. Opposed to this requirement, notably from the onset of the scientific revolution and the Enlightenment, was the demand for intellectual demonstration based either on logical reflection or empirical observation of the external world. The question "Where to go to find the source of Christian truth?" remained impaled on this highly dubious dichotomy.

And so it is still.

New Emotion, New Thought

The debate between belief and reason, as it applies to the contemporary quest for the "lost Christianity," will never end. One side stresses, and has always stressed, the need for emotional commitment to Christ, in which case there is little interest in new texts, new facts, new formulations—or, which comes to the same thing—in the rediscovery of ancient texts, lost patterns of Christian practice, hidden methods of inner discipline, etc. This approach makes no allowance for the distinction between *new emotions* (what Metropolitan Anthony called "feeling") and *old emotions with new objects*. This is a general problem of all human life, as we shall see it discussed in the writings of Father Sylvan. The problem can be simply stated as the illusion of a new or higher quality of emotion that accompanies what is merely a new object of emotion. This illusion is one of the chief factors, according to Father Sylvan, that keeps modern man in the state of what he terms "spiritual psychosis." I am sure that Metropolitan Anthony would agree, though with more moderate language perhaps.

The other side, the side of so-called "reason," stresses, and has always stressed, the need to understand, which means, in this context, the need for external confirmation and the distrust of emotional attraction or repulsion. In the Middle Ages, this approach urged the authority of Scripture and Church dogma with relatively little interest in inner experience. After the Renaissance, the Reformation, and the scientific revolution, this approach shifted to stressing logical demonstration and empirical evidence, while reliance on Scripture and Church authority passed over to the side of belief. In the present context, it may be seen as the great requirer of *credentials*—be they scholarly credentials, ecclesiastical, theological, historical or even political and ideological credentials. Here *lost* Christianity becomes *early* Christianity in the literal sense only. A person who goes to the representatives of this approach in search of the source of the Christian teachings will find not new understanding but the old understanding in new clothes, *not new thought but the old quality of thought with new things to think about,* such as unearthed

manuscripts or novel interpretations or hitherto unknown historical facts.

It is interesting to note that the difficulties associated with this
latter approach are exactly the same as those facing modern science in its efforts to understand the nature of the physical universe. New scientific theories and new data provided by techno-
logically sophisticated instruments provide new things to see,
but not a new quality of seeing.

For it is that, *seeing*, which is at issue. The old debate between reason and revelation, reason and belief, continues up to
the present day without either side suspecting that what is at
issue is the activation within the being of man of an entirely new
faculty of attention.

*The early Fathers observing what happened to them when
they were in a state of prayer:* this was the answer Metropolitan
Anthony gave to me when I asked about the origin of Christian
methods of spiritual struggle involving such elements as posture,
breathing, bodily sensing—those elements of the "lost Christianity" which so many people are now seeking.

Therefore, the following questions arise:

—This act of self-observation which Metropolitan Anthony
spoke of: is not this the seed of the real Christian *gnosis?* Surely,
this is not to be understood as the sort of "observation of oneself" that people engage in so commonly and which is actually
nothing more than thoughts and emotional reactions about oneself. Is not this seeing a level beyond the debate between belief
and reason that goes on within ourselves, as well as in the course
of history? Who or what in myself sees?

—The "state of prayer": why did he call it a *state?* Is observation, knowledge, of oneself only possible in a certain inner state?
Is knowledge that we gain in other states subject to distortion by
our emotions and thoughts? Is prayer a special struggle, a seeking, a condition of attention? If so, no wonder *gnosis* is "hidden"; no wonder the Alexandrine Fathers speak of it so guardedly, and no wonder that it never entered the mainstream of
the Christian doctine as it spread throughout the peoples of the
world. Salvational knowledge can only be acquired in a specific
state of consciousness!

No wonder the idea of dogma, which has become such a negative word for most modern people, developed in the way it did.

Mystery exists, the basic truths of the teaching exist, but they are hidden from us. But then, how did dogma become such an oppressive element for so many Christians? How did it change from being a system of ideas to guide one's search for relationship with the Higher into a rigid set of assertions that provoke the reaction of belief or disbelief?

And as for the question of the origins of Christianity, the early practices, the "lost" tradition, must we not say that these, too, are matters that cannot be settled by either the ordinary intellect or the ordinary emotions of man? Is not the question of the origin of religion itself a religious question—in the sense that it cannot be approached without at the same time seeking for the "origins" of Christianity within oneself? Could it be that the roots of Tradition can only be known in a specific inner state?

If so, then what becomes of all the information about the history of the Christian tradition that has been so prodigiously gathered, especially over the past century of Western scholarship and scientific investigation? Are there, as suggested earlier, two histories of Christianity, corresponding to the two directions that human life itself can take, two movements of life within human nature? What does the mass of outer information demand of us in terms of an inner search in order for this information to speak truly to us?

Chapter Three

Father Vincent

What Is a Priest?

Cold November afternoon. Skies gray and leaden; snow coming. My flight arrived early, and Father Dolan has not yet come to pick me up. I drift around the magazine stand, keeping my eye on Gate 32, finger a few newspapers, buy a pack of gum. I am nervous about everything. For five days I am to be the guest of one of the great Catholic universities in America and give five days' worth of lectures and seminars. They imagine they are getting a scholar of existentialist philosophy and psychology. And they are paying very good money.

I have warned them, but it didn't seem to matter. "It has been years," I wrote, "since I have been involved with the existentialists. I've become interested in Eastern systems of psychology and philosophy." No problem. Sounds very interesting. We will be interested in whatever you have to say.

But what I have not told them is that for years I have also been teaching courses in Christianity as well. Surely they will not want me, a Jewish professor of philosophy, to speak about the teachings of Christ to an audience that is not only Catholic but composed of theologians, nuns, priests, and even spiritual directors.

I peer down the corridor. Scurrying toward me is the person who is surely my host, a tall, rangy man of about fifty, wearing a tan mackinaw over a white knit sweater, his turned collar barely visible beneath it, and a tweed fedora. He recognizes me just as

I am recognizing him, and we exchange friendly smiles, warm greetings and good-natured complaints about the weather.

Driving from the airport, I feel surprisingly comfortable with this man. The reason is simple: he is an academic before he is a priest—at least he seems so to me. I had expected otherwise, which probably shows that I have gotten most of my picture of the clergy from the movies. I am surprised, and relieved, and faintly disappointed that I do not feel the alien ethnic identity of a priest of the Catholic Church. Little do I know that in the next five days this tiny, passing impression is to be replaced by a mammoth question obliterating every preconception I have had about the nature of the priesthood.

During the drive, I think about how little contact I have actually had with clergy, even of the Jewish faith. My only personal acquaintance with priests has been an occasional student in my classes or an occasional co-panelist at a symposium or academic conference. Odd.

And I saw that my image of the priest was of someone who had made some truly decisive sacrifice in his life—similar to what I understood of the monastic vow. As a teenager, I had felt similar things about rabbis, even after it was proved over and over again to me that it was a false assumption.

I was never sophisticated enough, or even sufficiently interested in the whole matter, to perceive anything like "hypocrisy" or "materialism" in the rabbis. My own Bar Mitzvah was, strictly speaking, a major fraud, a crash program of six months' cramming so that I could enunciate, without the slightest understanding, the necessary passages of the Hebrew Scriptures. My teacher, the neighborhood rabbi, was a sinewy old Russian who taught with an iron hand and who had rigid requirements of his pupils, making an exception with me only for the sake of my grandparents, who must have pleaded and implored quite a bit. Obviously, this was a man of enormous integrity and strength; but this was all before the days when anyone was concerned about making bridges between the old ways and the contemporary world. This rabbi was, purely and simply, an old Jew; you took him or left him as such. He was the Orthodox "tradition," solid and enduring, a rock. In the space of ten years, practically nothing of this world would remain.

The rabbis I saw as I grew older were so different from this one that I hardly even thought of them as rabbis. At the same time, in my head I did naïvely imagine that somewhere, somehow, there must have been a struggle, a spiritual encounter of some sort, a calling, a lifting—something of a higher order.

In any case, I never quite forgot the image of my Bar Mitzvah rabbi and the smile in his tough old eyes as I was intoning all the Hebrew perfectly, both of us knowing (as no one else in the congregation did) that I hadn't the slightest idea of the meaning of the language. That covert smile has remained with me through the years as a sign that although religious men and women were now literally trapped in stereotyped orthodox behavior and beliefs, behind it all was a spark—not of mere "warmth," but of a deep absence of hypocrisy and false idealism concerning the human condition. It has to do with the sense, which I soon lost and which I have only recently regained, that there exists somewhere a knowledge of the greatness of reality and the exact weaknesses of human nature, that deep within the feelings of man there is a love of reality and an attraction toward the Good, and that it is necessary to see human nature exactly for what it is, for this attraction toward Reality and the Good to become less hidden.

The rabbi's smile at my pretense and the fact that everyone else was being fooled, recognized me for what I was—and for what I wished to be, as if to say: "There is something beneath all these religious forms and 'good behavior' that has to do with the real God and the real man. And to reach that it is not necessary to pretend about anything. I give you that with this smile. What I cannot give, unfortunately, is the labor and struggle that is necessary for you to reach that deeply joyous level of real living and working. May you find it somewhere, somehow, in this life!"

To me, that is the cry of the orthodox ways in our time. But rare is the representative of tradition who can communicate that cry. I woke up twenty years later understanding the smile of my old rabbi, but of course I could never find him again.

As against this, the clergymen I had met, and the whole idea of a "priest," had come to represent the hypocrisy and impotence of "goodness." And then there was this allergic reaction I have always had toward anyone who speaks as if he knows precisely how God thinks and precisely what God wants.

Father Dolan quickly became "Ted" to me and I "Jerry" to him. He brought me up to the office of the Psychology Department and I met several of the faculty before proceeding to my living quarters. I was by then thoroughly at ease, and my curious mixture of disappointment and anxiety about the degee of "priestliness" was replaced by a feeling of respect for the savvy of the Catholic Church in allowing a university to be, on one level, simply a university, and a very good one in this case. In fact, I wasn't sure whether this was the result of wisdom that would allow secular values to be pursued against a containing background ambience of religion, or simply helplessness in the face of cultural change. Whatever it was, the Church was doing something more or less right, or so it seemed to me, whether by design or accident.

I was assigned to a special suite in the student dormitory. Ted had assured me that this would be extremely comfortable accommodations, plenty of privacy even though I would be rooming with two priests who were members of a missionary order associated with the university.

On hearing that, all my tensions returned, plus a few that I had not even known about. To have gone in one day from barely having ever spoken to a Catholic priest to the prospect of living for five days with not one but two priests, and missionary priests at that, was enough to bring back not only every fear and prejudice I had but all their relatives and grandchildren as well. How do priests eat? How do they sleep? How do they wash? Would there be some sort of rule of silence or some extended periods of prayer during which I would not be able to move around the room? Would I be obliged to participate in the prayers; would they be in Latin? Would the room be heated enough?

By the time I was putting the key in the lock, I was able to laugh at myself. My imagination had created the picture of a medieval cloister existing on the other side of the door. I half expected to encounter gaunt, kneeling monks, their heads bent in prayer, their fingers working rosaries, their eyes piercing into the depths of my flabby, non-Christian soul.

So I was thunderstruck by the tableau that met me as I opened the door: To my immediate right a slightly paunchy man in his fifties, wearing khaki trousers and a white T-shirt, slouches in a tan, vinyl-covered overstuffed armchair. Before him a TV set, color, tuned to a football game. Into that set he is staring without even lifting his eyes to me as I enter. In his left hand a can of Schlitz, and on the table next to him two empty beer cans. On top of one of the beer cans a burning cigarette struggles to stay alive in a bed of ashes and butts smoked down to their yellowed filters.

I prop open the door with my briefcase and drag my heavy bag inside. My "roommate" has still not acknowledged my arrival. The room is hot and stuffy; steam hisses from the radiators. Everything is plastic and lacquered wood. Big noise from the TV set, a touchdown. My "roommate" belches and leans forward in his chair, in order to perform which feat he has quickly to grind out his cigarette (wafting dead ashes down to the floor) and push himself up and forward, while uncrossing his legs, an operation which he does with great virtuosity and grace. Although I am already repelled by this man, I cannot help but register something special about his physical movements. He belches again, this time meditatively leaning forward to watch the instant replay.

To my regret, I am also now watching the game—with my overcoat still on. The point after touchdown is about to be attempted. It is important, a tie breaker. "Who're they playing?" I ask. "Green Bay," comes the answer without hesitation. Surrendering all my indignation, I sit down on the black vinyl couch and watch. The Packers block the point. My roommate shakes his head in disbelief. A commercial break.

This was Father Vincent. If after that first meeting someone had come up to me and suggested that eight years later I would be writing about him as I now wish to, I would have thought him crazy. For that matter, my impression of Father Vincent remained unchanged until the last day of my stay, when I began to understand everything about him in an extraordinary new way.

Once in my room, I washed up and began unpacking, when my second roommate happened by my door, Father John, a clean-shaven, fat, immaculately dressed and groomed priest, carrying a Bible and smiling that certain quasi-benedictory grimace that says far more about the man's professional training than about his interest in you or me. I recalled something I'd learned when I was being trained in clinical psychology. Our instructor advised us always to walk through the acute schizophrenic ward of the VA Hospital with our hands clutching our lapels—the "parson's posture." This way, you could most quickly put up your guard in case of physical attack by one of the patients. Walking through the ward in this posture, I was once approached by a new patient, who said to me, "Doctor, you are certainly a very thoughtful person!"

I had a cafeteria dinner with my two roommates and returned to my room to prepare the first lecture for the following morning. About Father Vincent I learned only that he had just returned from a long stay in Africa. Father John was much more communicative, but I remembered nothing of what he said even five minutes after he said it. About Father Vincent I remember even the food he selected.

Spiritual Psychology

During dinner, I attempted to try out some of the ideas I was going to speak about during the following days, but there was absolutely no interest on the part of Father Vincent and only a perfunctory, bored politeness by Father John.

I had a difficult time that evening. How to begin the series of lectures? I decided to concentrate on the idea of spiritual psychology, which the Eastern religions were bringing back to life in our culture. I would use the first lecture to try to define what could be meant by the term "spiritual psychology."

I felt that whatever I said would probably be controversial, but I did not want to be more provocative than necessary. I really was interested in understanding more about the possible interaction, on the deepest level of ideas, between Christianity and the traditions of the East. I was very familiar with the usual Christian reactions to such things as yoga, meditation, etc. One of the most familiar was to look upon the religions of the East, with their psychospiritual methods, as "Promethean." Appreciative accounts by Christians of Hindu or Buddhist forms usually ended by saying that the Christian must depend upon the grace of God, rather than his own efforts, and that spiritual methods of the sort taught by Eastern religions ultimately encourage man to rely too much on himself and not enough on God. Eastern religions are also often accused of "psychologism" or egoism, pointing man toward the experience of the higher within himself instead of opening him to the God above and beyond man, nature and the universe itself.

An especially clear statement of this attitude toward Eastern teachings I had found in the writings of Jean Daniélou, a cardinal of the Roman Catholic Church and professor of primitive Christianity at the Institut Catholique, in Paris. "In no way," Daniélou writes, "is it a question of deprecating the examples of interior life and of detachment which we find in non-Christian religions." But he goes on:

> China, along with the doctrines of Confucius, has brought us some admirable rules of wisdom for relations among men. India offers us the example of a people who have always seen in asceticism and contemplation the highest ideal. Nor can one read its masters, from the author of the Bhaghavad Gita to Aurobindo, without experiencing the feeling of the unreality of worldly goods and of the sovereign reality of the invisible world. It is understandable that, in our modern Western world, which is concerned only with harnessing the energies of the cosmos, and which has absorbed from Marxism the illusion that man can be transformed by changing his material living conditions, the wisdom of India attracts souls thirsting for silence and the interior life.
>
> But the fact remains that this assumes that man is able to reach God by his own powers. Christianity must categorically deny this, for two reasons. The first is the reality of original sin. This consists in a separation between man and God, which man cannot abolish by himself. . . .
>
> The second reason is that the Christian God is absolutely inaccessible. He alone can, therefore, introduce man to this participation in His nature which supernatural life is. For Hinduism, in fact, or neo-Platonism, the soul is divine by nature, and it only needs to move away from what is alien to it in order to find God by finding itself. . . . On the other hand, the first article of Christian faith is the doctrine of the Creator-God, that

is, the radical distinction between God and man. Accordingly, God alone is able to raise man to this participation in Him. . . . It is inaccessible to any human asceticism.

. . . For Christianity, the saved are those who believe, regardless of their level of interior life. A little child, a worker weighed down by his labors, if they believe, are superior to the greatest ascetics. . . . It is possible that there are in the world some great religious personalities outside Christianity; it may even happen that at a given time, the greatest religious personalities will be found outside Christianity. This is of no consequence. What does matter, is obedience to the words of Jesus Christ. . . .

Thus, compared with Christianity, the pagan religions seem out of date and distorted. Still, they contain some worthwhile elements. Would not their disappearance then be an impoverishment? Simone Weil feared that it would: "If the other traditions disappear from the surface of the earth," she wrote, "it would be an irreparable loss. As it is, the missionaries have already caused too many to disappear." Against this accusation, we must set forth the true concept of the Christian mission. Pius XII enunciated it thus in the encyclical *Divini Praecones:* "The Church has never treated the doctrines of the pagans with contempt and disdain; rather, she has freed them from all error, then completed them and crowned them with Christian wisdom."

This formula admirably sums up the attitude of Christianity. It does not treat the religious values of the pagan religions with disdain. But it first purifies them from all error, that is, it destroys the corruption—especially idolatry. . . .*

After one's strong reactions (positive or negative) to this statement subside, it is possible to take it as the basis of some ex-

* Jean Daniélou, "The Transcendence of Christianity," Chapter 9 of *Introduction to the Great Religions* (Notre Dame, Ind.: Fides Claretian, 1964).

tremely important issues now facing modern people in their search for meaning in life. And in my opening lecture I wanted to center this issue around the question of spiritual psychology. By this latter term, I meant in part to refer to the absolute necessity that modern man become free, if only a little, from his emotional reactions about himself.

I take this to be an essential element of what Metropolitan Anthony was speaking of, although of course at the time of these lectures I did not see things in quite those terms. The point is that emotional reactions, the desire-nature (to use a religious term), are an enemy of truth when they force thought and awareness into self-deceptions. Egoistic reactions about oneself, one's own moral or intellectual qualities, are surely translatable into some notion of a primal human error.

I take the aim of spiritual psychology to be the directing of our attention to what is really the case in ourself, free from egoistic reactions about ourself. Insofar, then, as the language of Christianity has become entangled with emotional reactions, rather than with the call of feeling (in Metropolitan Anthony's terms), it is necessary at an early stage for many modern people to have the language of religion restated in the scientific language of psychology—without necessarily buying into the view of human nature that modern systems of psychology are based upon.

Psychology and Scale

I shall touch on these ideas in some detail as we proceed in this book. The point I wish to make here, and the point I wanted to stress in my opening lecture, was that a number of the Eastern religions were offering themselves in this way, in the language of psychology.

These traditions themselves recognized the special problems this language can present, precisely those which trouble Father Daniélou. Psychology can reduce the scale of one's search and can lead to syntheses and crystallizations of a superficial kind relative to what is possible and what is demanded of man. Therefore every great tradition presents man with the constant encounter between himself and an infinitely greater objective scale of reality. This is true no matter what stage of the path the pupil or devotee has reached. In Theravada Buddhism, which to the outsider seems to stress only the individual's own efforts and his own awareness, this infinitely greater scale of reality is communicated through the urgency of the human situation, especially the fact of death and suffering. In Mahayana Buddhism, the objective scale is brought home through profound cosmological ideas, especially the notion of the Void, and through the imperative to strive for the salvation of all sentient beings throughout the universe. No matter how high an individual's spiritual attainment, it is as nothing when held against the need of the whole universal creation for liberation.

I intended to bring examples of this aspect from all the traditions. In Christianity, clearly, the salvational power of Christ and the Holy Spirit is an unimaginably vast and profound universal scale of reality, against which human effort pales to insignificance; and the degree to which man needs this miraculous help is also of such a scale as to reduce human efforts to help oneself to something worse than useless.

At the same time, however, the traditions have recognized that wrong emphasis on the greatness of God leads to passivity in man: the sin of sloth on the one hand or pride on the other. It is not hard to see how an excessive and emotionally heated reliance on God can lead to passivity in the sense of spiritual laziness and wishful thinking. One simply glazes over one's habitual patterns of living and reacting with the thought of "grace." But the egoistically manipulative side of human nature may also, paradoxically, be nourished by this wrong emphasis on an external God. This happens in all areas of human life where man is certain he has found the complete truth. The impulses to act, the factor of aspiration in man, become more and more outwardly directed and mix with the fears and desires that are always present in the human organism. Moreover, in order to correspond to the idea of the God's transcending greatness, the individual is drawn inevitably to seek a high level of intensity in his experiences. But, being what we are, the highest intensities of experience are usually one or another form of emotional violence, particularly as mixed with the energies of sex.

The Theory and Practice of the Search

My aim was to present the idea of spiritual psychology as the reconciling idea, for our time and place, with respect to the opposition between grace and effort. Beyond the passivity of theism on the one hand and the self-manipulation of psychologism on the other hand, there lies, as I saw it, the act of searching.

The *search*, in its real sense, is the property of a part of the mind, of the self, that neither modern psychology nor establishment religion acknowledges. To search means, first, I need Being, Truth; second, I do not know where to find it; and third, an action takes place that is not based on fantasies of certainty—while at the same time a waiting takes place that is rooted not in wishful thinking but in a deep sense of urgency.

I wanted to characterize spiritual psychology as the theory and practice of the search for truth—its necessary conditions, as well as the obstacles to it, within man himself. I intended to conclude by putting my point as forcefully as possible: "Without such a discipline, without such a search, even God Himself is powerless to help man."

But, in the actual lecture, I never even came close to that point. What interested people most—there were about 250 in the audience—was not the significance of Asian religions but the possibility that someone might be offering a new criticism of Freud. This was the East Coast, after all.

At first, it puzzled me. I was saying things and citing quotations from other sources that should certainly have aroused questioning, debate and perhaps even anger. For example, I played part of a talk by Krishnamurti in which he characterizes the genuinely religious life as the life of wholeness, a wholeness, however, that comes about precisely through observing, without altering, the fragmentation of our nature. I had not played the tape for some time and had forgotten many of the details of his talk—I simply knew the thrust of it, and I wanted my audience to hear how these things could be spoken about in a language understandable by modern people. But I nearly leaped out from behind the lectern to shut off the tape recorder when I heard him launching into one of his attacks on organized religion—in this case using Catholicism as his prime example of authoritarian conditioning of the mind, and going on to specify priests as the destroyers of the sacred in man!

I certainly had not wanted to come across as an attacker, not even indirectly. And as Krishnamurti went on with his extremely pointed criticisms of religion, I tried to think of what I could say that would bring the lecture around again to the spirit of inquiry, rather than argument. To my surprise, however, no one seemed upset in the slightest. Several nuns in the first row continued to take notes diligently, without once breaking stride. The others just looked on, attentive, interested.

What the hell was going on? Didn't they understand that this man was surgically pulling apart the very foundations of their own lives and beliefs? He was saying that the principal cause of human misery was the tendency of man to inflict mechanical thoughts upon the whole of his nature, resulting in all the conflict, violence and injustice of human history, and that organized religion was even more culpable than political ideologies in that it disguised its promotion of this process with "sacred" ideas such as God, salvation, spirituality, etc. So-called Christian love, for example, was only the head trying to tell the body and the feelings what to do, animated by the impulses of fear and greed. Real love, according to Krishnamurti, was impossible without freeing the energy of the psyche from the sway of mechanical thoughts, through an attention to oneself in all the conditions of living.

But no one was especially interested in that, and all the discussion centered around Freud and modern psychology. I promised my audience that the next day I would speak at length about Freud.

A Game of Cards

I returned to my rooms tired and a bit depressed around eleven that night, after having dinner at one of the faculty homes in the neighboring hills. Sure enough, there was Father Vincent glued to the TV. For some reason, this irritated me enormously, and I believe I walked past him without even saying hello. I went right into my room, threw my briefcase on the desk and my overcoat on the bed, and sat down on the chair trying to collect

myself. To no avail. I sprang up and went ~~back into the living~~
room en route to the kitchen. This time I did manage a perfunctory nod to Father Vincent, who raised his hand to me without
taking his eyes off the set. He was wearing a two-tone red-and-
gold windbreaker, like some overage varsity athlete.

I opened the refrigerator door, took out the container of or-
ange juice and sat down at the kitchen table. On the table there
was a deck of cards laid out in the middle of a solitaire game.
After drinking the juice, I started fiddling with the cards and
finally heard myself calling out to Father Vincent, "How about a
game of gin rummy?"

He immediately turned off the TV and came to the table. To
be truthful, I have never seen a person move faster or more
gracefully. Out of the corner of my eye, very faintly and very
fleetingly, I caught an impression: the suddenness with which he
had turned off the set; I had noticed he was watching a movie,
and I had even noticed which movie: it was *Paths of Glory*, a
good one.

And there he was, seated at the table as though he had suddenly materialized from another world.

I shuffled the cards and dealt, after reaching for a paper nap-
kin to keep score on.

Father Vincent scoops up the cards. "What are we playing
for?" he asks as he arranges them in his hand. This surprises me.
I assumed we would not be playing for money. I eye him—for
the first time all priest associations are gone from my mind. He is
a stranger and we are gambling.

Just for the hell of it I say, "A penny a point?"

"Are we playing California?"

"Sure," I say, turning up the knock card.

"Too steep. Try a tenth."

And that is exactly right: a tenth of a cent a point in Califor-
nia-style gin rummy, three games cumulative, schneider double.
If you schneider your opponent (prevent him from scoring any
points) in all three games, you can win a respectable amount,
and with good luck over a whole night's play, you could conceiv-
ably make thirty or forty dollars. Enough to make the game interesting.

I am a fairly good gin player, and after the first hour I begin
to worry that I will win too much from him. He handles his

cards very well, arranges them quickly and makes quick decisions, but occasionally he says or does something that indicates he is not as familiar with the game as he appears. I later discovered that it had been twenty years since he last played.

But his concentration is impressive, and as we enter the early morning hours, he begins to take large bites out of my lead. My sleeves are rolled up and I am now guzzling juice, coffee, crackers and anything else I can get my hands on. He, however, has remained fairly cool. As time passes, he starts to draw up even with me, and finally I find myself on the short end of a triple schneider!

And now my irritation with this man returns in full force, augmented by a wounded ego as I start losing with horrible regularity. Where did he learn to play like that? He seems to be seeing right through my cards, knocking when I am loaded with high cards, ginning just before I do, picking up cards from the pile in no recognizable pattern, and mysteriously withholding just what I need when there seems no possible way he could know it.

Two in the morning and I am down thirty-two dollars. By then, however, my irritation and anger had actually faded away. No, that is not exact. What began to happen is that, without having thought about it beforehand, I began to get interested in my own wounded ego. I think that is about as accurately as I can describe it. I was still trying as hard as I could to beat him, but at the same time something appeared in myself that was interested only in watching my own reactions of annoyance, disgust, resentment, injustice. The latter was quite a shock: I saw, as clearly as I saw the cards in front of my face, the origins in myself of the sense of injustice and outrage that governs so much of our inner life. I smelled the egoism in this sense of injustice! the hurt feelings—and I caught a fleeting glimpse of the huge, complicated thinking apparatus being called in to serve this wounded ego with all the ideas, arguments and amassed evidence at its disposal.

With that, my whole body suddenly came alive. My back straightened, my eyes opened wider, and I felt awake in every tissue of my body. Also, I began to win again.

Father Vincent—Vince—soon began showing signs of fatigue, and his eyes started drooping as we played on. Finally, it was I who called a halt. I paid him what I owed, eighteen dollars, which he accepted without fuss, and we both went to bed.

Seeing Father Vincent

At six the following morning, my eyes sprang open after only two and a half hours' sleep. I was certain I needed more sleep, but my body did not agree and there was nothing to do but get up and dress.

I moved quietly around the suite so as not to awaken my roommates, but to my surprise they were both up already. I saw them, on the way out, in the little chapel room situated off to the far side of the living room and separated by sliding panels, usually closed. I caught a glimpse of the bulky figure of Father John standing in profile in the semidarkness of the early morning, head bowed over an open Bible or prayerbook, two candles on either side burning brightly. A pale lavender light was just beginning to break through the single band of windows behind the head of Father John, illuminating his white collar. I caught an even more fleeting glimpse of Vince—somehow I was embarrassed to really look at what they were doing. The single-frame image of Vince is of him very clean-shaven and looking remarkably fresh. Magenta priestly robes. A silver crucifix hanging around his neck and catching a little of the candlelight. He is adjusting some things on the altar. I have never seen—and yet I have seen—quite the attitude as there was in him, in his face and posture. It is the attitude of someone who has done the same thing thousands of times, every day of his life. There is clearly something completely rote and mechanical about his movements. Yet it is all animated by something else as well. I know what it is! He is like a woman moving around her kitchen! She has done it thousands of times, she knows exactly what is next, and her body manifests it through a sort of overeconomy; too little is put into the movements. Yet she is also strangely serious, and though both she and the husband who comes home to her know his work is "more important," they both sense that her work exists at a deeper level than his.

I knew—or rather sensed, for I didn't really formulate it to myself—from that moment on that there was a quality to Father Vincent's life that I needed to understand. It is extraordinary how such a tiny, fleeting impression such as this can actually be the most significant event of an entire day, even a day filled with far larger, "more important" events and insights. Of course, the truth is that in that fleeting glimpse of Father Vincent, I myself was in a special condition of balance; one does tend to forget that these rare, fragile impressions, these "mustard seeds" point in two directions: toward the inner state of the subject and toward the new reality revealed in the object. Because we have lacked a language and a true science dealing with the former, we have for a long time had our interest taken up entirely by the latter. This has had especially negative consequences in the history of Christianity in the Western world.

"Acornology"

I began my lecture that morning from just this point. There is an innate element in human nature, I argued, that can grow and develop only through impressions of truth received in the organism like a special nourishing energy. To this innate element I gave a name—perhaps not a very good name—the "higher unconscious." My aim was to draw an extremely sharp distinction between the unconscious that Freud had identified and the unconscious referred to (though not by that name) in the Christian tradition.

Imagine, I said, that you are a scientist and you have before you the object known as an acorn. Let us further imagine that you have never before seen such an object and that you certainly do not know that it can grow into an oak. You carefully observe these acorns day after day and soon you notice that after a while they crack open and die. Pity! How to improve the acorn? So that it will live longer. You make careful, exquisitely precise chemical analyses of the material inside the acorn and, after much effort, you succeed in isolating the substance that controls the condition of the shell. Lo and behold, you are now in the position to produce acorns which will last far longer than the others, acorns whose shells will perhaps never crack. Beautiful!

The question before us, therefore, is whether or not modern psychology is only a version of *acornology*.

Freud and Human Possibility

Obviously, I went on, Freud was right in seeing that something essential in the development of the normal human being was being suppressed in modern culture. By pointing to the animal, sexual aspect of man, however, he made a theory about a force that cannot be seen by the mind. One cannot, according to the great traditional teachings of the world, of which Freud was largely ignorant, know the sexual force in oneself by the intellectual or emotional process. To know life, one must be able to see life and, as Zen teaches, and also as Christianity and Judaism teach, life moves more swiftly and subtly than the theoretic mind or the personal emotions.

The power to see may, however, be taken to represent the developmental force in man. Freud seems almost to have emphasized this; had he done so, a great deal might have been different. He taught that through insight the "cure" is effected. From what I am able to judge from my own personal studies of traditional teachings, what Freud meant by insight or self-knowledge is very far from what the traditions recognize as self-knowledge. Therefore no matter what, Freudianism by itself could never have led man toward the real development possible for him.

Nevertheless, taken *analogically*, Freud was surely right and his method surely a guide. It was the seeing, not the thing seen, that cured, that helped. Not realizing this, the whole movement shifted to theorizing about sexuality, i.e., life. Which brought the center of gravity of human existence back again into the suppressive mind, the theoretical mind imposing its products (its "insights") on life, the body.

As a result, in my opinion, Freudianism institutionalized the underestimation of human possibility. The neurotic suffering of man comes about, according to tradition, from his lack of self-knowledge, not from his suppression of sexuality; from the lack of relationship of his essential parts, not from the suppression of a form of sexual desire that is itself already a negative result of inner fragmentation.

At that point, I came to the end of my written notes, realizing in advance that before proceeding I would have to do a great

deal of defining and defending. Already there were several
hands waving impatiently. But I didn't want to stop. I felt on the
edge of understanding something—because my line of reasoning
had brought me to a point where I didn't know how to go on
and yet where I saw I absolutely had to go on. I wanted to speak
more about the suppression, the covering over of the organ of
deep learning in man; the part of the mind that receives experiences and impressions and takes them in. This has been the far
more serious repression in modern society. Deep in man, at the
core of his being, there exists the need for experiences of truth.
Around this need everything else in him is arranged like planets
around the sun.

There are countless stories and symbols in the traditions that
speak of this central need of the human organism, that which
distinguishes man from the animals. In the East, of course, there
is a very well-developed symbolism of what might be termed the
physiology of self-knowledge. There is a learning that takes
place in the cells and tissues, in the organic impulses of the
body; for the sake of this learning, man was created—so we are
told in many forms in the Koran, for example when the angels
doubt Allah's wisdom in creating man and Allah answers them,
"I know what you do not know." In Mahayana and Vajrayana
Buddhism, the doctrine of the chakras clearly informs us that the
human organism is, above all, a system of levels of mind embed-
ded or incarnated in matter.

I tried to answer questions about what I had said, while my
mind was racing around the subject of what I wanted to say. Because I was not paying the best attention to my questioners, but
was instead worrying about my own question, I soon found myself backed into a corner by some of the more practical-minded
therapists in the audience, who had gotten me on the horns of
some contradiction or other in what I had said about Freud and
psychiatry. I bid a reluctant farewell to my own thoughts about
the biological and physiological effects of self-ignorance in man
and tried to reply to my "attackers" (actually two very courteous gentlemen).

I was in a bit of trouble. I didn't know what my contradiction
was supposed to be, since I hadn't been following anything very
well for several minutes. Such situations occur very frequently in
the lives of professors, far more frequently than we care to

admit. It is usually a rather easy problem to solve; you say something like "Would you mind restating your question, please?" or "Did everyone hear that question—would you repeat it?" Or some such obvious fudge. I myself have never yet said, "Pardon me, I was more interested in something else and haven't heard a word you've said."

For some reason, I did none of this. Out of the clear blue sky, an approach to my own question sailed into view just as I was about to attend to my questioners. Through some short-circuiting of my brain, I put this new thought on my lips as the answer to whatever was being asked. I did not take even a second look at this new thought. Instead, I found myself saying, in a rather loud voice and with considerable posing—as though I had thought carefully about the question:

"Has it ever occurred to anyone that the whole corruption of religion, and therefore of civilization, begins when the work of self-knowledge becomes subjectively less interesting than sexual fulfillment?

I found myself looking at four slightly raised eyebrows as my interlocutors waited for me to continue and develop what they justifiably assumed was an answer to their question, whatever that was. To my surprise, I heard a penetrating voice from the audience amending the thought I had just begun to express:

"And when this fact isn't squarely seen and accepted!"

I looked over to the back of the hall toward the left. It was Father Vincent.

The Natural Attraction to Truth

In fact, I never did find out what the question to me had been. Although Father Vincent's response completely astonished me for many reasons, and encouraged me to go on trying to develop the idea, the audience would not allow it. Their response to the whole brief exchange between Father Vincent and me had been a rather insistent, though good-natured, laughter. Even my two elderly, courteous interlocutors seemed eager for me to go on to the next question. As I did so, I saw Father Vincent getting up in the back row and leaving the auditorium.

Of course, it had been stupid of me to express it in quite that way, but nevertheless the point was worth pondering: does there exist in man a *natural attraction* to truth and to the struggle for truth that is stronger than the natural attraction to pleasure? The history of religion in the West seems by and large to rest on the assumption that the answer is no. Therefore, externally induced emotions of egoistic fear (hellfire), anticipation of pleasure (heaven), vengeance, etc., have been marshaled to keep people in the faith.

The whole notion of sainthood, both in the East and in the West, has contributed to this assumption. The saint is often presented as though he were a being with an *unnaturally* strong impulse toward truth. The pictures of the saint's sacrifices and asceticism are so presented as to assure the rest of us that what he attained is impossible for us. This, of course, easily supports human passivity and wishful thinking, for at the same time that one is endowing the saint with an unnaturally strong impulse toward truth one might as well endow him, in the bargain, with a miraculous power to help the seeker without the latter making any real efforts of inner questioning and search.

This issue is faced directly in the great masterpiece of Tibetan Buddhism, *The Life of Milarepa*. Surely Milarepa's life goes beyond any normal human possibility if ever a life did. His feats of spiritual endurance, constancy of aim, bodily sacrifice and emotional renunciation are staggering; the degree of enlightenment he reached is incomparable, the help he transmitted to others inconceivable.

Toward the end of his life, he was asked by one of his close followers:

Lama Rimpoche, it seems to me that you are either the incarnation of Vajradhara Buddha and that you engage in all these actions for the benefit of sentient beings, or you are a great Bodhisattva who has attained the state of "Non-returning" and who has accumulated immense merit for many aeons. In you I see all the characteristics of a true yogin who sacrifices his life for the Dharma practice. We human individuals cannot even conceive the extent of your asceticism and your devotion to your lama, let alone practice it ourselves. If we dared to practice in this way, our bodies could not bear such an ordeal. That is why it is certain that you were a Buddha or Bodhisattva from the very beginning. And so, although I am incapable of religion, I believe that we sentient beings will be led toward liberation from samsara through seeing your face and hearing your words. Revered Master, I beg you to tell us if you are the incarnation of a Buddha or a Bodhisattva.†

To this, Milarepa answers—with, one may surmise, impatience in his voice: "I never heard whose incarnation I am. Maybe I am the incarnation of a being from the three lower realms. . . ." And he goes on:

Although this belief that I am an incarnation springs from your devotion to me, actually there is no greater impediment to your practice. It is a distortion of the true Dharma. The fault lies in not recognizing the true nature of the achievement of great yogins.

And Milarepa then speaks about the conditions under which there arises from within a man the "great longing for liberation." Finally, he says to this disciple:

It is possible for every ordinary man to persevere as I have done. To consider a man of such perseverance as the reincarnation of a Buddha or as a Bodhisattva is a sign of not believing in the short path. Put your faith in the great law of cause and effect. Contemplate the lives of enlightened teachers; reflect upon karma, the misery of the cycle of existence, the true value of human life, and not knowing the hour of death. Devote yourselves to the practice of the Vajrayana.

This issue, with respect to the idea of the incarnation of God in Christ, was well worth going into. And it was a very complex issue. Were I to go into it as the substance of the next lecture, it could lead to all sorts of theological debates about the divinity or humanity of Jesus Christ, and that I wanted to avoid, because the issue was not one of theology, but of psychology—that is, the

† Lobsang P. Lhalungpa (transl.), *The Life of Milarepa* (New York: E. P. Dutton, 1977), pp. 143–44.

question had to do with an exact knowledge of the whole of the human mind. If there is a natural attraction toward truth in man, how can it be reached and guided? Where in man does it exist? Why is it so deeply hidden? How to avoid the error of identifying it with some other impulse that is only an imitation or, at best, lower reflection of it—such as the desire for explanations? What kind of help does man need? And what must he—what can he—contribute from himself?

With only one slight change, of course, the issue falls into a nest of clichés: Is there a natural goodness in man? Or is he poisoned by "sin" down to the core of his being?

Well, these questions have preoccupied the Western world even before the days of the great heresies of Arianism and Pelagianism; the former holding that Christ is subordinate to God, the latter holding that there is a natural goodness in man.

Were the whole heresy business to come up in the lecture, everything would be thrown out of kilter. Not only was I not expert in the historical side of it, but the very aim of the lectures and the very idea of spiritual psychology as I understood it would have been thwarted. How to set aside all the past associations with these questions and try to approach them as questions about ourselves without unnecessary emotional investment in "answers" discovered by someone else a long time ago?

The question was, Is there in me a natural attraction toward truth and the struggle for truth? Had Christianity as we know it lost contact with this fact, if fact it is, of human nature? Had the Church, somewhere—and perhaps out of wisdom—acknowledged that it could no longer construct itself to reach that part in man and had fallen back on a lesser idea, the teaching of total sin, in order to forestall the forces of egoism in man, the imaginary belief in one's own powers, goodness and love of truth?

It was not such a bad way to put it: Was there an impulse toward God that is stronger than the pleasure principle? It could be spoken of in this way so as to relate to the general preoccupation with Freud and Freudian theory. Inevitably, of course, one would also have to face the notion of the sublimation of the sexual impulse, a notion that figured so largely in Freudian theory and which, in similar words at least, also formed an essential part in the great spiritual teachings of the world. And here the question would be, How to see for what it was the mechanical linkage of religious thoughts or images with the inner sensations of sex, and distinguish it from the actual, literal transmutation of sexual energy? The term "sublimation" was originally intended to refer to the latter process, as in the alchemical tradition. But how much of so-called mystical or religious experience in the Western tradition was only the former? In fact, how much of the whole of one's life was only the former? Had Freud, granted he was blind to the real notion of the transmutation of sexual energy, actually *not stressed enough* the role of sex in the pathology and ultimate meaninglessness of our unexamined lives?

This was getting interesting—to me, at any rate. Anyone who answered with a quick *yes* the question of an impulse toward truth that was equal to the pleasure principle would have to, as it were, defend himself against Freud. I was glad to have Freud as an ally, for once.

Conversation in Two Worlds

When I returned to my rooms after dinner that evening, I was at first disappointed to find only Father John. But I took the occasion to try to learn something about Father Vincent, who was intriguing me more and more.

After Father John told me enough to satisfy any normal amount of polite curiosity—namely, that Vincent had done missionary work in Africa for twenty years and would now be remaining in the States for a while—he circuitously tried to find out why I was interested in learning more. But how could I answer that when I myself did not know what it was about the man that drew me?

The answer began to appear when Vincent entered, at about ten o'clock. A part of myself came alive as he walked in and sat down among us. And then an odd thing took place. For the next hour or so, as the three of us conversed, I experienced a distinct division in myself. When I was addressing Father John, I was quite animated and articulate, to the point of developing some new ideas that would be useful in the next morning's lecture. But when my attention was directed at Father Vincent I stumbled for words and grew irritated. And when I said to Vincent that I was interested in his comment at the lecture, he did not acknowledge me at all; it was just short of actual rudeness.

Conversation proceeded; every time that Vincent spoke, I experienced a sensation of tension in my solar plexus.

Everyone began yawning at about eleven, and John was the first to excuse himself. That left Vincent and me. I was glad and nervous about this. Vincent was real for me, the most real person I had met in a long time, no matter how antipathetic in certain respects. I could not charm him, impress him, lead him onto my turf; I could not even be sure I was attracting his attention.

And yet, there was his quickness of response on the very few occasions when a response was really called for.

And there was this impersonal quality about him that seemed so . . . well, un-"spiritual," or un-"Christian."

It was really beginning to gnaw at me. Was it just myself? Was I only imagining things? Was he perhaps only some dull clod whose reactions just by chance were pressing certain of my subjective levers and causing me to project all sorts of qualities, negative and positive, upon him?

Vincent remained seated across from me, smoking a cigarette. He had a very clear, pink complexion, gray-blue eyes and closely cropped, silky white hair.

I stood up. I had no idea what I was going to do—turn on the TV? get a snack from the refrigerator? excuse myself and go to bed? Instead, I found myself sitting down again and saying, "Do you mind if I ask you a few questions about the situation in the contemporary Church?" I went for my notebook to make it look more or less professional. Of course, at that moment I couldn't have cared less about Vince's opinions on the Church.

He replied, without much hesitation: "A few deaths in high places are needed."

I stared at him.

Finally, I laughed and nodded my head knowingly.

But he did not laugh back. He looked at me as though he felt I hadn't understood what he'd said. "In very high places," he said.

Uncomfortable (for me) silence. What sort of creature was this Father Vincent? I sat back in my chair, and in my desperation to know what to say or how to be with this person, I decided simply to say whatever came into my mind, without editing it. As a result, there then followed one of the strangest conversations I have ever had in my life. I made no attempt to bridge one theme to another, no attempt to structure everything around the social graces. But inside myself everything was raging; all my upbringing, all my habits of speaking and dealing with people were constantly pulling at me. Yet there was simply no reason to obey these impulses. I wasn't trying to be "natural," or anything like that, not in the slightest.

I have of course had conversations with some remarkable people in the world, including spiritual leaders from other traditions and in other parts of the world. But because they had the "robe of office," were "officially" spiritual or religious teachers, I was able to suppress the ordinary conversational and social habits and talk more directly and with less fear of appearances.

With Vince it was entirely different. And I see now that those conversations, just mentioned, with official spiritual leaders, are open to suspicion. The conversations, not the leaders. I mean to say that my "spiritual personality" took over very nicely in such cases. My other personality was set aside—I should say blotted out—quite easily. I "knew" the people were "religious." With Vince I knew no such thing. He had no credentials. Even the thought that he had no credentials was absent. He was ordinary, ordinary, ordinary. And yet he was turning me inside out.

When I started to ask him a question dealing with spiritual or personal issues, the thought nagged at me that he was nothing very special at all. And when I spoke to him as an equal, the opposite feeling pulled at me.

And so, the question has arisen in my mind: What is the real meaning and function of hierarchy in a spiritual organization? What does a *priest* evoke in us? What does the office of the priest cover over and conceal in us?

The talk went on long into the night; to reproduce it here, even if that were possible, could not communicate its strangeness.

I will relate some of the interesting content concerning Father Vincent's life as an African missionary. But before presenting that material, I want to stress what it was that emerged from my knowing him and why I devote a chapter to him as an example of the questions relating to lost Christianity.

That evening, I saw with unforgettable clarity that the very least idea of the Christian tradition, and this surely applies to any authentic spiritual teaching, requires of man a quality of inquiry to which one may apply the term "voluntary suffering." Readers who are familiar with the writings of G. I. Gurdjieff will recognize this as his term, and I certainly do not mean to imply that I am using it in the precise sense meant by Gurdjieff. But no other words seem adequate to describe the persistent sense of "being-in-between" that accompanied my talk with Father Vincent. My religious side and my "worldly" side were both suspended—or, rather, both existed and pulled me, but neither by itself nor both together could prevail.

I discovered that there is an aspect of my nature that is neither spiritual nor worldly, and to be situated in that part of myself meant to experience a sort of suffering that simultaneously was new to me and had a flavor of familiarity, a distinct "my-own-ness." Also, and most important, I had constantly to *choose* it.

Had Vincent had more "credentials," had I been able to say to myself that he was "making me uncomfortable" as a form of "skillful means," my experience would no doubt have been very different—as it has been when I have met spiritual personages from the traditions, such as Zen masters, Tibetan lamas or Sufi sheiks.

What is this place in between my two natures? Why is it such bittersweet suffering to be situated there? Bittersweet because the sense of my-own-ness was really quite extraordinary. I was lost, uncertain, irritated, frustrated, and yet somehow I wished to remain in that state. I existed. And I must say, without being able to prove it in writing, that this wish had a completely different flavor from what usually goes under the name of desire or "interest" or "religious yearning."

I have since learned that this experience, unforgettable though it was, is only the merest foretaste of the reality between the two natures of man, and certainly only the merest brush with the suffering (the bitter) and the "voluntary" (the sweet) that it entails.

The issue here is that ultimate religious experience, "mysticism," brings man into the higher realms but is not in itself the fulfillment of his possible being. René Guénon relegates all mysticism to the realm of the *religious;* the realm of the esoteric is entirely different for him and points to a wholly different level of spiritual discipline and knowledge.‡ Father Sylvan, for his part, writes:

> The idea of levels of Christianity may never again be known in the West. There is an intermediate level of Christianity which teaches the way that the higher level becomes distorted. We need the intermediate level. We need to observe how we lose Christianity, lose mysticism, lose the energy of God. Here lies the origin of sin and repentance, on the border between heaven and hell.

The Life and Search of Father Vincent

Father Vincent related the following about his life as an African missionary. He told this story just after exclaiming to me:

"Christian? I'm not a Christian! There are no Christians!"

He began by telling me that his own youthful fantasies about Africa had nothing to do with "saving the heathen," although even he was surprised at how little "converting" went on. As a matter of fact, he had some interesting things to say about the whole missionary enterprise, how it needed to be reinterpreted in terms of human fellowship, rather than in the clichés about leading whole tribes or cultures into a new religion. "I learned from these people far more than I ever taught them."

No, his own dreams had to do with Africa as the origin of life, and of Christianity. The wish to help others was the main motivation, but the love of nature gave him strength and lent something necessary to his love of God and his love of human beings.

He spoke of several experiences, but with such brevity that I had to press him in order to get any details at all. One had to do with helping a medical team deal with a sudden epidemic and involved risking their lives to get people onto boats and down a dangerously swollen river. "I remember our broken-down boat—it would have been risky floating it in a swimming pool—charging down that river, people screaming and weeping; the crew—meaning myself and three other priests whose knowledge of how to handle a boat added up to half of nothing—managing some-

‡ See René Guénon, *Aperçus sur L'Esotérisme Chrétien* (Paris: Les Editions Traditionnelles, 1954).

how to pilot it to the neighboring village where the people not yet infected could be taken care of. We did that a dozen or so times within a forty-eight-hour span, carrying the boat back on our shoulders through the jungle each time.

"Toward the end of the second night, there was a moment just before dawn when the river was quiet and the people were all quiet. Suddenly, everything in myself became still, including my body, which had been in agony from stress and exhaustion. I felt the presence of God. The smells of the jungle and the river, the night sounds, the sensation of heat in the air—everything seemed part of the Oneness of God. Everything was motionless in eternity. All the things I had been afraid of—the sickness, the danger of drowning, of failing; all my personal revulsions and resentments—and there were plenty of them—everything appeared before me also as part of God. I felt an overwhelming gratitude toward God that He had given me this work to do. I prayed in a way that I had never before prayed; I knew it was the Son praying to the Father through myself."

This certainty never left him afterward, he said.

Another experience, not long after: "We had been working for over a year to build a school. It was damned difficult; no one knew how to do anything. For some reason, the elders of the tribe began to get angry with me, and just before the building was finished, they insisted that I leave. Why? I didn't know. I went to see the chief elder, who I had thought was a good friend. He would not even let me enter his house. But I remember his wife looking at me with pity when I stood at his doorway.

"Nothing that I understood about their religion could help me understand what was going on. Emissaries were sent, but with no effect. I had to leave, and soon.

"All the preparations for my departure were made, but the night before I was scheduled to go I had a dream unlike any I had ever had in my life. It was vivid as only nightmares are vivid, yet basically it was not at all frightening. I dreamt our planet earth had been 'captured' by another solar system. We people of the earth were all waiting for the new sun to rise, and we could see our old sun receding into the distance of space, small yet warm and inviting. A feeling of nostalgia passed over me—as strongly and unforgettably as any emotion I have ever experienced in waking life. At the same time, a kind of excitement, apprehension, and expectancy was equally strong. What would the new sun be like? Would it burn the earth and all of us when it rose? How big would it be? Finally, we began to see a beautiful, soft light on the horizon, and then the new sun appeared, breathtakingly. It was larger than the old sun, and its light was deeper and fuller. It cast an intoxicatingly beautiful magenta light on everything. We all took to the streets, giddy and excited, wanting to celebrate the new sun, yet feeling ever sadder and sadder for the old sun, which we could now see very far in the distance, hardly bigger than an ordinary star. And a new apprehensiveness appeared. We were told the people of the new solar system were in the streets, they were our new masters, and we were about to see them for the first time. When we first saw them, we at once realized there was nothing to fear. They were slightly bigger than we were, but their wisdom and gentleness reassured us and made us happy.

"I tell you this dream because it turned out to be a key element in what happened with the elders of the tribe. When I awoke the next morning, I was feeling completely at peace, and completely certain that I must not leave. This agitated all the brothers. Not only did I refuse to leave, but I went out to work on the school building. Strange to say, the tribesmen did not seem surprised in the slightest that I was back with them. But the brothers only became more and more disturbed. This went on for a week. I had never been as certain about anything as this, and eventually the brothers gave up trying to get me to leave; I told them I was now absolutely certain nothing bad would happen to me or to anyone because of my staying.

"The day came when the school was finished. A ceremony was planned involving all the tribe, but no one was sure if the elders would come. Mind you, there had been absolutely no communication with them all this time; the only natives whom we saw were the workers who came to help build the school.

"Well, we scheduled the ceremony; we ourselves cooked some food and made other preparations. And as one of the brothers stood up to give the invocation, sure enough down the way we saw a procession with the chief elder in front and—this is where it begins—holding on top of a pole an image of the sun which I had seen in that dream! I mean to tell you, it was an exact image: the color precisely the same shade of magenta, the same size, everything.

"Wait, that's not all. In the first place, no one had ever seen that image in any of their religious ceremonies before. Was it just made? Had it already existed, but was never used? No one knew. But here it gets even better. Behind the chief elder, all the other elders were wearing big wooden masks which were painted to look almost exactly like the figures I saw in my dream as belonging to the new solar system!

"When I reflected later about all this I was amazed, but at the time, as it was happening, I calmly accepted it and played my role perfectly, without having to think about it. The chief himself wore no mask, but his face was motionless and frozen, as though he of them all did not have to paint a godlike attitude on his face; he alone *was* godlike. I felt this meaning then, I didn't 'figure it out,' but it proved to be more or less accurate.

"It gradually dawned on me that we had badly misunderstood everything about the elders' actions. True, they had demanded that I leave, but they didn't mean it geographically. They had come to the decision that we—and especially me, for some reason —were 'people of the Father' (as they expressed it), and that it was time for *them* to admit *us* into their way of life. What I took to be anger was the only way they could act out toward me a certain ritual of passage. No one ever explained to me what went on with the dreaming, but frankly I don't need any explanations of that, so don't ask."

Father Vincent then spoke of how for the next two years, until he actually came back to the States for a temporary visit, his work as a Christian missionary took on an extraordinary new meaning, how his prayer life was constantly deepened and how he found he was able to act out of care for the welfare of others.

He also told of several other experiences—always in answer to my disconnected but deeply felt questions—involving not only relationships with the tribal families and their communal needs but confrontations with danger and death in the jungle. The notes I later made about these adventures could form the basis of a book in itself, as Father Vincent went long and often into the jungle, sometimes alone, and seems always to have drawn toward him, as he put it, "every unemployed evil spirit within a fifty-mile radius."

Through his special relationship to the chief elder, Father Vincent learned a great deal about the native customs and culture, mainly, he said, through understanding the language. "The language itself is a kind of textbook or scripture. They have no sacred books in our sense of the word. But the language itself is their sacred book.

"For example, I was surprised to learn that they have no word for what we call 'celibacy.' This surprised me only because among the elders and priests there are such strict customs regarding sexual activity. They do not have lifelong vows of celibacy in our sense, but there are definite periods for some of them when complete sexual abstinence is the rule.

"It turns out that the only word they have which refers to sexual abstinence for long periods is actually a prefix that is applied to the word meaning, literally, 'holy-power-of-the-second-birth' and applied, in actual, general usage, to the rituals of the hunt during the morning hours. They have different hunting rituals depending on what time of day it is. The morning hunting ritual is really amazing. At least, it was so to me. The ritual is very complicated; I saw it once from a distance. The amazing part of it is—they cannot hunt in the morning unless one of the men first faces the prey completely without weapons or resistance, and then allows it to go. I heard plenty of stories about rhinos or lionesses coming at the chosen hunter where it looked certain he would be attacked and killed. But I gathered that the hunter is only rarely hurt. The term meaning sexual abstinence is applied to this hunter and also to the ritual.

"Now, if you ask me, the reason for this sort of thing—and I'm no anthropologist, thank God—has to do with the native belief in the force generated by sexual life. For sexual abstinence there must be a situation outwardly of great force and inwardly of great force. Also, only the most admired and courageous hunters are given this position, although according to the chief the practice of choosing the most courageous hunter is beginning to be replaced by an occasional selection of men with other qualities— such as divine inspiration, and even material wealth. He gave this as the main example of the dangers theatening their tradition."

Father Vincent gave me several other extremely interesting examples of the tribal language and what it "taught" about the religion, metaphysics and psychology of the people, and on another occasion I plan to record these reports as well.

After eight years in Africa, he came back to the United States because of his mother's illness. He very well remembers that particular trip from Africa to Philadelphia, because, he says, "It was on that flight that for the last time in my life I had the opinion of myself as being a Christian.

"It began right at the airport. My sister-in-law met me at the plane. She was exhausted and nervous, what with all the family problems connected with my mother, but she filled me in on everything while we were waiting for the luggage. I was always very, very fond of this woman, and her anxieties even made me forget my own fears for my mother's life. I tried to console her, speaking as one Christian to another.

"While we were talking in this way, I took the car keys from her, and on the way out of the parking lot, I backed into the side of a parked car. It was somebody's brand-new Buick and it was pretty badly dented. I remember jumping out of our car like a jackrabbit. My heart was pounding and I started shouting at my sister-in-law through the closed window of our car. I was screaming something about insurance, calling the police, or whether we should drive away without letting anyone know. I was actually trembling with panic.

"My sister-in-law apparently had no idea of the state I suddenly was in; I suppose I was not manifesting it in any gross way. In fact she later told me how glad she was I was handling all that; she said such trivial mishaps always threw her into a fit and she was relieved that I took charge in such a calm and attentive way. Fantastic!

"The truth was that, inside, I, whoever I was, had disappeared into nothingness. Back in the car, after everything was on the way to being settled and after we were out of the parking lot, the thought of my mother's illness came back to me and also the thoughts of all that had gone on in Africa; I remember even searching my memory in order to relive in thought the experience of oneness I had been given on the raft during that epidemic I told you about.

"I soon dismissed this episode from my mind. But it kept coming back in the weeks that followed. At least once a day and then more and more often I would suddenly be stopped in my tracks by the overwhelming experience that my Christianity had disappeared *because I myself had disappeared!* It was almost always connected to something minor, some detail, some personal irritation.

"I began to become morbidly fascinated by this phenomenon, the way a person gets interested in what might turn out to be symptoms of a fatal disease. I spoke about it in a sort of indirect way to one or two friends, but they brushed it aside. But I really became wary of speaking of it at all. Perhaps I was making a mountain out of a molehill.

"Life went on. My mother began recovering up to the level of functioning that would be possible to her; she had had a stroke. Working with my brother, I had to settle a lot of details especially concerning my mother's will, which she wanted revised—that sort of thing. Also, I spent a lot of time with a group of theology students preparing for the priesthood, and I prayed morning, noon and night. My religious life flowered. I had quite a few good talks about my experiences in Africa, and a couple of the students formed a private little seminar group to work with me on a study of Teresa of Ávila, one of our female mystics.

"All along, I had this strange little secret, however. This strange little question, about the vanishing of identity in all these situations, whose number kept increasing and increasing. My religious experiences in prayer were deep and were getting deeper; the family problems were also pretty important. Yet this little question began to assume a completely different kind of importance to me. How to put it? It was certainly shallower than my religious experience, and certainly less pressing or obligatory than the family problems. Yet it was *my own question*. It was by far the most intimate, personal thing in my life. I have thought a good deal about this fact; the disease symptoms are a good analogy; another good analogy would be when a young man, say, suddenly begins to suspect that he is not the real blood offspring of his parents but only an adopted son, and while still fervently loving the parents he knows and while still feeling as deeply as ever the bonds of obligation toward their happiness, begins on his own, privately and in secret, to investigate the question of who his real biological parents are.

"This new question of mine did not seem to have any real relationship to matters of sin and guilt, or redemption and salvation, or service or anything else having to do with my interior Christian life. It was, in some new way, neither an inner nor an outer question. It was simply *my* question and I neither could nor wished to shake it off. And as I said, for some reason my inner experiences, connected both to my past experiences and to my present reading of Saint Teresa, became deeper and lasted longer.

"To make a long story short, during the last few days of my stay in Philadelphia, about a week before I was scheduled to return to Africa, I experienced a powerful sense of the love of God entering into me. And thereafter I had several strong religious experiences in my prayers and in the recitals of the Office. Yet, something completely bowled me over: I definitely experienced —not once, but a dozen times at least—that my identity did not even exist during these religious experiences.

"Now, this is where I get into trouble talking with people. People say, 'Yes, yes—the ego vanishes. The ordinary self disappears into the love of Christ'—or something along these lines. Crap! At least, as far as my own life is concerned—or was concerned then—crap! I can't ever explain, I gave up trying to explain, that the identity disappeared in the same way it disappeared when I rammed into that Buick. The same way it disappeared and was disappearing a hundred times a day in every petty annoyance or emotional outburst.

"I was disgusted with myself in a way that I had never before experienced. This not existing is despicable, it is not transcendent or anything mystical. If it is mystical, then you know what you can do with the mystics. No one was going to con me into that, at least. I didn't know what was going on, what secret I had stumbled onto, but no one was going to talk me into believing it was something good.

"People started worrying that I was losing my faith, so I had to force myself to stop talking about what I was discovering. It had nothing to do with losing my faith."

Father Vincent then spoke of what his life was like when he returned to Africa. In his absence, the chief elder had died, but he found himself accepted fully into the life of the people. And he made many interesting observations about their ways of life that would take too much time to recount here. One point, however, is directly relevant to the main issue, and needs to be emphasized. He felt that the difficult, primitive conditions of life in Africa supported the existence of a quality of human identity that opened people realistically to the teachings and practices of religion. He said that were he a scholar or philosopher, the main question he would be asking would concern the cultural influences within which Christianity or any true religion is introduced—but entirely from the point of view of the existence of the raw experience of human identity.

He felt that the Church had been wise to look askance at mysticism during the modern era. He said, in so many words, that it is better to have a Christianity for nonexistent people like himself than to encourage illusory higher experiences. But he felt it had gone much too far in that direction and needed now to organize a new monasticism, or some new rule of living, that could guide modern people toward the awakening of presence.

The full significance of Father Vincent's story became clear to me only later, when I was studying the journal of Father Sylvan. As will become apparent, Vincent had discovered the same "missing link" in Christianity as Father Sylvan.

Chapter Four

From the Journal of Father Sylvan

Tokyo, December 17, 1975. Passed a few hours yesterday at the Bangkok airport and on the plane with Jacob Needleman. He is a professor from California who is investigating the response of Christians to the invasion of Oriental religions. Interested in the problems modern people face trying to make use of Christian mystical literature, especially the new material that is coming to light from the early centuries.

It is true; it is a minefield. There is no order or plan in the way all these writings have come down to us. Which are the production of isolated individuals who have had one or two powerful experiences and have made a career out of them? Which are the expressions of a struggle for the attention of the heart? It is difficult to know, yet it makes all the difference.

It would be shocking for people to realize how many whom they revere as great mystics fall into the first category, and how few there are who know the steps that actually lead to the experience of Truth and can guide others. Most so-called "great mystics" give descriptions of results without exact understanding of the struggle itself. The Buddhists are good on this. They say, "Don't sell intoxicating beverages."

There are laws of grace. The Hebraic tradition stressed this. And there is the grace of the law, which the Christian tradition stresses. Grace and law: woe to him who chooses one of these over the other. People speak of it as a paradox, which only means they can't fit it into the computer program of the head. "Religious" people do not like to hear that there are scientific laws governing the movements of all forces, higher and lower. On the other hand, those who are attracted.to the idea of lawful precision do not like to hear that these laws are not subject to human manipulation. The problem is: how to move from the holy desire for God to the precise struggle for God without the intervention of the ego? No guide can give another man the holy desire, and no guide can give a man the contact with the higher. But what can be taught is the way to recognize and neutralize the initiatives of ego.

There must be many Professor Needlemans about to appear seeking to make contact with the interior of the Christian teaching. Would that I could help them. Would that I were nearer to the heart of Christianity. Maybe this whole notion of inner and outer religion needs to be thrown out. But who has a better word? How else to express the idea of levels of the teaching?

December 22, 1975 (*no location given*). Everything, absolutely everything about the Teaching must be experienced in ourselves and assimilated in our own being before we attempt to guide others. Call this mysticism, if you wish, real mysticism. Once, the Church understood this; there must be a perpetual mysticism, perpetual experience. This is the origin of the Church's distrust of so-called "mystics." Mysticism in the real sense is the natural state of the human mind. "Mystics" who have occasional "experiences" often end by mocking the human creature through treating these experiences as extraordinary. But what is extraordinary is the rarity of this level of experience.

The Church once knew about this. One of the consequences of its forgetting has been the fear and hatred of hierarchy among Western people. The organization of the Church originally reflected the organization of man and the universe. This organization had to be experienced within ourselves, constantly, "without ceasing." "Pray without ceasing" means pray *now*, in the present moment. In the present moment, now, seek the organization of the universe, of God in ourselves.

In ourselves: this means in our body. The Professor kept asking about what he called lost Christianity and about the place of the body. He is right: this is the thing most needed now, in order to begin. We are always losing it. Our mind, our attention, is the most lost thing of all. St. Gregory Palamas has written clearly about this:

> *Brother! Do you now hear the Apostle saying that "your body is the temple of the Holy Ghost which is in you" [1 Cor. 6:19], and again, that "ye are the temple of God" [1 Cor. 3:26], as God also says, "I will dwell in them, and walk in them; and I will be their God" [2 Cor. 6:16]? Who then, possessing a mind, will deem it unseemly to introduce his mind into that which has been granted the honor of being the dwelling of God? How is it that God Himself in the beginning put the mind into the body? Has He, too, done wrong? Such words, brother, properly belong to heretics, who say that the body is evil and the creation of an evil principle. But we regard it as evil for the mind to be concerned with mindings of the flesh, and not wrong for the mind to be in the body—for the body is not evil. . . . When the Apostle calls the body death, saying, "Who shall deliver me from the body of this death?" [Rom. 7:24], he means by this the minding of the senses and the flesh. . . . Therefore we fight against this law of sin, banish it from the body and establish there the mind as a bishop; and thereby we lay down laws for every power of the soul and for every member of the body as it is appropriate for it. To the senses we prescribe what they have to receive and in what measure—this practice of the spiritual law is called self-mastery; the desiring part of the soul we bring to that most excellent state whose name is love; the mental part we improve by banishing all that prevents the mind from soaring to God—and this part of the spiritual law we call sobriety. . . .

You see, brother, that not only spiritual, but general human reasoning shows the need to recognize it as imperative that those who wish to belong to themselves, and to be truly monks in their inner man, should lead

---

* Here and in several other places where Father Sylvan cites authors without offering precise references, I have attempted to locate passages from these authors that correspond to the material under discussion.

the mind inside the body and hold it there. It is not out of place to teach even beginners to keep attention in themselves. . . .

One of the great teachers says that since the fall the inner man usually accords with the outer (with outer movements and postures). If this be so, why not accept it that a man who strives to turn his mind within is greatly helped in this if, instead of letting his eyes wander hither and thither, he turns them inwards and fixes them in his breast? When the eyes wander outside, the mind becomes dispersed among things through seeing them. In the same way, if the eyes are turned inwards, this movement of theirs will naturally lead the mind too inside the heart in a man who strives to reverse the movement of his mind, that is, to recall it from outside and lead it inwards.

"Take heed to thyself," says Moses, "that there be not a secret thing in thine heart, an iniquity" [Deut. 15:9]. Take heed to yourself, that is, the whole of yourself; not so that you heed one thing and not another—you must heed the whole. With what do we take heed? Of course with the mind, for nothing else can take heed of the whole of oneself. Therefore set it as a guardian over soul and body, and you will easily be delivered from evil passions of the soul and the body. Thus stand on guard before yourself, stand over yourself, observe yourself, or rather watch, examine and judge. For in this way you will subjugate the unruly flesh to the spirit, and your heart will never harbor a secret word of iniquity.†

We must seek the bishop within ourselves. Only when I experience the natural hierarchy of Creation within myself, only when I directly experience supplicant, priest, bishop, archbishop and Divine King within myself do I consciously become part of the sacred Wholeness. Only when my lower nature is naturally attracted toward obedience to the higher, can I, as a human

† Text is from Gregory Palamas, *Triads*, Triad 1, Question 2, in E. Kadloubovsky and G. E. H. Palmer, *Early Fathers from the Philokalia* (London: Faber & Faber, 1954), pp. 401–6.

being in worldly society, voluntarily obey the Community of the Teaching or—as they used to say—the Elders of the Church. Through awareness of the attention of the body it is possible to see how even the instinctual desires obey the higher instantly, without violence. They have only needed contact for this natural obedience, this innate love of the Higher, to become active. Ego prevents contact between the various sources of attention within the human organism; that is its evil and it is only that about it which needs to be destroyed. It is, however, a very difficult task.

The body is sacred because in it we may, with diligence and persistence, come to experience directly the hierarchy of God and the confusion of the ego's striving. Through the body we may study and destroy at the root the illusions and initiatives of my social self, the self I assume to be myself but which is only the smoke of the ego. No person in the Church dare speak or act with respect to another without knowing whether in that moment he is or is not experiencing the truth about himself and the Creation. It is not demanded of us that we always be in the state of the heart which grants us vision and self-mastery. It is only demanded of us that we know the state we are in.

But this is difficult. So difficult that it requires everything of us. It is difficult because it is in fact what is realistically possible in this moment for us human beings: to know our state. What is ultimately meant for us is something else, something of an inconceivably high level. But what is possible for us now, in the present moment is not what is meant for us—that is our tragedy, our situation, which was once precisely defined by the word *sin*, a word which is now empty of meaning. To imagine that what is possible for me now is the same as what is ultimately meant for me is the dangerous illusion of ego, the religious ego which is the most dangerous of all. It is the same as imagining that the words "salvation came through Christ" means that "I am already in the state of salvation" or safely on the way to salvation. These are the sorts of truths which will inevitably result from honest and sincere people poking into higher levels of the tradition. They should be warned. It is going to sting.

Professor Needleman asked again and again about what happened to the Church. He kept coming back to the Albigensian Crusade. And to Bernard of Clairvaux. "How could a great mystic, a master of the contemplative life, have also endorsed the slaughter of hundreds of thousands of people?" He has a theory that this was the turning point in the history of the Church, where it began to go down.

I answered him that in that era there may simply have been too much "mysticism" going on and I accused him of believing too much in history and linear time. Too much emphasis on inner experience inevitably provokes resistance and a swing toward outer institutional organization. The free exploration of the inner life to the relative exclusion of the outer lawfully provokes a counter movement to tidy up the tradition outwardly, just as happened in thirteenth century Tibet—though far less violently, I believe.

In fact, there is no such thing as a turning point in the real world. There are only forces and their interaction. The idea of God acting in history, which is such a fetish for Western religious thought, is originally a symbol of the play of fundamental forces (God) everywhere and in everything.

The professor agreed about the danger of taking symbols literally, but he did not seem satisfied with this way of understanding the play of forces within the epoch of Bernard of Clairvaux.

He makes too much of this whole question of literal or allegorical understanding of scriptures. In fact, the distinction is beside the point. What is the point? The point is the origin of the symbols. A symbol is a token left by one of greater understanding to record what he experienced. Through his compassion and exact psychological understanding, the Founder leaves just these symbols and no other for our guidance. The symbol is meant to act on us as we are, in our condition of mental, emotional and bodily rupture. The symbol is meant to guide the arising of the unifying force within ourselves, the force which can bring our aspects together, the force called "the Heart," the holy desire.

The symbol obliges us to begin by recognizing the low level of our own inner state and understanding. Our work in front of the symbol is to become still and allow the symbol to arouse echoes in us and to observe how it is acting upon us. This is not a stage to be passed through, it is the perpetual demand that the symbol makes upon us, the water of the root of the perpetual mysticism that is actually possible for man.

Therefore, what is a symbol for the Founder must be taken as a metaphor for myself, a metaphor of my inner condition. Allegorical or literal is not the point; the point is to regard the symbol as a metaphor of myself. The Founder understands the symbol in a great way, it expresses his visionary power to see things as they are in objective reality. But we, who do not even live at the level of a normal human being, far less at the level of the Founder, presume to think we understand the symbol's truth and proceed to try to fit reality into it, thus creating the evils of dogma. I begin by seeing that in myself I crucify my Lord and I end by crucifying you in the name of the symbol of the cross. The causes of religious violence, including inquisitions, lie in this tendency to leap impatiently from metaphor to symbol. One struggles to live according to the Teaching and gradually a certain level of understanding is reached. One begins to feel and know, to a certain degree, how important the Teaching is to mankind. One is truly devoted, let us say, to Christianity.

This is a most critical moment in the life of a community or individual. An error here can cause everything to be lost or twisted. Enthusiastic about the truth of the Teaching, one then forgets the metaphorical nature of the symbols. Which is to say, one forgets that I myself need the Teaching even more than the world does.

Professor, do you see this point?

Washington (undated). Dr. M. took me on a tour of the public buildings today. He and his friend are interested in our teaching and asked intelligent questions. I saw how their state changed when we walked through the Lincoln Monument and past the Capitol Building. They became quiet, without even noticing it. The same thing happened in the evening at a concert.

Like many elements of culture, love of country originates in the holy desire which then combines with something else, another energy, in human nature and becomes twisted. The desire to serve the higher is at the origin of patriotism but there it gets distorted and confused. Tradition recognizes this and seeks to remind man of the two worlds and the two forces within him. But only the *gnosis* can guide man to study the distortions of the sacred impulse down to its roots within himself.

I laugh at all this interest now in what is called "gnosticism." I laugh because no one is ever going to be able to disentangle what happened in the early centuries of the Church. Ideas, symbols and rites come into existence out of great experience and are offered both as guides to the study and destruction of ego and as forces acting on the heart. Inevitably, and very quickly, new religious movements are invented by who knows what individual acting on God knows what understanding. Defenders of the faith mount their steeds and do battle with the heretics. May God preserve us from both.

Who knows how a great teacher lives, where he goes, whom he sees, how he sows the Teaching? An órthodoxy forms, but behind the scenes, perhaps very far away, are others who have also received the Way in different conditions with different accents. Later, they may appear. Or they may never appear, but their influence may still become decisive.

Did not the Buddha teach to kings and householders, who did not or could not become monks in the narrow sense of the word? Later, that form of the teaching manifested as *tantra*, and who is to say that its origins are really later in time than the Theravada? Historians cannot say; they are locked in a house and only record the facts that wander past and knock on their door.

Where did Christ go? whom did He teach?

In any case, I have visited places where I have heard the Manichaean myth told with such inner feeling and understanding as I would only wish for every follower of the Way in each of its manifestations. The *presence* in these followers of Mani gave the meaning to their language.

Of course, those who trust words without sensing the being behind them will not see the nature of this teaching. Furthermore, the Manichaeans throughout their history no doubt had as many impatient and unprepared followers promoting their ideas as did the Church.

Being, and the laws of Being, do not care much, I think, about words. The only issue is what helps and what does not help.

No serious person in the history of the world ever held the notion of dualism which is considered by theologians and scholars to be a central tenet of so-called "gnosticism." What is called dualism, the idea of a good and evil force in the universe, is connected with the task of discriminating different directions of energy, and of recognizing that the struggle for inner perfection involves cosmic principles that operate within and outside of human nature. If the term esotericism is going to be used, it should be reserved for the study of energy within oneself; it has nothing to do with words and formulations as such, or rituals as such, or social practices as such.

And the study of development and degradation of energy within oneself requires the long and difficult development of the force of attention, which is the soul in its infinite gradations within ourselves.

Behind what the world calls virtue there lies the hidden squandering of the sacred energies in man. This truth can never be popular and those who have been touched by it must be cautious in speaking about it, both for their own sake and for the sake of others. The "gathering of the light" may seem to conventional minds to be outside the realm of morality. But it is the only basis for true morality.

Above all, it must not be spoken about in ways that encourage improvised and invented imitations. How many of what are now called "gnostic sects" were actually such "improvisations"?

To understand history requires the same intuition as to understand nature or my neighbor, or myself. There exist messages from others which tell us what they have discovered about the world; and there exist messages from others that help us to discover the truth for ourselves. Only he who has the second can make use of the first. Without my own power to discriminate, to inquire for myself, I will be fooled every time by history, facts, nature herself. It is not the fault of nature or of the facts. It has to do with the arrangement of energies and sensations within the mind. Yes, this is what is not realized. Correct or incorrect information, true or false theories, right or wrong pictures of reality or history or whatever—this is all just a screen over the movement of energies within man. I believe because of forces, I do not believe because of forces. Subtle forces, perhaps, invisible, undetected by me—but they are there nevertheless. I am moral or I am a criminal because of forces. This is the "law of my parts" which is the real cause, as St. Paul said, that drives me.

Therefore the greatest enemy is what the world calls "virtue." Not even God Himself can help a man who has no attention.

People say that the Eastern teachings will open the West to the inner practices of Christianity. Yes, but then this will turn into a movement of reform, and on whatever scale will become like other movements of reform with consequences that are bound to be either unpleasant or uninteresting.

In the first place, who really cares about Christianity? A billion people, you say? Absurd. A very tiny part of a very large number of people adds up to a rather small measure. A billionth of the mind of a billion people—perhaps one serious person altogether, for the purposes of record.

But look at the time they devote, the money, the passion, the energy! Beside the point. It is the smallest part of the mind that brews the biggest fantasies. Technology has become the instrument of huge collective daydreams and nightmares. The whole idea of a religious revival in the modern world is on the level of thought energized by fear and the wish for comfort, the craving for belief systems. Books, electronic media, newspapers, jet planes—all this has become the instrument of modern man's collective egoism. Who sees unity in this phenomenon, who sees a "planetary consciousness" sees only a daydream which the instrumentalities of science allow everyone to share in.

In the second place, reform movements throughout the centuries have been the result of someone seeing one thing that is wrong and then trying to correct it. May God preserve us from improvements!

If we would infuse new life into Christianity, it is necessary first and last, to occupy the body of the old Christianity, just as Christ occupied the body of the old Adam. Who is there who sees and *accepts* both the truth and the falsity of modern Christianity?

It is not necessary to change anything. That is, not until one witnesses exactly how our tradition became what it became; what each and every idea and ritual is for and how—precisely and from what causes—these elements have gotten twisted. How each and every indication for living has become thrown into the ambiguities of everyday, aimless life and has been associated with the language and conceptions of meaningless "ordinary" life. For example, the sin of "sloth"—what is called laziness, something the puritans don't like—means something only if one is actually going somewhere. For most of us, it is not sin to be lazy simply because we are not going anywhere that is good in the first place. Would you call a man lazy who drags his feet on the way to the electric chair?

I admit to feeling a little uneasy speaking about Christianity in this way. I like Kierkegaard's distinction between Christendom and Christianity, the former meaning what man has made of the latter. But "Christendom" has wrong implications in an era where political rule throughout the Western world is so disassociated from religion. Practically speaking, of course, one doesn't really need this distinction between Christendom and Christianity, between broken Christianity and real Christianity. We only know broken Christianity, so why worry about a word for the real thing?

We must occupy the body of the old Christianity, the mortal body of the immortal Truth. Criticism is not the point. Presence is the point, awareness of the gap separating the ideas and the actual situation. Moments of such presence are not enough, not nearly enough. In fact, such moments when one confronts the separation between what ought to be and what is are in themselves a great danger because if one does not value these moments rightly, the impulse to correct things takes over and one immediately and unconsciously loses contact with the helping force of the Holy Spirit. Such is the origin of Protestantism. But it has existed and dominated within the Church as well, long before Luther or Calvin or Wesley or Fox experienced their moments of presence.

The overwhelming problem is one of attachment to the teaching itself; the "love" of one's own religion, spiritual egoism—it can be called many things. Within each teaching, the same thing happens with respect to this or that thrust of the teaching. I become attached to this or that idea or method that has helped me in the past. I do not see how it is connected to everything else in the teaching, and in fact, everything else that I have been given to experience. I do not see how certain elements of the teaching which I judge negatively have actually been necessary, that without them I would never have come to the understanding I now have. "God created the earth and said it was good": this applies—first and foremost—to the teaching, the Word, the path, the Torah. Until we can guard this, we cannot become guardians of anything else.

However, the tradition we now have must not be equated with the teaching in this sense. The tradition as it now faces us is the end result of a million efforts to make improvements or to eradicate or assimilate others who were making improvements. Which of these changes throughout the two-thousand-year history of the Church are the result of the operation of the healing force or presence, as when Jesus heals the sick not through human reaction, but through the reconciling force of the Holy Spirit?

How many of the prayers of the Christian teaching are actually guides for seeking the appearance of this holy force, the "peace of the Lord"? Through confrontation of the higher and the lower and through an ontological silence in the very heart of this confrontation the "peace of the Lord" may appear.

It is extraordinary to think how much of the intellectual activity of man is actually a beginning contact with this force, this third Person of the Holy Trinity. All efforts to think, being the call for confrontation between levels, are a first step toward the prayer to the holy reconciliation of Presence. Thought begins with seeing, but ends, unfortunately, with slavery to the mechanisms of conceptualization. Out of these conceptualizations, which are only the records left in the nervous systems by moments of seeing, and which are needed as instruments of the energy of the spirit existing in the world, or the lower reality—out of these neural results of the spirit man erroneously tries to imitate the work of the spirit. But only the spirit can do the work of the spirit.

Thought, which means in essence seeing, exists on these many levels. There are no esoteric thoughts or esoteric ideas, as such; but there is esoteric thinking, an inner action which carries the energy of harmonization and reconciliation between levels. We may gladly leave the words "consciousness" and "self-awareness" to the Aquarian people of the day; good luck to them! But may we continue to seek, and may we find, a language that can guide us in the occupation and seeing of the whole of ourselves. "Consciousness" and "awareness" will suffer the same fate as "thought" and "mind," terms which originally signified the possible action of the Holy Spirit within the structure of human nature.

But who is there who can occupy the tradition in order to reconstruct the teaching? Where are the few Christians who can become, so to say, the "subtle body" of the Church? I take it as my aim, but God knows it is beyond my power, to call out for such people. I invoke these spirits, if I may so express it!

It can only begin with individuals who can occupy their own being. I travel throughout the world, I try to see and accept what has become of Christianity; I try not to give all my force to the reactions of like and dislike which constantly well up in me. But who do I think I am? Only in rare moments can I be toward myself what I wish to be toward the tradition. And if I cannot be a forgiver of myself, how shall the power of forgiveness ever enter toward Christendom itself? Forgiveness is the seeing that carries the holy force of reconciliation. God forgives; Christ forgives; but actually the power of forgiveness lies with the Holy Spirit. I begin on a tiny scale, first with thought that seeks a freedom from the obvious egoistic reactions of like and dislike, a thought that is to some extent independent of desire. Thus I begin as a self-scientist.

One hears it said that religion, at its heart, is practical psychology. But, just because something works, it does not mean that it is comparable to modern science. True metaphysics works; true philosophy works; true mystery works. True magic works—through the phenomenon of resonance. One must know the exact words to say and one must say them in exactly the right place and the right time; and then forces may be called down from heaven.

However, to be sensitive to the law of resonance beyond the realm observed by the senses, it is necessary to bring a great intelligence to one's petition—either that or a very purified emotional state. Or an extraordinary degree of bodily suffering, pure bodily suffering without the admixture and intensification of personal emotion.

Your Christianity must have magic in it; your magic must be Christian.

Christianity shows man his helplessness apart from God; magic brings about physical results that are lawfully caused by the sacrifice of spiritual illusions.

Christianity empties a man; magic fills him with the power to act from his vital center as a being made in the image of his Creator.

All real religion produces physical results. But the question of how to be toward these results is the most easily lost element in a teaching. It is the very first thing to go when a tradition begins to disperse. But both magic and religion are necessary components of every complete teaching.

Without magic, Christianity turns man against nature, the creation of God, and eventually against God himself.

Without magic, Christianity abandons the inner physical sensations that support the forces of hope and love. Religious man may know he is nothing under God, but without magic he no longer physically tastes the goodness and the warmth of this hard truth, no longer applies it to *himself* out of the instincts of his heart. Instead, he applies the Truth to his neighbor's weaknesses, and eventually he may kill his neighbor. Without magic, without inner results that can be sensed, man loses the sense of wonder before the Creation that is within himself, the movement up and down of his own inner energies. Only this self-knowledge can generate real compassion for my neighbor and real knowledge of him and a true sense of justice toward him. Those who love justice without long experience of these inner forces will never bring about anything but more violence and hatred.

Man must have results, real results, in his inner and outer life. I do not mean the results which modern people strive after in their attempts at self-development. These are not results, but only rearrangements of psychic material, a process the Buddhists call *samsara* and which our Holy Bible calls *dust*.

Without religion, however, magic by itself draws man fatally under the thrall of influences which pervade the earth and for which human emotional forces are nothing more than fuel. These influences were called demons. The word no longer has anything but a childish meaning, however. The general idea can be roughly stated in modern, scientific language, always remembering that our language is not based on actual experience of such forces.

What we call the universe is the creation of Mind descending, or dividing, into form and substance.

Consider a nerve entering a muscle in the human body. The nerve transmits a psychic energy which is transformed by the muscle into mechanical energy. We see the external movements of living beings for what they are—patterns of material mechanism. What we do not see is that a law of descent is at work, from the psychic to the material. This particular transition is biological life.

In the human animal, as well as in all higher animals, the fundamental psychic energy transmitted to the muscles is twofold: instinctual and emotional. The transmission or transformation of instinctual psychic energy into matter takes place on a very general scale through the species structure of all living beings. It cannot vary in individual animals of the same species. But the emotional psychic energy is different; it is the central power of all higher animals, those which Buddhists of certain lineages call "sentient beings."

There are many gradations of energy within the band of transition between the mechanical and the psychic. But the main point is that the world of life is to a great extent created and maintained through the expression of emotional energy. It is this energy through which magic operates. Results that are the effects of magic are always the products of a certain level of emotion. People will never believe in the reality of magic who are not well acquainted with this quality of emotion.

The control and manipulation of emotional energy is the secret of all magic, for good or evil. The evil magician agitates the mind until a certain intensity of emotional force is evoked in people. From that point, he can make them do or see whatever he wishes; for, in the state of mental agitation, the controlling power of attention—the specific quality of attention that distinguishes man from the animal—is absorbed by each passing thought-association and the passion to act which accompanies it. In such a state man is even more than usual the prey of suggestion. An external manipulator, concentrating on a specific aim, can control the mind and the perceptions of another person. However, in the prevalent conditions of modern life, external suggestions do not often follow one straight line. There is only a crisscross of suggestions coming from countless sources.

Christianity does not work with either mechanical or psychic energy, but with a different level of force to which the name of "spirit" or "spiritual energy" is given. The same is true of all the God-given teachings. Christianity becomes Christendom when it begins to revolve around psychic, biological and mechanical energies, no matter how much it retains the language and the forms which were originally created to channel spiritual energy. Sensitivity to qualities of energy is the one and only touchstone for determining the level or authenticity of Christian practices. The discipline, way of living, ideas, practices, that enable a man to acquire this sensitivity in the whole of himself stands as the esoteric tradition at the heart of every revelation. Only there may one speak of the unity of all man's religions. Every other attempt to identify similarities among traditions is false ecumenism.

On both the individual and collective levels, the Spirit does result in attainments in all the realms of human life—mind, social forms, culture, an enduring sense of personal worth and the normal psychological comfort which accompanies it. Spiritual energy can and must descend, as God's grace, into these forms of goodness on earth—such is the nature of God's power and "magic." But, on the individual and collective level, when these successful forms, which are results, are repeated beyond their term and without understanding of the causal energies behind them, the product is the transition of Christianity to Christendom—in other words, magic without religion. This whole process must be observed in ourselves as an irreplaceable component of the inner teaching. May I occupy my own tradition in this way. In order to do this I must have the humility to occupy my own body.

To awaken spiritual emotion is the work of religious discipline. This comes about through sacrifice. The sacrifice of what? What is the inner purpose of sacrifice? I must sacrifice attachment to results of the spirit—*even as they are taking place in me*. Religious man may become a magician, but through becoming such he sees only the greatness of God and the insignificance of his own being. The energies of egoistic emotion, the psychic and mechanical energies, that, through the inherent structure of human nature, are bound to his inner or outer results are immediately separated from these results and are transformed upward and therewith connected to the Tree of Life, the conduit of the power of God. Thus sacrifice brings union with God. Without this understanding, both self-indulgence and asceticism are equivalently inhuman.

Modern man's prayers have no effect; they do not reach God. It may be said that way, although what this means is far from simple. People's prayers have no resonance, no power. But it need not be that way.

Here we may learn from Buddhism. In the history of Buddhism, there is an "argument" between two schools, Hinayana and Mahayana Buddhism. The first says: seek your own liberation; the second says, work for the liberation of all sentient beings. Out of this so-called clash there appear two kinds of higher men: those who have reached the inner freedom for themselves and those who are working for others.

In Christianity there is also a Hinayana and a Mahayana. But Buddhism teaches us that to be Mahayana we must first be Hinayana. To work for the other we must first work for ourselves. A higher Buddhism then teaches that really to work for my own liberation is to work for the liberation of others. But why? How? Is it true for Christianity? Is my first duty to myself before I can love my neighbor?

May all those who preach love of neighbor, love of this and that, kindly put down their guard and become quiet, quite still, and try to think, attempt to bring reason into the position of activity over emotional reactions, as was enjoined unto us by Isaiah when he said "Be still and know that I am God," and by our teacher Socrates who taught Plato and the Western world that it is necessary to be inwardly still so that there can appear a power of intelligence and love of the Good which all the parts of our nature will willingly and happily obey as servants; and as was taught by the ancient skeptics who urged us to separate our sense of self from all thoughts and logical reasoning in order to reach the relative void from which the certainty-that-has-no-name may speak.

I seek for myself. I struggle for myself. This produces such a neurosis, such a terrible egoism that to be told, "love others, serve others," releases me from neurotic striving and brings me into either hebephrenia or a glazed sense of self-justification, or simply the normal human recognition that there are ideals which are not made by me and to which I may seek a relationship. But to step from any of this to the notion that I am serving God, the Highest, that my prayers actually reach Him, or that He actually reaches into me: about this one must be very, very careful. It is true, but it is not literally true and upon that fact hangs every-thing, including the violent deaths of men in the wars of religion, which means, actually, all wars.

But think: To seek and work for my own liberation means ac-tually to seek and work for contact with God; God in myself. To work for myself means nothing other than to seek to know God. It cannot be otherwise. Thus the spiritual father takes away all results; thus religion makes its appearance in its stricter sense. Religion tears away your so-called "work for others," your so-called "service," which is ultimately nothing other than the search for emotional self-justification. Religion turns you upon yourself; the guide, if he is really a guide and not a religious madman, turns you upon yourself, which means leaves nothing but God for you to work with and seek, God in your own being. You must be brought time and again to the end of your rope, which you cannot do by yourself. Life can do this to you some-times and, truly, when this happens, even the least of us experi-ences some kind of contact with God.

The guide needs to train us how to understand what happens when we are at the end of our rope, what laws are operating when this in fact occurs. This is real religion. Then when this takes place, when power does appear as a result, he instructs in the way to study this also and not be fooled by it. He then be-comes our magician.

Christians must bring back Hinayana and give up their infatu-ation with their neurotic Mahayana. It is childish to wonder what God is doing to him or to her or to the world or to the Rus-sians or the Chinese or the French. Let the Eastern religions bring us more and more of their teachings, their ideas, so that we may find live metaphors for our inner search. We need Hina-yana, we need the "lesser vehicle," the lesser Christianity in order not to be driven crazy by the "greater vehicle," the Mahayana. We must work to know what God is doing in ourselves and then God will enable us, through power, to love my neighbor. We need power, energy, to love, that is, to not get absorbed by our emotional reactions to the other. This energy—this magic—cannot appear without self-struggle of a specific, revealed nature. All revelation is the revelation of how to search, how to struggle. It is not the revelation of results.

May the Hindus not drive us all even crazier with their Brahman-Atman doctrine that has broken off from its immense moorings and is running around like a mad dog making people believe they can start from what is actually the highest state of consciousness. But can we reasonably expect that courtesy of the Hindus when we Christians have not acted with any more consideration, setting off our doctrines of grace, contact with God, salvation, and all the rest, as though telling the world it can start with what is actually the highest state of will possible for man?

But now, think, consider: all these high ideals have been let loose in the world like packs of marauding dogs. What to do? How to understand this whole situation? Perhaps we can make use of all this, without being driven crazy by it. How?

The answer is: through the law of resonance. All these high teachings may be taken as so many scripts for conscious man. We who do not have this consciousness, this being, can become actors playing the role of perfected men and women.

But here there is danger. Great guidance is needed. We must play these roles without believing in them. We must keep one half of our attention on our failure to be what we are impersonating. This must be done internally. Externally, we must act as virtuous men and women. Internally we must watch and study the details of our sinfulness, our failure to correspond to these outer roles.

These outer scripts must be "memorized" when we are children. That is why we must teach them to our children. But we have taught them all wrong; in fact we have taught about them in a way that makes them poisonous. We teach our children in a way that infects them with fear and guilt, which is the virus carried by these dogs. And after this happens, when the whole civilization becomes infected with this illness, then the highest ideals that can be offered reach no higher than therapy, a therapy that can bring people no farther than to be where Adam was after he was expelled, namely, at the beginning of the search for God, although modern people mis-identify this as the end. Thus Christianity becomes equivalent to psychiatry. To hell with it!

First, before we go too far with these scripts, although after we have studied and memorized them, we must then enroll in the study of the laws of resonance. This can only be done in the quietest states of being; and this, nothing else, is the primal function of meditation—or "sitting." With the body still and natural, relaxed and alert, the eyes closed, let us say, all by oneself, we must be helped to acquire the tools to study the laws of resonance. Our lower nature can call to our higher nature, to God, only if there is a bridge between them, an attention that can serve as the medium of transmission by means of which the imitation Christ can be gently superseded by the real Christ.

Therefore one must even before this learn how to prepare, how to become quiet in the midst of all the inner movement in our lower nature. May God preserve us from all forms of meditation that do not lead us precisely from the outset, in orderly, logical fashion, but logic in the sense of spiritual logic, not mental logic which kills. To whom shall we turn for this spiritual logic?

Thus meditation is the heart of civilization, and the learning of meditation is the heart of meditation. But in this world everything has gone backwards. It cannot go on like that for long, no more than a shepherd can allow for very long that his sheep fail to produce the wool he needs.

Purity of intention is to seek and struggle for one's own self. This is a science, the sacred science of all ages. Call out to a higher God, an external God, if you must. But at the same time ask yourself in a quiet inner place: who is calling out? And study until you are shaken by the answer that it is the ego calling out. When you are so shaken, completely, in a way that through a quiet body you can receive the energy of this truth about yourself, then and only then is it possible for the law of resonance to be activated.

Tehran, December 29, 1975. Today, sitting down to the morning practice, the first thing I hear is the traffic already starting up in front of the hotel. I close my eyes and try to bring my attention into myself, but it is constantly drawn outward to all the noise. A struggle begins. The traffic is overwhelming. Across the street a radio starts playing, or is it a television set? Irritation, and then fear that I will not make contact with the Truth. What to do? What to do?

I give up fighting the noise and, without moving my body at all, I begin to listen to the sounds of the traffic without mentally identifying what I am hearing. Suddenly, behind all that noise, from very far off—so faintly that it is barely audible—I hear the call to prayer from some distant minaret. Although I have heard this call countless times in Moslem countries, this morning it is as though I am hearing it for the first time.

It fades in and out. I hear it for a microsecond and then nothing but the trucks and cars outside my window. Again and again. The temptation arises to try to direct my attention away from the traffic and strain to hear the muezzin whose call fills me with hope. But no sooner do I do that than the sound of the call disappears. Only when I accept the street noises does the call to prayer break into my awareness. Even the wish that the noise were less prevents my hearing the call.

For some, religion cannot exist in the contemporary world; they would take away all the traffic in order to hear the muezzin loudly and clearly, so much so that the call to prayer becomes a warning, an admonition, and even a threat. But when they ask me, I say to these people that I too have my reward. Although I may not hear the call as often or as loudly as they, yet when I hear it the whole of myself hears it; I have no need for ethical rules at that moment, because all my parts become obedient without the passage of time; the holy desire has blended with the energy of a universal attention within myself.

Their way requires time, the whole of our aeon. Not until the last days, the end of this cycle, will salvation come for them—or the judgment. Then there will be the resurrection of the dead, and a new phase will begin for the whole of our planet; this is the end of the world.

As for the path we follow, it exists in a different mode of time, subjective time. Our way is for people who are impatient. Ours is the rapid path.

You see, Professor, your question about the hiddenness of Tradition is only the beginning of the question. Tradition is never hidden for long; nor does it need protection. Tradition itself hides the rapid path from us, mercifully. The spiritual danger of the present moment is not the loss of Tradition, but the confusion of Tradition with the rapid path.

Tradition is the ideal held up to humanity; it does not change over thousands of years; its forms can remain throughout the aeon, for it is the salvation of humanity that is its principal concern. Our way changes, sometimes from moment to moment and woe to those who find our way before the activation within themselves of the holy desire. Therefore our teachers, such as

Socrates, have made their central work the arousal in man of the holy desire.

Our teacher in *The Cloud of Unknowing* speaks of this in the language of the twofold nature of humility. For the sake of the weakness of mankind, the Tradition could not demand of man the constant experience of this twofold humility. For the sake of salvation, only one humility was demanded. But the rapid path, the attainment of the Kingdom in this life, requires both.

‡Let us then consider the virtue of humility so that you will understand why it is perfect when God alone is its source and why it is imperfect when it arises from any other source even though God might be the principal one. But first I will try to explain what humility is in itself and then the difference will be easier to grasp.

A man is humble when he stands in the truth with a knowledge and appreciation for himself as he really is. And actually, anyone who saw and experienced himself as he really and truly is would have no difficulty being humble, for two things would become very clear to him. In the first place, he would see clearly the degradation, misery and weakness of the human condition resulting from original sin. From these effects of original sin man will never be entirely free in this life, no matter how holy he becomes. In the second place, he would recognize the transcendent goodness of God as he is in himself and his overflowing, superabundant love for man. Before such goodness and love nature trembles, sages stammer like fools, and the saints and angels are blinded with glory. . . .

The humility engendered by this experiential knowledge of God's goodness and love I call perfect, because it is an attitude which man will retain even in eternity. But the humility arising from a realistic grasp of the human condition I call imperfect, for not only will it pass away at death with its cause but even in this life it will not always be operative. For sometimes people

‡ I have selected Fr. William Johnston's translation of the relevant passages: *The Cloud of Unknowing* (Garden City, N.Y.: Doubleday/Image Books, 1973), pp. 65–67.

well advanced in the contemplative life will receive
such grace from God that they will be suddenly and
completely taken out of themselves and neither remember nor care whether they are holy or sinful. . . .
Nevertheless, I am not suggesting that the first motive
be abandoned. God forbid that you should misun-
derstand me, for I am convinced that it is both profita-
ble and necessary in this life.

Although I speak of imperfect humility it is not because I place little value on true self-knowledge. Should
all the saints and angels of heaven join with all the
members of the Church on earth, both religious and
lay, at every degree of Christian holiness and pray for
my growth in humility, I am certain that it would not
profit me as much nor bring me to the perfection of this
virtue as quickly as a little self-knowledge. Indeed it is
altogether impossible to arrive at perfect humility without it.

And therefore, do not shrink from the sweat and toil
involved in gaining real self-knowledge, for I am sure
that when you have acquired it you will very soon come
to an experiential knowledge of God's goodness and
love. . . .

In all conditions and at every moment to experience in ourselves both the Eternal Presence and the fallen ego—that is our
way and our possibility, just as our teacher Moses experienced
both the Absolute Force and also the treachery and weakness of
the multitudes, and just as the Master experienced God and
human nature within Himself.

But it is very difficult. Why? Because the experiencer is absent
and needs to be born and grow within us. We have Spirit within
us and sometimes it calls to us. "Mystics" take the call of the
Spirit for the end and the goal of human life, and they have their
reward. We, however, seek something else.

PART TWO
THE LOST DOCTRINE
OF THE SOUL

In selecting Father Sylvan, Metropolitan Anthony, and Father Vincent as examples of contemporary people who in my judgment have made personal contact with lost Christianity, I by no means wish to imply that they are the only Christians I have met who have so struck me. Nor, by any stretch of the imagination, do I wish to claim that I have adequately surveyed the worlds of contemporary Christianity and have identified all those people who are part of what I have earlier referred to as "the second history" of the Christian tradition. The preposterousness of such a claim would be obvious not only from the quantitative point of view but even more so from the qualitative point of view. It is even pretentious to make such a disclaimer, but the printed word has these days assumed such exaggerated importance that I feel it is necessary to state as plainly as possible that this book represents the thoughts and observations of only one, very limited, observer—limited, that is, both physically in the ability to go places, read books and investigate historical, linguistic, theological and anthropological materials, and limited spiritually in the ability to see what is really taking place within another human being and to sense from whom and from where new life is appearing. In short, this book, like everything else that involves the human heart, exists at a certain level of sensitivity and intensity of thought, and it would be foolish to expect of it more than what can exist at this level.

It is not my aim to offer anything like a "catalogue," although I do intend in this part of the book to point out some of the principal people and places that warrant the attention of anyone seeking to assess the present ferment within the religions of the West. I wish also to call the reader's attention to certain philosophical and psychological aspects of the Christian teaching, and raise specific questions about its historical development. All of these aims would be meaningless to me and to the reader, however, were there not some *feeling* about the ideas which have been lost to Christianity, and which need to be brought back to the center of our civilization.

It is through such people as Father Sylvan, Metropolitan Anthony and Father Vincent that I myself have come to feel and sense, as well as cognize, certain of the ideas relevant to lost Christianity. I have written about these ideas in this way specifically so as to portray, and perhaps even reproduce in the reader, something of the feeling and the sense of weight that these lost ideas have. To be precise, it is the mode of cognizing the ideas that is lost, quite as much as the ideas themselves.

In saying this latter, I find myself paraphrasing Father Sylvan, whose formulations and attitude have, for better or worse, become the chief influence upon my approach to this whole subject. I therefore intend to allow Father Sylvan to continue speaking through his journals where appropriate to the subject at hand and also, when appropriate, to explicate and apply some of his ideas, which I have already introduced without comment.

Chapter Five

Christianity and Eastern Meditation

Christianity and Buddhism

There is perhaps no better place to begin this more systematic treatment of our theme than with an examination of some current attempts by Christians to make use of the specifically Oriental methods of meditation. Writing in 1972 of the present confrontation between Christianity and Eastern religions, Father William Johnston sees it as an event of even greater potential significance than the epoch-making interaction that took place between Christianity and classical Greek culture in the early centuries of the Church:

> Starting as a Jewish religion, founded by a Jew, and proud of its Jewish origins, Christianity was destined to break out of its Hebrew framework through dialogue with a Hellenistic world. . . . So it was that there came into existence a Hellenistic Christianity. The men who built the Western Church were Hellenistic in background and education—Augustine, Gregory I, Bernard of Clairvaux, Aquinas, and the rest.
>
> Hellenism contributed vastly to the enrichment of the Western Church. The insights of Plato and Aristotle and Plotinus, and even of Homer and Virgil, gave life and energy to the schoolmen and artists of the Middle Ages. But . . . Catholic theologians now feel (and rightly, I believe) that Catholic Christianity got an overdose of Hellenism. Thanks to a Greek way of think-

ing, theology tended to categorize, to see things neatly, to conceptualize, to rationalize. And, alas, in the years after Trent, *growth stopped*. Or it almost stopped. Christianity in both its Catholic and Protestant forms became incapable of opening itself to other cultures. Great missionaries such as Robert de Nobili in India and Mateo Ricci in China who attempted to enter into serious dialogue with Eastern religions were sadly reduced to silence. The inability of Christianity to recognize the beauty and validity of the Chinese rites is a tragic episode in her history.

Together with Vatican II and the end of the post-Reformation period, however, came a purification of Christianity from Hellenistic exaggeration and a return to the biblical sources. And now we see a world-wide Christian Church preparing for a second great dialogue: the dialogue with Oriental religions and culture. This will surely be even more earthshaking and even more enriching than the Judaeo-Hellenistic encounter. Where it will lead no one knows. But it has begun and nothing can hold it back.*

Father Johnston is a Jesuit who has lived in Japan for thirty years and whose experience with Zen Buddhism has made him, after the late Thomas Merton and along with Aelred Graham in England, one of the few committed Catholics who have long believed that Christianity must show itself to be an expression of the same truth as the great Eastern teachings. In his book *Christian Zen*, he describes how he understands the need among Christians for methods of prayer involving physical posture, breathing, attention and separation from the train of automatic thought associations. The book describes the erect sitting posture of *zazen* meditation and the method of counting the breath and several other elements of the Zen practice that Father Johnston has sought to assimilate into the prayer life of Christians. "It seems to me," he writes,

* William Johnston, S.J., "Christianity in Dialogue with Zen," in Jacob Needleman and Dennis Lewis (eds.), *Sacred Tradition and Present Need* (New York: Viking Press, 1975).

that Christians can profit greatly from Zen methodology to deepen their Christian faith, and here in Japan an increasing number of Christians, both Japanese and Western, are discovering this. . . . Surely it would be a good thing to take up this methodology and start once again teaching people how to pray. For the sad fact is that, while Catholic monks and nuns are teaching all kinds of things from botany to business, not many are teaching people how to pray. . . . Western civilization has become horribly one-sided and unbalanced, so much so that serious people cannot see the distinction between a computer and a man. When this happens, and when the contemplative dimension existing in every man becomes starved, then people go berserk and do crazy things. And this is what is happening. Moreover it is ghastly to think that it is happening even among some monks and nuns. Here are people whose lives are geared to *satori,* yet they feel that all is meaningless unless they are moving around the place making noise in the name of Christian charity.†

Similar thoughts were being expressed nearly a decade earlier by Dom Aelred Graham in his pioneering book *Zen Catholicism.* There Dom Aelred, the prior of a Benedictine monastery in England, pointed to key aspects of Zen Buddhism that Western Christianity desperately needed to make its own in the sense of rediscovering something essential that had been lost. "It may be," he wrote, "that the West has something to learn from the East on the importance of 'mindfulness,' that is, bringing one's mind completely to bear on whatever confronts it."

What is called for is not intense concentration, with a knitting of the brows, but, rather, the opposite, an awakening of the mind without fixing it anywhere, the quietness of pure attention. . . . What we may need to learn is that merely to look at things as they are, with bare attention, can be a religious act. We are thus enabled to apprehend God's creation as it is, our minds

† William Johnston, *Christian Zen* (New York: Harper & Row, 1971), p. 19.

unclouded by egoistical emotions, and so made more aware of God Himself.‡

Zen Catholicism was written well before the so-called "spiritual revolution," with its proliferation of new religions, and before the arrival in the West of most of the Oriental spiritual leaders who are so influential today. But writing in 1974, well after "new religions" began to establish their impact in America and Europe, Dom Aelred is, if anything, more convinced than ever of the need for Christianity to absorb methods and ideas directly from the religions of the East. The very future of the Christian tradition may depend, according to Dom Aelred, "on reviewing its basic doctrines in the light of religious insights now being made available from the East."

> Here it is worth recalling that the first-century break between the New Israel and the Old—probably the greatest single tragedy, in itself and in its consequences, in the history of religion—was due to an over-anxious conservatism incapable of assimilating apparently alien doctrines. . . .
>
> Possibly the simplest way to discuss this problem is to raise the question whether the Church has not been too much concerned with religion *about* Jesus, too little with the religion *of* Jesus. In Mahayana Buddhism, for example, the faithful are encouraged to believe that the Buddha's luminous state of consciousness, what is held to be his supreme degree of wisdom and compassion, is open to everyone. This is the prospect which is attracting so many in the West to Buddhism today—to which must be added its apparent harmony with much that is disclosed in the sciences of physics and psychology. . . .

Dom Aelred therefore urges that the contemporary Christian seek after the attainment of a transformed quality of consciousness in himself, "the God-centered consciousness of Jesus," just

‡ Dom Aelred Graham, *Zen Catholicism* (New York: Harcourt, Brace & World, 1963), pp. 143–44.

as the Mahayana Buddhist strives to attain for himself the same level of being as the Buddha.

> That this happens to be what Christianity is all about is rather more than hinted at in passages from both the Pauline epistles and the Fourth Gospel. . . . Could it be that in striving to attain the Christ-consciousness, as here indicated, we have the only effective foundation for Christian renewal?
>
> To achieve "the mind of Christ" may well demand a profound re-thinking of Christianity's prayer life. Telling God, reverentially, what he should do, and people, indirectly, how they ought to behave, together make up a good deal of the Church's vocal prayers. They are hardly enough for those who believe themselves to be sharers in the divine nature, who wish to realise experientially such a state and make it known to others.*

Only a few years ago, Aelred Graham and William Johnston were nearly the only Catholic writers calling out for an exchange, at the level of practice as well as doctrine, between Buddhism and Christianity. And they were certainly among the very few who were attempting to carry out this exchange in their own prayer life. Now, however, the situation is quite different. Throughout America one may find devoted Christians from many denominations bringing Zen Buddhist forms of meditation into their spiritual practices. When Father Johnston began giving instruction in *zazen* at the Jesuit House of Prayer in Tokyo, he justifiably felt himself as something of a pioneer. But today one may find similar instruction being given at Catholic retreat houses from New England to Texas to California.

How to regard this whole phenomenon? In recent years, not only *zazen*, but other forms of Buddhist meditation as well, have begun entering the practices of both religious and lay persons at key places in the Western world. *Vipassana* meditation, which emanates out of the Theravada Buddhist tradition of Ceylon and Southeast Asia and which stresses the discipline of mind-

* Aelred Graham, *Contemplative Christianity, An Approach to the Realities of Religion* (New York: Seabury Press, 1974), pp. 120–23.

fulness, has lately begun to attract serious modern seekers, not a few of whom are Catholic priests and monks, while Tibetan Buddhist meditation has already become a profound influence in the spiritual lives of a surprisingly large number of Americans, largely through the work of two Tibetan lamas, Chogyam Trungpa and Tarthang Tulku, now living in the United States. The sort of impact that Tibetan Buddhism can have upon Christians has been provocatively described by Harvey Cox in his book *Turning East*. Cox writes:

> My own experience, mainly gained from the type of meditation I learned from Trungpa and his students, is that, far from luring me away from active participation in the world (as some critics claim it does), it enables me to think and act more decisively, to see things and people in sharper focus, and to suffer fewer regrets and recriminations. I came away from Naropa convinced that a sitting-type meditation is perfectly compatible with Christian life. Eventually it might even provide a modern equivalent of something we have lost from our heritage, the idea of a Sabbath or a stated time to cease, to do nothing, to allow what is to be. . . .

Cox goes on, however, to cite certain reservations he has about the Buddhist teaching as it was presented to him. Principal among these is that "despite its emphasis on not trying too hard, it seems to lay out a very long path," "a stupendous mountain the seeker must eventually climb in order to become enlightened." Put off by the complexity and intricacies of the Tibetan teachings, which remind him of ritualistic accretions that damaged Catholicism, he nevertheless concludes:

> But the sitting meditation remains the core. No teaching should be discarded either because of the excesses of its students or the pretentiousness of its interpreters. Learning to meditate does not entail ingesting the entire corpus of Buddhist ideology, doctrine and world view—or any of it. In fact, I believe there is no reason why it cannot become an integral part of Christian dis-

cipleship. I returned from Naropa convinced that it would be part of mine.†

Thomas Merton

Of course, it is impossible to go further on this subject without considering the work of Thomas Merton, though it will probably be many years before we can gain the necessary perspective concerning this remarkable person. Many of his writings are still unpublished and available only to scholars; many biographical data remain unexamined, and, most important, a great many people who knew Merton are still to be heard from, while those who have already spoken out present a picture that is complex, many-faceted and often self-contradictory.

Merton's deeply moving autobiography, *The Seven Storey Mountain*, published at the age of thirty-three, only seven years after he first became a monk, stops long before he was drawn into a sustained spiritual study of Eastern religion. The popular success of that book and the now accelerating influence of all his writings have made the general outlines of Merton's life widely known. Born in Prades, in southern France, in 1915, the son of a New Zealand artist and an American mother, Merton was raised and educated on two continents. At the age of twenty, he entered Columbia University, where he was plunged into the life of intellectual and moral experimentation that characterized the young American intelligentsia in the years leading up to World War II.

Even in this early autobiography, Merton relates that it was his friendship with a Hindu that opened his mind to Catholicism. This young Hindu seemed to Merton to embody in his character the truth of religion, as opposed to the then (and now) intellectually fashionable materialist philosophy. He urged Merton to study the Catholic mystics. "Now that I look back on those days," Merton writes, "it seems to me very probable that one of the reasons why God had brought him all the way from India, was that he might say just that."‡

† Harvey Cox, *Turning East* (New York: Simon & Schuster, 1977), pp. 60–62.

‡ Thomas Merton, *The Seven Storey Mountain* (New York: New American Library, 1941), p. 195.

Merton looked in the books of Christian theology and mysticism with completely new eyes. He began to feel living ideas in material that had thitherto remained closed or even contemptible to him—such as medieval scholastic metaphysics and psychology, long the butt of jokes among modern academic philosophers, with their strong commitment to positivism and British empiricism. Shortly thereafter, he converted.

In the quarter of a century that Merton lived as a Trappist monk at Gethsemani, Kentucky, he delivered a tremendous body of written work dealing with Christian mysticism, the contemplative tradition, monasticism, and the Eastern religions, particularly Zen, which he felt had a crucial role to play in the West by revealing the contemplative, mystical core of normal human life and therefore of the Christian tradition as well. One of Merton's last essays, "The New Consciousness," begins:

> One would like to open this discussion with a reassuring and simple declaration, to say without ambiguity or hesitation: Christian renewal has meant that Christians are now wide open to Asian religions, ready, in the words of Vatican II, to "acknowledge, preserve and promote the spiritual and moral goods" found among them. *

But "it is not that simple." Merton proceeds to list the strong activistic, secular and antimystical tendencies that militate against the recovery of contemplative Christianity in the West. Zen, to Merton, is the best hope because it rejects all doctrinal dispute and offers itself as something completely unclassifiable in familiar Western theological, moral or philosophical terms. "The real drive of Buddhism is toward an enlightenment which is precisely a breakthrough into what is beyond system, beyond cultural and social structures, and beyond religious rite and belief. . . . What this means then is that Zen is outside all structures and forms." (*Zen and the Birds of Appetite*, pp. 4–5). Zen, according to Merton, offers us the pure act of seeing, pure consciousness. It is this, Merton writes, that is the real meaning of *knowledge* in meditation and contemplation leading to salva-

* Thomas Merton, *Zen and the Birds of Appetite* (New York: New Directions, 1968), p. 15.

tion in Christ. Like most modern scholars and theologians, Merton has a horror of such terms as gnosis and esotericism. They suggest to him a secret, pseudo-system of ideas which not only bars the majority of men from the help of God but also intellectualizes the spiritual quest, leading to the egoistic "inflation" that the saints warn is the inevitable companion of so-called "higher knowledge."

Merton died in Asia in 1968, exactly twenty-seven years after entering the Trappist Order. The extent of his attraction to Eastern religions has been much disputed and is of course an extremely sensitive issue. Some who knew him claim that he was on the verge of "converting" to Buddhism, but even if that is so, it is a simplistic way of putting the point and, in the light of Merton's own written statements, would by no means imply any apostasy from Christianity. In fact, there is a common thread in his writings about Eastern teachings that indicates he placed even the highest forms of Oriental religion beneath the level of the Christian revelation. That thread is the Scholastic distinction between the order of grace and the order of nature, a distinction that allows Merton to praise the Eastern religions as the highest achievement "within the order of nature," while reserving the action of grace for the Catholic Church.

Certainly, there is a great difference between Merton's early and later statements about Eastern mysticism, a great deepening of his understanding and appreciation. In *The Seven Storey Mountain* he tells of his youthful enthusiasm for Oriental mysticism but admits that all he could take from its teachings was "a variety of auto-suggestion, a kind of hypnotism or else simply muscular relaxation. . . ." And he concludes:

> Ultimately, I suppose all Oriental mysticism can be reduced to techniques that do the same thing, but in a far more subtle and advanced fashion: and if that is true it is not mysticism at all. It remains purely in the natural order. That does not make it evil *per se*, according to Christian standards: but it does not make it good, in relation to the supernatural. It is simply more or less useless, except when it is mixed up with elements that are strictly diabolical. . . .†

† *The Seven Storey Mountain*, p. 185.

It is a far cry from this sort of opinion to Merton's later statements about Zen, one of which we have already cited. In an essay entitled "A Christian Looks at Zen," written only a year or two before his death, Merton identified the specific contribution of Buddhist meditation, and its unique value as a sign of what must be recovered in Christianity, in the following way:

> Buddhist meditation, but above all that of Zen, seeks not to *explain* but to *pay attention*, to *become aware*, to be *mindful*, in other words to develop a certain *kind of consciousness that is above and beyond deception* by verbal formulas—or by emotional excitement. (*Zen and the Birds of Appetite*, p. 38.)

Nevertheless, even when Merton is most appreciative of Zen, he almost always qualifies his stance by confining Buddhism to the "natural order." In the same essay, he writes:

> Zen is then not Kerygma but realization, not revelation but consciousness, not news from the Father who sends His Son into this world, but awareness of the ontological ground of our own being here and now, right in the midst of the world. (*Zen and the Birds of Appetite*, p. 47.)

And in the last public utterance of his life, delivered on the day of his death in Bangkok, he said:

> And I believe that by openness to Buddhism, to Hinduism, and to these great Asian traditions, we stand a wonderful chance of learning more about the potentiality of our own traditions, because they have gone, from the natural point of view, so much deeper into this than we have.‡

‡ *The Asian Journal of Thomas Merton* (New York: New Directions, 1973), p. 343.

Intermediate Christianity

But now let us pause to take stock and try to identify the essential issue in this encounter between Christian spiritual leaders and, in this case, Zen Buddhist meditation.

How are we to understand that sensitive and gifted Christians are opening themselves to Buddhism, while at the same time many among these claim that the only complete spiritual fulfillment for man is offered through Christianity? And how to assess the effort to select from Eastern teachings only those aspects, such as particular meditative practices, that seem to fill a certain gap in our lives? What is the real need that is being felt and expressed by the writers we have just cited—Johnston, Graham, Cox, Merton—as well as by the efforts of thousands of Christians in the Western world to make use of Eastern meditative practices? This question must be put even to those who are now turning solely to the contemplative tradition of Christianity (and Judaism) itself. What do they (we) want? And what do we need?

We have seen it stated that what is lacking is direct experience of God: mystical experience; that one must move from the theory and doctrine of God to the inner knowing of what these doctrines speak about. But I question whether this is really the basic issue or the basic need. I question whether the really lost element in Christianity is mystical experience as so characterized.

In my opinion, it is not the experience of God that is drawing Christians to contemplative practices, but the experience of existing as such: my own existence. The discovery is being made that our lives, even at their best, even at their most "virtuous," do not bring us the experience of our own existence. And the concomitant discovery is being made that in a hitherto unknown place—within the sphere of my own stable attention to myself—I find that I can exist. I see that everything else, no matter what grandiose or pious names we use—be they religious names, ethical, social or artistic—has been and is a substitute for my existence and therefore conceals the fact that I *am* not.

This point requires clarification. It has nothing to do with modern psychological notions of self-identity or existentialist

theories of selfhood. I am referring to an idea on a completely
different scale, which throws a radically new light on the fate of
the Christian religion throughout history. This need that is being
felt by some modern people points to a "missing link" of Christianity which for centuries has simply not been recognized as such
in the Western world. And now that the idea of it, at least, is
again surfacing, there is a great danger that it will not be perceived with sufficient precision and honesty. If it is packed in too
quickly under the name of mysticism, a momentous opportunity
may be lost—this time forever.

I wish now to give this "missing link" a name: *intermediate
Christianity*.

The name is not my invention; I first came across it in the
journals of Father Sylvan, in an entry from which I have already
excerpted a few lines. Here I reproduce this entry in full:

> The idea of levels of Christianity may never again be
> known in the West. There is an intermediate level of
> Christianity which teaches the way that the higher level
> becomes distorted. We need the intermediate level. We
> need to observe how we lose Christianity, lose mys-
> ticism, lose the energy of God. Here lies the origin of
> sin and repentence, on the border between heaven and
> hell.
>
> Modern people do not understand that the Christian
> ideals to which half the world attempts to conform
> comprise a description of the results of a specific inner
> act and inner inquiry. Mysticism is a result, a great re-
> sult perhaps, of the inner inquiry; but everything is cor-
> rupted when I confuse inner work with the results of
> inner work.
>
> To experience love for God or my neighbor, even for
> an instant, is no less a result than mystical experience.
> To be virtuous is a result. To have faith is a result.
> Similarly, wisdom and compassion are results.
>
> All corruption of tradition begins with the confusion
> and mixing of inner work with the results of inner work.
> Jesus saw that the Judaism of his time had fallen into
> this confusion and that no one was practicing the inner

discipline free from the expectation or assumption of results.

These observations correspond very closely, of course, to Father Sylvan's discussion of magic and religion, which I have already reproduced. In that case, however, he was addressing himself to a quite different aspect of the modern situation. The issue there, as I read it, is the general sense, perhaps unconsciously felt by millions in the modern world, that Christianity simply has no force, no power to bring about change. Christianity as we know it does not produce Christian results, either in the individual or in the world. We shall discuss this later in detail, along with the observation that the wrong association of the Church with the political and economic (and lately scientific and psychiatric) currents in society covers over and conceals the inherent lack of results in modern religious practices.

However, the issue here is rather different, though of course related. When Father Sylvan speaks of the need for an *intermediate Christianity*, he is in effect saying that the teachings of Christianity as we know them were not intended to be put into practice without what he calls elsewhere "the accumulation of the force of inner attention." He writes, in rather atypical aphoristic fashion, "Stone must become water before it can flow." The pathos of Christendom, and here he is perhaps referring to the condition of most religions in the modern world, is that of preaching to stones that they must flow into the ocean. In the same passage, he says also: "In a certain sense, the problem of Christianity is not that something has been hidden, but that not enough has stayed hidden." In other words, in our present psychological condition, we are like stones, and the Christian virtues do not represent what is possible for us until we become as water.

In my opinion, this is also the message—the cry—of Thomas Merton and other Christians who are reaching out to Eastern forms of spirituality. The language they use is not attuned to put this message with philosophical precision, and their statements are perhaps mixed with other elements which do not correspond to the idea of an intermediate or preparatory Christianity. Yet, as I hear them, that is the essential petition in their writings and their search. Let us look once again at the works of Merton and we will see that such distinctions as that between the order of grace and the order of nature can usefully be approached in terms of levels of Christianity in the sense expressed by Father Sylvan.

In one of Merton's earliest writings about Zen—an exchange of essays with D. T. Suzuki—he roughly equates the term "purity of heart," as found in the teachings of the Desert Fathers, with the term "emptiness," as used by Dr. Suzuki. Both terms are taken to refer to a certain inner state—a state of consciousness—in which a man is "free of alien thoughts and desires . . . all images and concepts which disturb and occupy the soul. It is a favorable climate for *theologia*, the highest contemplation, which excludes even the purest and most spiritual of ideas and admits no concepts whatever."

Merton continues:

> One thing, and this is most important, remains to be said. Purity of heart is not the *ultimate end* of the monk's striving in the desert. It is only a step towards it. . . . It is, in fact, only a return to the true beginning. The monk who has realized in himself purity of heart . . . has still not ended his journey. He is only ready to begin. He is ready for a new work "which eye hath not seen, ear hath not heard, nor hath it entered into the heart of man to conceive." Purity of heart . . . is the intermediate end of the spiritual life. But the ultimate end is the Kingdom of God. This is a dimension which does not enter into the realm of Zen. . . . Purity of heart establishes man in a state of unity and emptiness in which he is one with God. But this is the necessary preparation . . . for the real work of God which is revealed in the Bible: the work of the *new creation*, the resurrection from the dead, the restoration of all things in Christ. This is the real dimension of Christianity, the eschatological dimension which is peculiar to it, and which has no parallel in Buddhism. (*Zen and the Birds of Appetite*, pp. 131–32.)

Several years later, reviewing *Zen in Japanese Art*, by Toshi-mitsu Masumi, Merton quotes with approval the author's state-ment:

"Christianity is a manifestation of the Incarnation of God, whereas Zen is intensive, inward enlightening of the divine being which the Japanese has apprehended as Nothing, and which must be supplemented, uplifted and completed by means of the manifestation of the In-carnation." (*Zen and the Birds of Appetite*, p. 92.)

Still later, Merton characterized the teaching of the Buddha as "an opening to love." There is something within human nature, a "primal consciousness" or "inner self," which needs to be awak-ened before the teachings of Christ can "take on flesh," that is, actually enter the heart, muscle and bone of a man's day-to-day living.

I am informed that toward the end of his life Merton was see-ing even more in the Eastern teachings than his published writ-ings reveal. Apparently, he realized that, in the Oriental tradi-tions, when the "Self" is spoken of in a certain way it is equivalent to the Christian teachings about God. And certainly were one to criticize Merton's accounts of the Buddhist tradition, or Eastern traditions in general, one might well begin by point-ing out how far short his writings fall from presenting the full scale of the spiritual traditions of Buddhism and Hinduism. But that is not what is at issue—and, in any case, who among us re-ally *sees* the full scale of even our own traditions? (Merely prais-ing a teaching as the "highest" does not in itself count for much in this respect.) Furthermore, it seems clear that unlike many promoters of "ecumenical mysticism," Merton's valuation of Eastern teachings was based on the hard-won understanding that arose out of his own inner struggles, rather than on specula-tive comparisons of written accounts of religious systems. Fi-nally, we must remember how much new material about Eastern religions has become generally available even in the past five years.

But the main point is not Merton's degree of competence as a comparative religionist. His aim was to become a better Chris-tian, and this, surely, dictated what he sought from the East as clues to the missing essentials of the Christian tradition. And I am persuaded that, for Merton, the magnetism of Eastern religion lay not in the promise of a methodology of mystical experience, but in the idea of an intermediate state of consciousness, an intermediate condition of man, as it were between sin and salvation. This intermediate state Merton saw as the state of Adam in Paradise; only in such a state was a relationship with God possible. Such a relationship was the beginning of service to God, rather than the end. In any case, for men as they are—as we are—to imagine we are in connection with God is to imagine, fantastically, that we are still in Paradise.

Once again, readers familiar with the Gurdjieff ideas will recall his extraordinary emphasis on what he called "the third state of consciousness," to which he gave the name "consciousness of self." According to Gurdjieff, this third state, which lies between "waking sleep" (our present, "fallen" condition) and "objective consciousness," is man's real *birthright*. It is only in that state that the great ideas and ideals of sacred tradition can be rightly received and acted upon. But if man in the state of sleep gets hold of sacred ideas or "techniques," he merely builds them into his egoistic subjectivity, his waking dreams. Therefore, for Gurdjieff, the aim of any serious man is first of all to awaken to himself. From this point of view, the term "esoteric" must be reserved, at least initially, for ideas, practices and methods of living that support the process of awakening. It has nothing to do with the exotic, arcane or "occult," as such. Gurdjieff is reported to have said to one pupil:

Dr. X., are you a Christian? What do you think, should one love one's neighbor or hate him? Who can love like a Christian? It follows that to be a Christian is impossible. Christianity includes many things; we have taken only one of them, to serve as an example. Can you love or hate someone to order?

Yet Christianity says precisely this, to love all men. But this is impossible. At the same time it is true that it is necessary to love. First one must be able, only then can one love. Unfortunately, with time, modern Christians have adopted the second half, to love, and lost

view of the first, the religion which should have preceded it. . . .

. . . It is naive, dishonest, unwise and despicable to
wear this name [Christian] without justification.*

In the language of Father Sylvan, the ability to love is a "result."

A result, however, of what? As Father Vincent discovered, in
order to say, *I am a Christian,* a man must also be able to say, *I
am.*

What is the way that leads to this? We need to go into this
question more thoroughly.

* G. I. Gurdjieff, *Views from the Real World* (New York: E. P. Dutton,
1973), pp. 153–54.

Chapter Six

St. Joseph's Abbey

The Primal Christian Act

What is the foundational act of Christian spirituality, and why is it so easily lost? This is the question brought to us in the writings of such men as Thomas Merton, Aelred Graham, William Johnston and a growing number of other Christians now investigating the religious systems of the Orient. And it is a question being lived in an exemplary and highly instructive way in a Catholic monastery sixty miles west of Boston, St. Joseph's Abbey, a Cistercian community in Spencer, Massachusetts.

Before looking at this important experiment in contemplative Christianity, it may be useful to remind ourselves of the weight of this question of the foundational act of Christian spirituality, the actual inner movement that makes possible the contact between man and what is higher than man. We need to recognize that we are not speaking about only one or another aspect, major or minor, of a tradition. To Christians such as Thomas Merton, the outcome of this search for what has been lost will determine the future of the whole Christian tradition. And we who are looking in from outside, trying to understand the need they feel, may be shocked to realize that upon this issue may depend our own future as well, and indeed the very life of man on this planet.

The search is not for some new theology, nor for the return of ritual forms, nor for a considerate relationship to other traditions, nor for any broadening of doctrine to accommodate the changing problems of contemporary life. The search is for something "smaller" and at the same time more basic than any of these things, desirable though they may be from certain points of view. Even concepts dealing with different states of consciousness have already become so psychologized in our culture that they do not convey the immensity and centrality of this "intermediate awakening," without which no truth or moral power can enter into the life of man.

Once one has learned to identify this awakening, one begins to see it spoken about in many traditions throughout history, and one begins to distinguish it from descriptions dealing with the highest states of inner spirituality. Many apparent contradictions between traditions and within a tradition itself are resolved when it is realized that in one place the struggle to awaken is being spoken of, while in another the attainment of Union is in question.

It becomes clear that throughout history as we know it, the very first idea that disappears from tradition when it begins to lose its power is this teaching about gradations of the being of man. When this happens, it is no longer possible to distinguish elements of a teaching meant to support the developmental process toward awakening, from descriptions of the results of awakening; far less is it possible to see the real distance that separates ordinary human life from the moral and spiritual powers that are actually associated with the highest states of presence but which, through a terrifying irony, have been assumed by whole societies to be the innate characteristics of every human being just by virtue of his physical existence. Thus, before one can speak of the extraordinary powers and gifts (to use the traditional Christian term) associated with the highly developed spirituality of the saintly, one will have to speak of such things as freedom of choice, clear intelligence, and goodness of will (altruism) not as given characteristics of our being but as themselves results of inner discipline. These latter characteristics may be said to be a necessary condition for the higher reaches of spiritual attainment, and they may also be said to be aspects of the birthright of man insofar as natural man is defined as the "likeness of God." And from this point of view, the distinction between nature and grace must be read to position our present level as not even at the level of natural man. We are subnatural men. Yet the teachings of the great religions as we know them are meant for natural man, in whose essential nature there lies an activated disposition toward God. "Before the Fall, Adam was able not to sin."

Father Thomas Keating

St. Joseph's Abbey is situated among rolling hills just off US 9 ten miles west of Worcester, Massachusetts. I swung my car around the wide, circular driveway in front of the main building, a large, handsome stone structure with magnificent low gables and commanding an expansive view of the New England countryside. It was a brilliant October afternoon, just past the peak of the autumn coloration. As I was a bit late for my appointment with the abbot, I only glimpsed the sweep of the well-tended grounds.

I was graciously ushered into a small, paneled drawing room where three men were waiting for me, two in the black-and-white robes of the Cistercian Order. Abbot Thomas Keating introduced himself and then presented me to Father Basil Pennington and to Dr. Ewart Cousins, of Fordham University, who was visiting as a guest lecturer.

I had heard a great deal about Thomas Keating. A gifted young divinity student in Berkeley, who had himself explored many Eastern teachings both in America and Asia, spoke of him as his own spiritual guide and of St. Joseph's Abbey as a place where, under Keating's direction, Catholicism was meeting the challenge of the new Oriental religions in America. I had listened with great interest to a taped lecture recently delivered by Father Thomas to the monks at St. Joseph's. The lecture was an incisive historical analysis of how Western Christianity had lost the method and meaning of contemplative prayer and how, due to this loss, the truth of Christianity was no longer able to penetrate into the lives of modern people.

Contemplation as Knowledge

According to Father Thomas, the Christian sense of the term "contemplation" is rooted in the biblical teaching about knowledge. The Bible uses a specific term to refer to the level of knowledge about God that is possible and necessary for man.

The word in the Greek Bible is *gnosis*, which translates the Hebrew word *da'ath*, "an extremely intimate kind of knowledge involving the whole man, not just the mind."

This immediately caught my interest. In the first place, the term *da'ath* in the Jewish mystical tradition refers, among other things, to divine omniscience—not only in the sense of knowledge about everything but of a knowing (or awareness) that penetrates into all the realms of the universe, a knowledge that lives and moves in everything. By application to man, the microcosm made in the image of God, this term, then, refers to a quality of knowing that suffuses and harmonizes the whole structure of human nature, and this in turn rests on an understanding of the human organism as in itself a many-faceted mind, of which the mind we know is but one small aspect.

This touches directly on the metaphysical teachings of the Western tradition, which have been so poorly understood in the modern era. Just as *gnosis* has been mistakenly identified with unusual objects of ordinary mental processes (i.e., new objects of knowledge), rather than as referring to a new or higher faculty of knowing itself, so, in the metaphysical aspect of the Western tradition, higher realities have been mistakenly identified by modern critics as invisible or extraordinary *things*. But, in both cases—with regard to the structure of man and the structure of the cosmos—the higher refers to levels of consciousness. The harmonizing and governing power of *da'ath* (in the Kabbalistic and Hasidic cosmic scheme) has its counterpart in the unfolding within man of the harmonizing power of consciousness, the growth of a new attention.

The "Middle" and Its Neglect

Keating's lecture, however, turned immediately to the notion of love. The higher, experiential knowing comes only through love, the love of God—in two senses: the love or striving that a man feels toward God and the love that God directs to man.

But here, too, an issue of central importance cries out for separate consideration. In Christianity, perhaps more so than in the Asian teachings as we are familiar with them, the ultimate good, the reconciliation of man and God, is constantly stressed. The only real value, the basic meaning of all life, inner and outer, is never lost sight of. In the human realm, psychologically, all changes and developments possible within the structure of man—developments of power, perception, etc.—are secondary to the ultimate good, which is man's union with God. Similarly, in the metaphysics of Christianity the whole realm of nature is always seen in its subordination to the ultimate goodness of God. Therefore, both in man and in the cosmos, the middle realms have tended to become neglected through an unbalanced emphasis on the ultimate or final reality in life. So concerned was the Church that man not be diverted by that which, while higher than ordinary man, is still secondary to God, that it neglected the intermediate world, both outwardly and inwardly: Outwardly, the world of nature in its many levels; inwardly, the world of the "third state of consciousness." Outwardly, the realm symbolized by medieval angelology; inwardly, the realm of intrapsychic energies and forces. Outwardly, the precision and flexibility to adjust its symbolism and expressions to the changing subjectivity of the modern world while at the same time retaining the essential "sound" of the Christian teaching; inwardly, the use and constant rediscovery of spiritual technique for the purpose of ontological growth rather than emotional satisfaction. Throughout Western history, the Church has tended to emphasize the goal of man's life and to underplay or neglect the instrumentality by which the goal may be reached. Perhaps only thus, as René Guénon has observed,* was it able to rescue the Western world from complete submersion in the tides of barbarianism and materialism throughout the centuries; it offered pure and real ideals as well as patterns of living that oriented the whole of Western civilization. For two thousand years it has been a "hearth of hope." At the same time, however, enormous confusion is bred when purity of intention (love of God, love of the Good) is demanded of man without a compassionate and workable psychological knowledge of everything in the individual human being that resists or covers over such purity of heart.

At the very outset of Thomas Keating's lecture, I therefore experienced a shock of recognition. Both Christian love and the Judaic knowledge of God could not be understood as starting points in the usual sense; they could not simply be assumed to

* In *Aperçus sur L'Esotérisme Chrétien*.

exist in man. *They could not be commanded!* Or, rather, if they
are commanded, it can only be within the context of a precise
and complete method of inner development. And then such
terms must have distinctly different meanings, depending on the
level of development of each individual man. How much of the
religious hypocrisy and unnecessary suffering of this world was
rooted in the failure to see this point?

Knowledge and Love

Keating's lecture proceeded to a general historical outline of
the discipline leading to this "knowledge of God that is impreg-
nated with love." In fact, the very word *contemplation* originally
meant such knowledge, and this meaning remained, according to
Keating, until the end of the Middle Ages. Throughout the Middle Ages, the key element of the Christian inner work, the discipline that could result in the contemplative knowledge of God,
was what Keating called "an exercise in listening." "The method
of prayer for these monks . . . consisted in a practice known as
lectio divina (the Latin literally means *divine reading*). . . . For
the medieval monks, *lectio divina* meant reading Scripture, or
more exactly, listening to it. They would repeat the words of the
sacred text with their lips so that the body itself entered into the
process. . . . It was primarily an exercise of listening. Listening
can be at different levels. It can be with the bodily ear, with the
imagination, with the heart, or with the whole being. The monks
sought to cultivate through *lectio divina* the capacity to listen at
ever deepening levels."

But around the twelfth century things began to change. With
the founding of the great schools of theology, the analytic faculty of the mind began to receive more emphasis and was eventually brought to bear on spiritual life and prayer as well. The
lectio divina began to be organized and compartmentalized into
various systematic methods, although contemplative knowledge
of God still remained the ultimate goal.

However, by the sixteenth century historical and cultural
events were accompanied by "a general decadence in morals
and spirituality." Prayer began to be used "as a means of
(moral) self-discipline in an age when institutions and structures
of all kinds were crumbling." Keating adds: "While prayer can

certainly be used for this purpose, it is not its primary function. Prayer is response to God. It does not come into being because we want to do things with it. But during this period of much needed reform, prayer began to be used primarily as an instrument for moral formation."

Along with this development, the tendency to systematize and compartmentalize prayer resulted in the division of methods according to the part of the self that was most active. "Mental prayer itself came to be divided into *discursive meditation* if during prayer thoughts dominated; *affective prayer* if the emphasis was on acts of the will; and *mystical contemplation* if graces infused by God were the predominant factor." Each method had its own methods and its own separate aims. The goal of contemplative knowledge of God was moved into the background. "It did not fit into approved categories. . . ." This, says Keating, was "a disaster for the Church's traditional teaching."

The Fragmentation of Contemplative Prayer

Keating's message was that the loss of the meaning and wholeness of contemplative prayer effectively barred Christians from the direct experience of God within themselves. Mystical experience became somehow suspect, if not even "unholy." Christians were systematically cut off from the possible experience of the divinity within human nature.

The Renaissance and its influence added to the problem. With pagan elements "taking over Christendom," it seemed necessary to "reconquer the world for Christ," with the result that outer action, rather than inner experience, came to be the dominant value of religious life, just as it was beginning to dominate all other values of Western civilization. Here the influence of the Jesuits was decisive. Whatever may be the full meaning of the *Spiritual Exercises*, developed by Ignatius Loyola (the founder of the Jesuit Order), they came to be employed almost exclusively in the service of Christian action, rather than contemplation: the aim was to "serve God," rather than to "taste God." Keating's point of view, however, is clearly that the aim of serving God through action cannot be separated from the independent struggle to experience God in one's own being.

Other events of great significance drove the Roman Church ever farther from the aims of contemplative prayer. The spread of Quietism in the seventeenth century brought mysticism of all forms into great disrepute. Quietism was a teaching that placed complete emphasis on an individual's inner intention of surrender and did away with the need for continued effort in prayer or in the outer life. It was condemned as false mysticism by Pope Innocent XII in 1687.

Certainly since the Protestant Reformation the Catholic Church had clearly drawn itself up against individualist spiritual experience. But Keating did not discuss the situation as it developed within Protestantism itself. Instead, he made a brief but telling observation about the influence of the Jansenist controversy on the whole of Catholic spirituality in the past three centuries. Jansen, a seventeenth-century French bishop, argued for the utter corruptness and spiritual impotence of post-Adamic man. According to the Jansenists, man was totally unable to love God and was so under the sway of sin that nothing in his inner or outer life was good. Only divine grace, which was not guaranteed to all, could save him.

Although Jansenism was eventually condemned, "it left behind a pervasive, anti-human attitude that perdured in many parts of the Church throughout the nineteenth century and on into our own time. . . . The pessimistic form of piety which it fostered spread with the émigrés from France at the time of the French Revolution to many English-speaking regions, including Ireland. Since it is largely from French and Irish stock that priests and religious in this country [the United States] have come, the Jansenistic spirit of narrowness and exaggerated asceticism has deeply affected the psychological climate of our seminaries and training centers."

The Scale of History

I had replayed Thomas Keating's lecture several times before this present meeting. It had been a great help in bringing to mind the vast historical stage upon which Christianity has developed since becoming the "state religion" of the Western world. For nearly two thousand years the ideas and the language of this teaching had entered into every social, political, and cultural experience of much of the world's population. I was forcibly struck by this fact, which one so rarely *feels*. And because one does not often feel the weight of this fact, one is tempted to say the word "Christianity" and imagine that the essence of the teaching is right there, between one's eyes. In any case, Keating's taped lecture had helped me to sense the stupendous fact that two thousand years after Christ walked the earth, and after the birth and death of how many nations, how many wars, how much violence and torturing of the forces of human life, after how many cultural upheavals, how many revolutions, how many ideologies and philosophies, how many movements of peoples and races across the face of the globe—that after all of this there were still serious people who felt within reach of the inner core of the path of Christ. To know even a little of the mad history of the human race and to be even slightly sincere about the knots and twists of the human psyche is to be brought to respectful silence by this possibility. Even if one holds a worm's-eye view of history, the question that still baffles the mind long after all theories and explanations are considered is, What was the shock that Christ brought to humanity and that still reverberates two thousand years later?

The Centering Prayer

Father Keating solicitously pointed me toward the sofa and offered me a cup of tea. He is a tall, thin man in his late fifties. His movements are slow and regal, his large, gentle features full of warmth, his voice a rich, wavering vibrato. Seated to my left, Father Pennington presented a strong contrast: big and robust— a man of about forty—with obviously great physical energy. His long, full beard, streaked with gray, poured over the black scapulars and called to mind the bearded monks of Eastern Orthodoxy. I soon learned that he had, in fact, recently traveled to Greece and had lived for an extended time at the monasteries of Mount Athos.† On the chair to my right was Ewart Cousins, whom I knew by reputation as one of the leading scholars of me-

† Fr. Pennington has published selections from the journal he kept during this retreat, a movingly written document of first importance for anyone seeking to understand how the church perceives its present need: M. Basil Pennington, *O Holy Mountain!* (Garden City, N.Y.: Doubleday, 1978).

dieval Christian spirituality. Only some months later, in a private meeting with Cousins, did I learn of his own pioneering efforts to bring the ancient contemplative teachings into relationship with the current "consciousness" movement. At this meeting, however, he modestly refrained from speaking much about his own work—and this particular quality of his lingered at the back of my mind after I left St. Joseph's.

Seated with such men, there was no need to beat around the bush, and before five minutes had passed we were in the thick of the subject. I discovered that here, at St. Joseph's Abbey, an approach to contemplative prayer was being attempted that was beginning to have influence beyond the walls of the monastery. Called "the centering prayer," it was originally designed for people outside the monastery who were seeking a more simplified kind of prayer than is generally taught in parishes and Catholic educational institutions. The name disturbed me, but I brushed aside my initial reaction. After all, anyone who has lived as long as I have in California and observed the way very big words are applied to very little things is bound to develop certain allergies.

As the rationale behind the centering prayer was explained to me, my skepticism began to give way to a sense of anticipation, especially after hearing this new technique of prayer likened to the method described in *The Cloud of Unknowing* and compared to the disciplines of the great masters of the Hesychastic tradition such as Nicephorus the Solitary!

Was it really so?

Was it here, in Spencer, Massachusetts, that the "invisible history" of Christianity was being carried forward into the twentieth century?

I turned on my tape recorder and began the interview by asking, "Do you think there is a renewal of the contemplative spirit of Christianity in the West, in America?"

"Emphatically yes," said Keating. "It's been percolating over the last few years in various places—not only individuals, but centers; it's almost an . . . explosion."

"But isn't there some particular difficulty," I asked, "due to this being the twentieth century, where people are constantly exposed to such things mainly through books and the intellect, rather than through the total environment of a more traditional culture? Is there a danger of a superficial spirituality that does not really penetrate to the root of the human condition? The problem certainly exists among the Eastern traditions that are now coming in."

Father Pennington answered me: "We're in a whole new era," he said. Recapitulating the points Keating had made about the intellectualism that began to stifle medieval Christian spirituality, he went on to say that today's young people are no longer bound by that problem. "I think that just in recent years, because of multimedia, the whole TV culture and everything that goes with it—because of all that, the error of intellectualism has passed or is passing. It's much more a *total* thing now, as it was in the earlier time, when our order flourished, in the twelfth century. And so we find that the young people today are ready to go into nonconceptual prayer very quickly. We've found, for example, that older priests and religious who have been through the seminary have an awful time getting out of their heads; they are very caught on that conceptual error and have to fight all the way when they try to learn something simple, like the centering prayer. But the young people are different. . . ."

I wanted to interrupt Father Pennington by saying that my sympathies were entirely with the older priests. My own experience with television and the younger generation corresponded not at all with what he was claiming. Quite the contrary. When I first came across such views about television in the writings of McLuhan and others—the idea that television engages a different aspect of the self from books or newspapers—I was intrigued and made a number of experiments to find out if it was true. I saw, and this was confirmed by friends who were also interested in this question, that, opposed to everything McLuhan claimed, television was directed to precisely the same part of the mind as novels and newspapers. Interestingly enough, this issue had also come up at one point during my conversations with Father Sylvan in the Bangkok airport. I had asked him specifically about the influence of journalism and media. He agreed with my assessment and added, "People do think television can reach the heart more easily than the written word, but that is not true. Both are taken in by the associative mind. But economic forces make people fool themselves about it. The television industry has to prove it is appealing to a different part of man from newspapers or books, and this it does by programming with sex and violence. But it is really the same thing as newspapers. Because people are drawn more to sex and violence, they begin to believe what they are told about television's power to engage the feelings." This observation was followed by an extremely interesting discussion about the emotions that are part of the associative mind. "This part of man has imitation feelings as well as imitation thoughts. It is easy to be fooled by it. One has to awaken an attention that can 'geographically' discriminate the sources of perception in the human body. . . ."

Father Pennington went on to cite the need many young people feel to come home to their own tradition after having explored Eastern spiritual disciplines. They are therefore well prepared for Christian spirituality. To meet this need, in the terms in which it is being felt and according to the preparedness of today's spiritual seeker, the centering prayer was developed. It was in this context that the name of Maharishi Mahesh Yogi was first mentioned—to my surprise. I soon discovered that the methods of the Transcendental Meditation movement were a principal stimulus and standard of comparison of the centering prayer.

Father Pennington must have noticed my puzzlement about this. "I've always been impressed by Maharishi Mahesh Yogi's ability to get to people. He meets people where they are. He took a scientific approach to Americans, because that's where they are. He very quickly gives people a deep experience and then explains it and develops it, builds on it, and then leads people to community and responsibility. And I think we have to look at that carefully. Today you have to take the chance of leading people into an experience and then building from that. But, sooner or later, the person has to pay a price. The biggest problem is fidelity, staying with it, looking for the God of experience, rather than only the experience of God. That's the key, that's the dying and suffering . . . but experience is the best way to move toward that. I agree with Maharishi; if you can just get them started, practicing regularly. . . ."

I offered my own opinions about television and my suspicion that such methods as TM might, like television itself, support a certain passivity of the mind that was not related to the inner stillness of which the contemplative traditions speak. Father Pennington said he did not wish to place too much stress on television—he had watched it only two or three times. He took it merely as one of many signs that young people are seeking to be reached in other ways than by books.

One could hardly disagree with that.

Obviously we had reached, and quickly, the question of the emotions: *What are the emotions of a Christian?* And what is the bridge that can lead a man from the state of submersion in the egoistic emotions to that incomparable range of life known under the simple term "the love of God"? Is the present hunger for "experiences" only, as Metropolitan Anthony warned, a misleading attempt to mask the pursuit of ordinary emotion?

It seemed the right moment for me to ask about the conversation I had had with Metropolitan Anthony on this subject. I repeated, in detail, what he had said to me about the years it had taken for his people to begin to understand the difference between "emotion" and "feeling."

Apatheia, *or Emotional Freedom*

As a matter of fact, not long after that meeting with Metropolitan Anthony I accidentally came upon the writings of the fourth-century spiritual master Evagrius Ponticus. These writings gave strong voice to the distinction between emotion and feeling, and explained a great deal about the historical distortion of the Christian teaching about the nature of human emotion.

The key term is the word *apatheia*, which translates into our word "apathy" but which is as far from the meaning of our English word as diamonds are from broken glass.

I should mention here, before proceeding to Evagrius' characterization of *apatheia*, that for many centuries this extraordinary author was officially condemned as a heretic by the Church, principally because of his writings about the cosmic nature of Christ.‡ This aspect of Evagrius' teachings is referred to as "Neoplatonism," a term that is as badly misunderstood by many scholars as the term "gnosticism." Evagrius was a pupil of Clement of Alexandria and Origen, who was also condemned. Origen, in his turn, is thought to have been a pupil of the mysterious Ammonius Saccas, under whose powerful influence the teachings

‡ See the illuminating Introduction, by John Eudes Bamberger, in Evagrius Ponticus, *The Praktikos—Chapters on Prayer* (Spencer, Mass.: Cistercian Publications, 1970), pp. xxiii–xciv.

we now call Hermeticism entered the stream of ideas in both Western and Eastern Europe. The immense significance and force of these ideas are now beginning to be recognized.

Apatheia means, literally, "without emotions"—or, more precisely, freedom from emotions. Its quality of being an *intermediate* state of the soul, the above-mentioned bridge, is characterized by the translator in the following way: "*Apatheia* . . . marks a decisive turning point in the spiritual itinerary of the Christian. It is the door to contemplation, or more exactly, its vestibule." And Evagrius himself writes, "Now this *apatheia* has a child called *agape* [love of God] who keeps the door to deep knowledge of the created universe. Finally, to this knowledge succeed theology and the supreme beatitude."*

It is interesting to note that immediately after this statement about the nature of *apatheia*, and before proceeding to discuss the practical aspects of the Christian spiritual discipline, Evagrius writes of the hidden, or (in our definition) esoteric, nature of these teachings:

> We shall not, to be sure, tell everything that we have seen or heard, but as much as we have been taught by the Fathers to tell to others. . . . So as "not to give what is holy to the dogs or to cast our pearls before swine" some of these matters will be kept in concealment and others alluded to only obscurely, but yet so as to keep them quite clear to those who walk along in the same path.†

The most influential of Evagrius' practical writings may be taken as general guidelines for the arduous inner struggle to break free from the sufferings and illusions brought to man by the emotions. Emotions and the thoughts that support them are often given the name "demons." This term, which sounds so naïve to the modern mind, has a meaning that is anything but naïve. Man is a microcosmic being; he lives and moves within a field of forces and influences spanning the entire ontological range of forces in the universe. These forces have a direction—a vertical direction toward or away from unity with God. And the

* Ibid., pp. lxxxvii and 14.
† Ibid., pp. 14–15.

transactions of these forces take place within the mind and heart, within the "soul," as well as in the external universe. Seen from this point of view, modern man has absurdly underestimated the reality and the ontological direction of the energies within his own psyche. We say, "I am angry" or "I feel happy," without realizing or seeing that in that moment a specific energy transaction is taking place that is as much a part of the order of nature as the turning of the earth or the movement of lightning. Moreover, our fundamentally Cartesian view of nature as a play of nonpurposive motions prevents us from discriminating the direction of the forces within or outside of ourselves. The term "demons" suggests that man, without extraordinary help, can no more control the basic course of the emotions and change their direction than he can reverse the rotation of the earth.

The *Praktikos* of Evagrius begins with the listing of eight kinds of "evil" or "passionate" thoughts: gluttony, impurity, avarice, sadness, anger, *acedia*,‡ vainglory and pride. By calling them "thoughts," Evagrius is referring to an exceedingly important element in the early-Christian teaching about the emotions. This element—which has been completely forgotten or only crudely guessed at in modern times—reveals why emotions have such negative power over us; at the same time, this forgotten knowledge about the emotions points to the single weak link in the armor of human egoism, the precise place where, though difficult, it is actually possible to struggle against the emotions. "It is not in our power," Evagrius writes, "to determine whether we are disturbed by these thoughts, but it is up to us to decide if they are to linger within us or not and whether or not they are to stir up our passions."

In short, thoughts, impulses, associations appear within the psyche, but as such *they are not yet emotions*. It is only when these "thoughts" are given something by ourselves, some energy, some specific psychic force, that they take on the nature of emotion—passion—and assume their overwhelming power in our inner and outer lives. The struggle against egoistic emotions is thus precisely located at that exact interval or "space" before a

‡ No single English word adequately translates this term. It has been variously rendered as "laziness" or "despondency" or "boredom." Perhaps it is best rendered as "the desire to give up."

thought, impulse or association becomes an emotion. But this is immensely difficult and supremely subtle work.

The Location of Freedom

I am certain that it is this aspect of the emotions that Father Sylvan refers to at one point in his writings where he says, "The Church long ago mis-identified the locus of human freedom. Because of this error, the whole of Western civilization is crashing against a brick wall." Once a "thought" becomes an emotion, it is impossible to destroy it; one can only suppress it or mask it with another emotion, or hypocritically give it a false name, or simply turn one's awareness away from it and its effects. All these helpless alternatives have characterized what we know of our culture's relationship to the emotions, including the most recent—namely, modern psychology's identification of certain emotions as "the unconscious."

Having begun the *Praktikos* in this way, Evagrius goes on to speak at length about the inner warfare that is necessary in order to touch the state of *apatheia*. As in all of the writings of the early Fathers, the impression given is that this struggle is the labor of a lifetime, requiring the supernatural grace of the influence of Christ and His teaching, the precise guidance of a holy teacher, and extraordinary persistence and spiritual desire on the part of the monk.

I only cite all this now in part to explain to the reader my bewilderment at what Father Keating said at this point in the interview. After I had repeated Metropolitan Anthony Bloom's remarks about the difference between emotion and feeling, Father Keating answered: "Our life here is something like an extended meditation. Some of the principles of meditation are applied to everything we do. . . . So, our approach to spirituality is quite different from what someone might need in order to get started outside, in ordinary life. When they come here, when they get this far, they've already gone beyond this period of emotion that you're speaking of. . . ."

Father Keating went on to speak about the low-keyed daily life of the monastery, the long-range daily routine, the environment of brotherhood, religious symbols and prayer quietly acting on the monks over a period of many years. And as a matter of fact, the conversation then went in many interesting directions.

But, perhaps because the subject under discussion was the emotions, I was suddenly aware of my own emotions carrying me away. Why did I assume that my understanding of the Christian teaching was along the right lines? Why was I so certain that there is no one who ever "goes beyond emotion" in any degree whatever, except in brief moments and then only after exceptional struggle and search? Why did I imagine that this man, Thomas Keating, for whom I already felt enormous admiration and respect, and even affection—why did I imagine that he would agree to the way I saw the issue? I have never felt more an outsider and intruder in what was none of my business than I did at that moment and for the rest of the interview. And why this sadness that I felt?

After an hour, when the interview was over, I left. I could have stayed longer; I might have been invited to stay the night and perhaps participate to some degree in the life of the monastery. Perhaps I could have experienced the centering prayer for myself. And ordinarily, I would have jumped at the chance; that was always the way I worked when investigating these things. It always proved invaluable, a necessary element in my efforts to understand.

What Does the Church Really Want?

But, instead, here I was in the late-October afternoon driving back toward Boston. Before reaching the turnpike, I turned into a side road and parked my car for a few minutes. I smoked a cigarette and watched the leaves falling. One phrase kept revolving over and over again in my mind: "What do they want? What does the Church really want?"

By the time I got back to my hotel in Cambridge, I had regained my composure. I went out to dinner with an old friend who was not the slightest bit interested in religion, and when I returned to my room that night I took out some of the cassette recordings that they sell at the monastery gift shop.

There was a set of three tapes by a Father William Meninger, who, I had been told, originated the centering prayer. The cassettes were intended to guide beginners in the actual practice of this form of meditation. I stacked two folded blankets and a bed pillow on the floor, sat down, and started the tapes. The first was a general introduction recapitulating what Keating and Pennington had said about the present need for contemplative prayer: For too long the faithful had been led to think that the direct experience of God was at best a rare event reserved only for saints or "mystics." Speaking very simply, Father Meninger compared contemporary Christians to poor immigrants on a ship, carefully rationing the meager provisions they brought with them and completely unaware that in the dining room a banquet is waiting for them three times a day. Others are simply turning away from the banquet the Lord has provided and going to "other tables—to gurus from India, to esoteric cults, to witchcraft and even the dope scene, although certainly these things are by no means to be considered of equal value."

"The unfortunate thing," according to Father Meninger, "is that many of the people doing this are Catholics or were Catholics, and don't realize that Mother Church is not Mother Hubbard and . . . is able to give an experience of God that far surpasses anything that could be found elsewhere." In this respect, he goes on, the Church—meaning "ourselves"—has been a failure. The aim now is to correct that failure by means of a simple technique that any person can employ, a technique that can very quickly bring about an experience, the "first course" of "the sumptuous banquet that the Lord has provided."

After discussing the various levels of Christian prayer—theology, mental prayer, affective prayer and contemplative prayer—and summarily relating them to everyday religious experience, and after revealing how as a seminary student he, too, had gone years without imagining that the experience of God was for anyone but the saints, Father Meninger describes how he hit upon the centering prayer, which he explains as "a way to dispose yourself to enter into contemplative prayer."

The tradition he draws upon is expressed, he says, in John of the Cross and Teresa of Ávila. But it was beautifully expressed prior to them in the fourteenth-century treatise *The Cloud of Unknowing*. "The author," says Father Meninger, "is an anonymous monk of the Benedictine Cistercian tradition. He expresses this tradition beautifully, but somewhat haphazardly. And I have systematized it a little bit to make it a bit more comprehensive and somewhat easier to teach. Something else I have done also, which the Church has always done; and that is, when it is convenient and helpful, to look into other traditions, even into traditions outside the Church. For example, if something in the Hindu or Zen tradition could help us in methods of disposing the body, to make prayer easier, then we ought to be able to utilize this. The Church has always done this, by the way. She did it in the second and third century through Clement of Alexandria by absorbing into herself the whole Hellenic culture. She has done it in every new culture she met along the way. She has taken what is good and what is true in them, and so she continues to do this. And we have a perfect right to do so, because all truths belong to us and all truth is supportive. This, then, is what we will do next: We will share with you this very, very concrete tradition of contemplative prayer—in such a way that I think you will experience something of what it is even after your very first attempts at it—as it is expressed in *The Cloud of Unknowing*. . . ."

Shortly after this, the first tape ends. Before changing cassettes, I got up from my pillow and walked around. Perhaps because it was a tape and not a man talking, I did not feel troubled as I had that afternoon at the monastery. It seemed clear to me that here Christians were facing the same pattern and the same dilemma that the new religions of Eastern origin were facing. I knew *The Cloud of Unknowing* very well. To call its method "simple," in the sense of "easy," is as misleading as it is for the followers of Zen to speak of breaking through the dualistic mind as "simple," "easy." It is not easy; it is stupendously difficult, however easy it might be to talk about it or imagine one is experiencing it. And to call the arrangement of *The Cloud* "somewhat haphazard" is as misleading as it is for many new religionists to speak without hesitation of "systematizing" and "updating" sacred texts, rituals, or even whole traditions. Is not every spiritual work of art a rhythm as well as a statement? a sequence of open spaces, of unheard sounds, a field of forces and tensions as well as a series of ideas or "instructions"?

But what made me think of the new Eastern religions was, more than anything else, the drive to bring that which is hidden into the open, with all the good intentions that accompany this effort among the followers of the new religions. The problem here is immense. The *hidden*, the *secret*, the *esoteric* refers not to the exotic or bizarre but to the hidden part of man, the part of ourselves that is covered over by the emotions of the ego. To touch that hidden part of ourselves, a certain language is needed, and an arrangement of impressions that obeys a spiritual logic incomprehensible to the exoteric mind.

The new Eastern religions, in my experience, often sacrifice entirely the hiddenness of their traditions. That is, they often restate the ancient teachings in ways that evoke recognizable emotions or "experiences." They see clearly enough that the old language and the old forms touch nothing in us and have no action in our lives. But they then sometimes swing over to the other extreme in order to make themselves known.

How to call *both* to the ego and to the unknown in ourselves at the same time? Those representing the purer, unchanged traditions discover how difficult it is to reach the inner feelings of man directly, and with tears in their eyes they watch people turning away from the ancient truths. But to appeal principally to the emotions or the thought without setting up a silent and troubling inner vibration—to what does that lead?

Such writings as *The Cloud of Unknowing* or the *Philokalia* are the "East" of the Christian tradition, corresponding to the "East" within our own nature. In his journals, Father Sylvan writes:

> The really necessary dialogue is not between East and West, but between parts of ourselves that are kept separated and unrelated by numerous influences both in secular and organized religious life. The whole question of fecundation by the East is a metaphor which Westerners must bring to themselves even if they never open an Eastern text or attach themselves to a guru. In myself there is the East, a source of light hitherto unconscious; and a West, where I hide what I have made of the great truths. Who can bear to accept that his life is what it is because of ideas which are poorly digested, ignored or altered in order to ever accommodate passing desire?

It was not until the following morning, after a night's sleep, that I listened to the rest of the tapes. The third tape led one through the actual practice of the centering prayer (which was in fact remarkably similar to Transcendental Meditation) and offered additional comments by way of practical rationale and explanation. It was this tape that strengthened my conviction about what Christians were really looking for under the name of "contemplation" and "mysticism." They were seeking *the next step* beyond faith (in its ordinary sense), the next step beyond ethical conviction and intellectual assent. They were seeking intermediate Christianity. Realizing this anew, I could not help but feel a sense of comradeship with them after hearing these tapes—quite the opposite feeling that I had had the day before. I, too, in my way, was seeking the *how* of truth, the next real step beyond conviction and appreciation. And certainly I, in my way, had seen a thousand times how difficult it is to remain focused on such a search, how easily and imperceptibly one slides into the old thoughts and emotions under the name of God or Higher Consciousness or Transformation or any of the dozens of words and concepts that can so effectively mask one's actual state of incompleteness and ignorance.

Chapter Seven

A Search for Conscious Christianity

The phrase "conscious Christianity" occurs several times in the journals of Father Sylvan, most strikingly when he is speaking against contemporary representatives of what he calls "mysticism without a soul." It is clear that he equates "conscious Christianity" with his other term "intermediate Christianity." The single dominant thread in his writings is the idea that the lost element of the Christian tradition lies in between mysticism and belief; something "more subtle than the experience of God: the experience of myself; more easily twisted than the knowledge of God: the knowledge of myself; more needful to me than the power of God: the power of listening from myself."

It is the thesis of this book that it is precisely this intermediate, or conscious, Christianity that is being sought by the numerous Christians turning now toward Eastern teachings or responding to the challenge of the new religions by delving into the Western contemplative forms and texts that have survived over the centuries.

Jesuit Spirituality

I brought this general point of view as a question to Father Daniel J. O'Hanlon, of the Jesuit Theological School of Berkeley. Father O'Hanlon has drawn upon extensive personal contact with the religions of Asia to deepen his understanding of the *Spiritual Exercises* of St. Ignatius, founder of the enormously influential Society of Jesus in the sixteenth century.

Although the caricature image of the Jesuit (bloodless, inquis-
itorial, knife-edged, manipulative intellect, etc.) has softened in
recent years, few Westerners outside the Jesuit Order realize the
extent to which the order is based on contemplative discipline.
The *Spiritual Exercises* is in fact an extended thirty-day series of
carefully guided meditations and psychological efforts intended
to bring the individual into direct contact with the divine Will.
In his essay "Zen and the *Spiritual Exercises*,"* Father O'Hanlon
points out that historical factors, such as the Church's general
suspicion of private religious inspiration, inclined the Jesuits to
emphasize the element of external application and service in
their spirituality and to soft-pedal the inner, experiential component. Eastern teachings, such as Zen Buddhism, can now serve,
he feels, to right the balance by bringing the meditative essence
of the *Spiritual Exercises* into clearer focus. Speaking in general
of the dialogue that has now begun between Christianity and the
religions of the East, he concludes:

> Some of us would not be surprised if what comes of this
> exchange, now beginning with a seriousness not found
> in all the centuries of their histories, turns out to be the
> most significant religious development in the centuries
> just ahead of us.

I asked Father O'Hanlon if he felt that contact with Eastern
traditions such as Zen would help to counter what has been
called the "excessively muscular" form of spirituality in the Jesuit Order.

"I think most serious students of the *Exercises* would agree
with me," he said, "that the real heart of what is going on there
is that although they *are* exercises, the whole point of them is to
create a receptivity and openness; and what happens in that
openness is the principal thing.

"For instance, the *Exercises* are geared toward coming to a
proper kind of decision about your life. But if you look carefully
at the way in which St. Ignatius is trying to help you bring that
about, it's not by reasoning it through and working hard at it,
but mainly by getting you sufficiently unhooked from your preju-

* *Theological Studies*, December 1978.

dices, your agenda, your own way of going at it—so that then what moves in you, the Spirit of God, can be trusted."

I then asked Father O'Hanlon specifically about the "intermediate": "It seems," I said, "that much of the contemplative in Christianity is being taken by people in the same way that the Oriental mysticism is being taken: in terms of experiences which actually imply a relatively high inner state. And what I gather from what you and some others are saying is that what is really missing is some kind of intermediate state. Not so much the big experience—but something without which the big experience leads to illusion or distortion of some kind. People seem to have gotten stuck in the all-or-nothing approach; either you are experiencing nothing less than God directly, or you are hopelessly fallen. Aren't you speaking of an awakening of some power or faculty of openness which we mistakenly assume is already active in us?"

Father O'Hanlon agreed, but wished at the same time to stress the process of *testing* that is a key element in the Ignatian *Exercises*. If one is truly open to the Spirit of God, certain feelings arise and persist, positive feelings that are the assurance of valid spiritual experience.

Frankly, I did not wish to get into a discussion of these feelings, the sensitivity to which in any case would have to be considered a result of some inner movement initiated by the individual. This elusive inner movement was, to my mind, of central importance—here and everywhere in the search for lost Christianity. I referred to a sentence from the *Spiritual Exercises* that Father O'Hanlon had cited in his essay, where St. Ignatius writes: ". . . it is not within our power to acquire and attain great devotion, intense love, tears, or any other spiritual consolation; but that all this is the gift and grace of God our Lord."

"Obviously," I remarked, "there is something the individual has to do; equally obviously, we are doing the wrong thing. We can't be totally passive in the dream that grace will just come down upon us. Nor can we be active in the way we are accustomed to be. It's the same question that arises out of St. Paul: we are helpless and weak; there is nothing we can do. Yet there is something we *must* do. Just what, exactly, is within our power?"

Father O'Hanlon approved of the formulation of this question and answered using the same term that Thomas Keating had used—and, of course, Thomas Merton as well: *disposition.*

"To answer that," he said, "just look at the title of the *Exercises.* These are *exercises* in order to *dispose* us to be free of attachments. The exercises are ways to reveal to yourself all the ways you are attached, helping you gradually to loosen your clinging to all sorts of things, with the confidence that that is much more effective than simply directing you to, say, acts of love."

"Actually, then, it's the confrontation with my attachments that is the channel for something freeing?"

"Right."

"Because," I went on, "I see that there is a tendency when I confront an attachment, to try to get rid of it—as a sort of act on my part—and I wonder if this is a danger too; I want to be very sure that I understand what you're speaking about."

Father O'Hanlon paused and reflected for a moment. "It does get very subtle," he said. "The willingness to let go"—here he smiled—"even of the trust in your efforts to let go, brings you to a point of . . . maybe despair is too strong a word . . . but a point where you simply . . . give up."

I smiled too. But we were both quite serious.

I persisted. "But it's just there, when I am giving up, that something must be maintained. A kind of vigilance? There's a way of giving up that is a kind of sinking. . . ."

"It *is* subtle," he said, "and I think you find these two elements emphasized in the two principle Zen schools, Soto and Rinzai. The Soto school is, Do nothing, sit there, get rid of the gaining mind. On the other hand, the Rinzai people say, *Strive* for enlightenment! And they're both true, in a sense. You have to be simultaneously alert, which is a kind of a striving, and relaxed, which is a letting go. And at a certain point, after a while, you begin to know what it is to stretch and relax at the same time, a point where you realize that to be alert and to relax are actually the same thing. You begin to see that the striving is a letting go.

"I can remember one week when I was meditating at a *wat* in northeastern Thailand. An American there loaned me a book: Shunryu Suzuki's *Zen Mind, Beginner's Mind.* I started reading it and I thought, 'It's kind of crazy; it doesn't make sense; it's kind of beautiful, but it doesn't hang together; he says one thing here and another thing there. . . .' Anyway, I sort of set it aside, but then. . . . When I was sitting, doing the kind of meditation he talks about, at a certain point I'd say to myself: 'Ah! *That's* what he's talking about! That's right!' You know? Something was verified somehow or other in the experience, without being able to be totally articulated.

"Now, I'm not talking about some huge mystic thing. Because I haven't had that kind of experience. I'm talking about just a very modest sort of entering into a different kind of orientation.

"And I think the same thing is true in the *Spiritual Exercises*. I think that what happened over a period of time was that, with the suspicion of the mystical, with the suspicion of the 'letting go,' the business of Quietism in the seventeenth century, and of course with the coming of the Enlightenment and all of that, the more 'muscular,' more 'Pelagian' kind of things that liberal Protestantism has fallen into—out of synch with what Luther was talking about—tended to take over. At the moment, however, the principal interpreters of the *Exercises* are trying to restore the balance."

I then took out my copy of Father O'Hanlon's essay and put it on the table. I opened it to a page where I had scrawled the words "a big *If*" in the margin next to a quote from Hugo Rahner's study, *Ignatius the Theologian:*

> According to Polanco, if the exercitant "places himself" simply and humbly in God's presence and follows this method of nondiscursive cognition, he will find the *sentire* for that to which God is calling him. Henri Pinard de la Boullaye has shown that this *sentire* is a key word in the Ignatian theology of prayer. It has nothing to do with emotional, let alone sensual, impressions; it is a completely intellectual mode of cognition, though it is certainly higher than discursive reasoning and must be ranked among the "spiritual senses."

"Isn't that a rather large assumption?" I asked. "*If* I could be 'simply and humbly in God's presence,' I would already be half-way home, or more—wouldn't I?"

"Exactly," he answered, "and that's why so many "devious"

means are used in the *Exercises*—to "catch you out," to show that to you. Just when you think, 'Well, here I am, I really have reached something,' then an exercise will be sprung on you and you'll say to yourself, 'Oh! I guess I'm not really where I thought.' So, in a sense, you're quite right; that *is* a huge *if*. And practically everything that is in the *Exercises*, in terms of concrete things to do, is intended to bring you to that point—"

"The confrontation with one's own weaknesses?"

"One's attachments."

"And illusions?"

"That's right," said Father O'Hanlon. "But attachment is one of the key words, and also *indifference*."

My eyebrows lifted. I thought immediately of the term *apatheia* in this connection.

"Indifference," he continued, "is not a very good word in the English language. In the Ignatian sense, it does not mean a kind of blasé or uncaring attitude. It refers to nonattachment, to not being ruled by your own self-centered desires. The example Ignatius gives is that you become like the balance scales that are evenly weighted on both sides; you're not pushing down this way or that way; you're simply resting there, waiting for the indication of the Will of God. He just puts a little speck of dust on one side and you are so open. . . .

"Now, that doesn't mean that you are not fully involved. But the involvement is not your own private, self-conceived agenda. That little speck shows you the direction your life may take, and you go with that. Ignatius himself was obviously a fantastically energetic man."

"It seems, then," I said, "that this is more a way of living, rather than a once-in-a-while experience. Surely, the human condition is such that the moment this happens, this openness, then in the next moment you're back into ego—"

"Right. You have to keep at it constantly."

"But as I understand the *Exercises*, it is a relatively infrequent undertaking, sometimes only once in one's life."

"Of course," Father O'Hanlon answered, "the *Exercises* in their historical form were geared toward the moment of a particular decision about the whole direction of your life, the choice of a form and vocation of your life. That's what they were originally for, and one of the problems of adaptation is that such a decisive moment doesn't occur every second Thursday in an individual's life. So, when you're using the *Exercises* as an annual event, you need to be much more flexible about a number of things, to adapt it from this kind of gearing everything to that once-in-a-lifetime decision—adapted more toward a constant creating or maintaining, recovering that kind of openness which may be there at moments of great decision but which really must be there in all of the follow-through."

I asked: "Then, is there an equivalent to a kind of constant inner work of this kind, even in the midst of life's activities? and is that being sought after in the Jesuit Order today?"

Father O'Hanlon replied to this question by explaining that the framework in which the *Exercises* exist is the structure of the Society of Jesus as drawn up by Ignatius in the latter years of his life. "This community is generated by the *Exercises* and includes a whole process of prayer, spiritual practice, living together, which are the means of supporting the experience of the *Exercises*.

"But," he continued, "when you ask about how this is done by the ordinary person who is not a member of such a group—well, in a way, Ignatius made a beginning toward that by freeing his religious community from the obligation of regular choir, wearing certain kinds of clothes, living all their lives in one place—a beginning toward the idea of maintaining the proper attitude and spirit wherever you are, whatever you're involved in.

"But the further application of this to the reality of lay life, married life, everyday life as most people know it—this remains to be worked out."

Attention and Virtue

My interviews with Dan O'Hanlon and other Jesuits who are exploring Eastern spiritual disciplines helped me to appreciate why Father Sylvan so often uses the rather colorless term "intermediate Christianity." Such a term effectively takes the issue out of the realm both of theological dispute and one's own subjective associations. It is not until considerably later on in his journals that he begins to associate it, as I have indicated, with the phrase "conscious Christianity," and with the especially heavy-laden term "soul."

It is interesting to note that the Ignatian term *sentire* in the passage quoted above leads to this very issue. Jesuit scholars generally agree that this is one of the most central ideas of St. Ignatius and at the same time the most difficult to define. It is an old Spanish word which on the surface means simply "feeling." But, as one Jesuit characterized it to me, it is "a feeling that is not ordinary feeling; and a knowing that is not ordinary knowing." Yet it is not anything like "mystical ecstasy."

The point seems to be that something has to be awakened in man that is both highly individual yet at the same time free from mere subjectivity, something both intensely my own yet free of ego. It is referred to, in ancient language, as "that which is between God and the animal." It is "the intermediate." Other traditional descriptions speak of the need for something to be "formed" in man; or "collected" (as "light" is collected); or "purified."

By calling this "something" the "intermediate," Father Sylvan is striving, it seems, to prevent our associating it with familiar subjective experiences of thought, emotion or sensation. The "intermediate" in man is not mind or reason as we ordinarily experience them; not familiar emotions, no matter how intense or how exalted their object; not "personal identity" in the sense of the social self.

In Father Sylvan's hands, this notion takes on the distinctly revolutionary character that it has in certain Christian writings themselves, a character that has become covered over by modern interpretations, literal, theological and psychological. Without the appearance of the "intermediate," the teachings of Christianity—the morality, the call to faith and to love, the work of sacrifice or service—simply cannot enter into a man.

Extraordinary notion! Unless we become "intermediate men," the teachings of Christ can have no real action on our being, however much we believe or strive or give ourselves in action in the world, or even undergo mystical experiences. All of this is, in Father Sylvan's words, "unconscious Christianity," or—to cite another of his disturbing expressions—"Christianity without Christians."

Various terms, terms that sound familiar to us psychologically but that we must now guardedly examine, seem to cluster around this notion of the intermediate: *openness, sensitivity, consciousness, feeling*—but, above all, the terms *presence, attention* and *seeing.*

"Openness," writes Father Sylvan, "is purity of attention." He then goes on to cite a passage from the tenth-century Eastern Orthodox figure St. Simeon the New Theologian. This particular statement is, in fact, quoted no less than three times in his writings. No other passage, apart from certain scriptural references, is ever cited more than once in the whole body of Father Sylvan's journals.

In order to appreciate the full force of this particular passage from the writings of St. Simeon, it is necessary first to recall to mind the beatitudes of the Sermon on the Mount, the words of Jesus that have served over the centuries as the essence of the Christian ideal:

> And seeing the multitudes, he went up into a mountain: and when he was set, his disciples came unto him:
> And he opened his mouth, and taught them, saying,
> Blessed are the poor in spirit: for theirs is the kingdom of heaven.
> Blessed are they that mourn: for they shall be comforted.
> Blessed are the meek: for they shall inherit the earth.
> Blessed are they which do hunger and thirst after righteousness: for they shall be filled.
> Blessed are the merciful: for they shall obtain mercy.
> Blessed are the pure in heart: for they shall see God.
> Blessed are the peacemakers: for they shall be called the children of God.
> Blessed are they which are persecuted for righteousness' sake: for theirs is the kingdom of heaven.
> Blessed are ye, when men shall revile you, and persecute you, and shall say all manner of evil against you falsely, for my sake.
>
> (Matthew 5:1–11)

The passage from St. Simeon the New Theologian is as follows:

> He who does not have attention in himself and does not guard his mind, cannot become pure in heart and so

cannot see God. He who does not have attention in himself cannot be poor in spirit, cannot weep and be contrite, nor be gentle and meek, nor hunger and thirst after righteousness, nor be merciful, nor a peacemaker, nor suffer persecution for righteousness' sake.†

Father Sylvan does not cite the statement immediately following this passage, which reads: "Speaking generally, it is impossible to acquire virtue in any other way, except through this kind of attention."

I spoke to another Jesuit priest about this passage and its distinctly revolutionary significance. "How many people," I asked, "will even entertain this idea that the familiar Christian virtues, by which half the world seeks to live, presuppose the development in oneself of a quality of consciousness that is actually extremely rare and difficult to acquire?"

I was intensely interested in what this man's response would be, as he himself was not only a scholar of traditional Christian spirituality but had seriously investigated some of the most powerful "non-Christian" psychospiritual disciplines now to be found. His answer could almost have come from the pen of Father Sylvan: "Not only is virtue impossible without the development of attention," he said, "but also, without attention there is no real sin."

He went on to explain that, in his opinion, the traditional Christian teaching about mortal, or deadly, sin refers to a relatively developed individual. He enumerated the three characteristics of mortal sin: it must be of a serious nature; it must be done consciously, with "full knowledge"; and it must be deliberate. Until a man has the power to act consciously and deliberately, his sinfulness is of an entirely different nature, as described by St. Paul in Romans: the sinfulness that is in me but is not my own act, the original sin that represents the general human malaise. "It is destructive, but not conscious."

This idea, he said, is what lies behind the teaching about the fallen angels. "There is no automatism in an angel. When they fell, they did it consciously. The fallen angels stand for that which is consciously against God."

† E. Kadloubovsky and G. E. H. Palmer, transl., *Writings from the Philokalia on Prayer of the Heart* (London: Faber & Faber, 1951), p. 158.

Where are all such thoughts leading? What conclusions are rising before us?

Certainly, two points need to be understood. In the first place, the intermediate in man actually represents the source of all the attributes that generally define human nature as distinguished from animal nature: free will, consciousness, moral power and rationality (in the sense of independent reason). And, inasmuch as we are not intermediate men, the classic definitions of human nature do not, strictly speaking, apply to us as descriptions of what we are, but only as descriptions of what we ought to be.

In the second place, the development of what we are calling attention, consciousness, openness is neither an easy nor an unambiguous enterprise. Inner, psychospiritual discipline of any kind, certainly the reaching out for "mystical experience," is an endeavor fraught with false directions—and a mistake in this sphere is of an immensely more serious nature than the usual so-called "sins" or errors that we customarily suffer over in our everyday lives. In fact, from this general point of view, it is actually incorrect to speak of "mistakes" or "sins" at all in any basic sense, just as it is incorrect to speak of any "virtues" or successes, unless and until there is activated in man the intermediate principle of human nature.

The conclusion is that the teachings of Christ as we know them are meant for people of a higher level than we ourselves. And the lost element in Christianity is the specific methods and ideas that can, first, show us the subhuman level at which we actually exist and, second, lead us toward the level at which the teachings of Christ can be followed in fact, rather than in imagination.

In brief, there are levels of Christianity. Failure to understand what this means has led to the distortion of the Christian teaching, with all that that implies in the collective history of Western civilization.

The Attention of the Heart

As I have come to understand it, this whole point of view can be best clarified and assessed in terms of the Christian teaching about the nature and destiny of the human soul. It is here, I believe, that we can precisely locate the question of lost Christianity in the language of the tradition itself and link that language to terms that are more understandable to the modern psychological temperament. At the same time, a fresh look at the Christian doctrine of the soul can bring us toward the cosmological element that is so lacking both in modern psychology and, by implication, in the way we think about ourselves.

Before turning directly to the traditional formulations about the soul as the intermediate principle in man and in the cosmos, it will be helpful to return to Father Sylvan's use of the citation from St. Simeon the New Theologian concerning the primacy of attention in the acquisition of virtue.

As I have mentioned, Father Sylvan copies out this passage several times in his journals. Yet nowhere does he explicitly describe the context in which this passage occurs in its original setting.

At first, this omission puzzled and disturbed me, because the context of this passage seems of utmost importance if we would grasp the real scale of the term "attention." Until we do so, the Christian doctrine of the soul will drift toward the same clichés and superstitions that have eroded the power of this idea over the centuries. As we shall see, the world of attention is the world of the human soul.

The passage in question occurs as part of St. Simeon's discussion of what he terms the "three methods of attention and prayer." His aim is to show that there are various kinds of attention within man and a different kind of inner struggle associated with each. The first method of attention and prayer is characterized as follows:

> . . . a man stands at prayer and, raising his hands, his eyes and his mind to heaven, keeps in mind Divine thoughts, imagines celestial blessings, hierarchies of angels and dwellings of the saints, assembles briefly in his mind all that he has learnt from the Holy Scriptures and ponders over all this while at prayer, gazing up to heaven, and thus inciting his soul to longing and love of God, at times even shedding tears and weeping. . . .‡

‡ Ibid., p. 153.

Of this method, however, St. Simeon says that it can lead to a man's being driven out of his mind or committing suicide. At the very least, he writes, an individual who takes this method as his principal form of prayer will remain all his life without success in spiritual life.

Why? And why is this kind of praying called a "method of attention"?

The "second method of attention and prayer" is this:

> . . . a man tears his mind away from all sensed objects and leads it within himself, guarding his senses and collecting his thoughts, so that they cease to wander amid the vanities of this world; now he examines his thoughts, now ponders over the words of the prayer his lips utter, now pulls back his thoughts if, ravished by the devil, they fly towards something bad and vain, now with great labor and self-exertion strives to come back into himself, after being caught and vanquished by some passion.

Yet this method too is condemned by St. Simeon. "The distinctive feature of this method," he writes, "is that it takes place in the head, thought fighting against thought." He goes on to say:

> In this struggle against himself, a man can never be at peace in himself, nor find time to practice virtues in order to gain the crown of truth. Such a man is like one fighting his enemies at night, in the dark; he hears their voices and suffers their blows, but cannot see clearly who they are, whence they come and how and for what purpose they attack him; because he himself remains in the head, whereas evil thoughts are generated in the heart. He does not even see them, for his attention is not in the heart,

Again: why? What is being spoken about? Could it be that what I call my "attention" is not attention, consciousness, at all? Or, rather, is it such a shallow level of consciousness that any attempt to know myself through the employment of this faculty is doomed to failure and self-deception?

But if that is so, are these masters of the Christian contemplative tradition also speaking about something at such a high level that one might as well return to the old descriptions of mystical ecstasy, which are also in fact so high and removed from my ordinary state of being that to cultivate them is little more than a form of spiritual psychopathology?

We are looking for something practical here, a bridge that is real and that actually relates my present psychological and moral condition to the possibility of tangible inner change. Father Sylvan speaks about this incessantly: the real, practical bridge to becoming myself. And the bridge, the intermediate work, has to do with this factor of attention, awareness, presence. Promising, full of hope. Yet, here we seem to be presented with a power or force of attention that is itself far removed from what I am and how I can in fact search. Is even Father Sylvan talking over our heads?

Now I begin to think there is a good reason why he has not quoted the words of St. Simeon that provide the context of the passage about attention being the precondition for virtue. But let us see what St. Simeon says about "the third method of attention and prayer":

> Truly the third method is marvelous and difficult to explain; and not only hard to understand but even incredible for those who have not tried it in practice. They even refuse to believe that such a thing can actually be. And, indeed, in our times, this method of attention and prayer is very rarely met with. . . .

So, I think, even in the time of St. Simeon, Christianity has become "lost." Or perhaps this particular form of inner search must always be discovered, even within the structure of the established forms of tradition in all their authenticity. Again, and again: what is being spoken of here? There is something, some approach, some struggle within myself, some activity within myself, that is very "high," very necessary and possible for me. Yet it is "unbelievable"; even the appointed elders of the tradition may not believe it is possible, may not dream of its existence both as a power and as a *way*.

After speaking of how this third method has become lost along with the real meaning of obedience to the teacher, St. Simeon writes:

> The beginning of this third method is not gazing upwards to heaven, raising one's hands or keeping one's mind on heavenly things; these, as we have said, are the attributes of the first method and are not far removed from prelest.* Neither does it consist in guarding the senses with the mind and directing all one's attention upon this, not watching for the onslaughts of the demons on the soul from within.

And so St. Simeon the New Theologian proceeds. The reader (myself) follows the text with great anticipation, fully expecting to hear the third method of attention, the true method, described with direct precision. But no such thing happens. Instead one reads:

> But you, beloved, if you want to be saved, begin to work thus: having established perfect obedience in your heart, which, as we have said, you must have toward your spiritual father, act in everything else with a pure conscience, as though in the presence of God; for it is impossible to have a clear conscience without obedience. You must keep your conscience clear in three respects: in relation to God, in relation to your spiritual father and in relation to other men, as well as to things and objects of the world (of life).
>
> In relation to God it is your duty to keep your conscience clear, permitting yourself no action which, to your knowledge, is distasteful and unpleasing to God.
>
> In relation to your spiritual father do only what he tells you, allowing yourself to do nothing either more or less, and proceed guided solely by his will and intention.
>
> In relation to other people, you will keep your conscience clear if you refrain from doing to them anything you yourself hate or dislike being done to you.

* A Russian term untranslated in the English text. The term is a rendering of the Greek *pláne:* "wandering" or "going astray."

In relation to things, your duty is to keep your conscience clear by always using them rightly—I mean food, drink and clothes.

In brief, do everything as though in the presence of God and so, in whatever you do, you need never allow your conscience to wound and denounce you, for not having done your work well.

Bewilderment! And extreme disappointment! Expecting to find a practical bridge, a step toward the intermediate in myself, I find only a list of actions and intentions that are impossible either because the external conditions of monastic structure no longer exist or, more basically, because these very rules cannot apply to a fragmented, contradictory being such as myself in the inner and outer conditions of contemporary life. I would, for example, gladly follow my conscience if only I could make contact with it; but the whole problem is that I do not hear my conscience! And so, yet again I ask: What, why, how to understand? What is the principle behind all this? Can it be rediscovered here and now in our present world?

Only after listing all these requirements does St. Simeon proceed. And as I read on, I begin to sense something. What St. Simeon has given is a summation of all the aspects of one's life that need to be contacted at the same time that one is *searching* for the necessary level or quality of attention in oneself:

Proceeding in this way you will smooth for yourself a true and straight path to the third method of attention and prayer which is the following: the mind should be in the heart—a distinctive feature of the third method of prayer. It should guard the heart while it prays, revolve, remaining always within, and thence, from the depths of the heart, offer up prayers to God. (Everything is in this: work in this way until you are given to taste the Lord.) When the mind, there, within the heart, at last tastes and sees that the Lord is good, and delights therein (the labor is ours, but this tasting is the action of grace in a humble heart), then it will no longer wish to leave this place in the heart . . . and will always look inwardly into the depths of the heart and will remain revolving there, repulsing all thoughts sown by the devil. (This is the third method of attention and prayer, practiced as it should be.) . . . Therefore our holy fathers, harkening to the Lord Who said: 'For out of the heart proceed evil thoughts, murders, adulteries, fornications, thefts, false witness, blasphemies' and: 'These are the things which defile a man' [Matt. 15:19, 20], hearing also that in another place of the Gospels we are instructed to 'cleanse first that which is within the cup and platter, that the outside of them may be clean also' [Matt. 23:26], have renounced all other spiritual work and concentrated wholly on this one doing, that is on guarding the heart, convinced that, through this practice, they would easily attain every other virtue, whereas without it not a single virtue can be firmly established. Some of the fathers called this doing, silence of the heart; others called it attention; yet others—sobriety and opposition (to thoughts), while others called it examining thoughts and guarding the mind.

It is only now that the passage occurs of which Father Sylvan is so fond and which, as I have indicated, he cites several times without once describing the context. I begin to understand why. Because there is something underneath the words of St. Simeon that is so urgently important; and at the same time, the words themselves, if taken literally, would spell death for a modern person seeking the necessary inner struggle "without which a man can never pass from the hallucinations of Christendom to the perceptions of Christ." (Father Sylvan)

What is it that is underneath the words? I am certain that I have discovered it, almost at the very end of St. Simeon's letter, a line that I passed by several times before sensing its importance. Having stated that this third kind of attention, the attention of the heart, is the primary aim of spiritual work, and having then reiterated that everything else in one's inner and outer life must be subordinate to this aim, and having explained certain specific methods that may lead to error (omitted in the Russian and English versions), St. Simeon then writes:

Keep your mind there (in the heart), trying by every possible means to find the place where the heart is, in order that, having found it, your mind should con-

stantly abide there. Wrestling thus, the mind will find
the place of the heart.

With this, suddenly, I am known for what I am. I do not know
the place of the heart; it is that which I must find. It is not something that I can assume. *But this point is almost never made in
all the literature of Christian mysticism.* Or, rather, if it is made,
it is in a language and form that we modern people cannot recognize. We falsely assume we can find the place of the heart, or
that we are already there.

Thus, the third method of attention and prayer is meant to
guide us toward the heart, the center of our being; it does not
start from the heart; it leads to the heart.

Attention as Prayer

But what form of attention or inner struggle breaks through
and into every circumstance of my life here and now, in the conditions of the modern world? How is the heart, the center of the
feeling of myself, to be sought in the life I lead?

We are asking about a mode of attention or consciousness that
is a bridge between our present level of being and the level of
being described not only in the contemplative literature of Christianity, but in the mystical and contemplative literature of all the
traditions. We are not speaking only about the development of
the inner world, but of the balance between the inner and the
outer world. We are not asking only about higher experiences,
but about that in ourselves which can receive the energy and
vision of such experiences and transmit this energy into the
whole of ourselves. We are asking about the soul, the intermediate principle in man.

Merely using such words as attention, consciousness, presence,
awareness or openness is not enough, though of course it is a
great discovery to recognize and identify such factors as the essential "dispository" elements in human nature. This, certainly,
the contact with the Eastern religions has given us through the
exceptional insights of such men as Thomas Merton and now so
many others as well. But this insight will be utterly wasted if
such terms are now associated with qualities of mind that do not

manifest or do not lead to the bridging of levels of being within myself.

Thus, in man there are many things, not merely one, that can be called "attention"; many things that are "openness," awareness; there are many kinds and degrees of consciousness and presence. Having identified these aspects as essential—this is the approach to lost Christianity—the problem becomes one of knowing exactly what we are looking for and why. Otherwise we shall repeat the same process by which Christianity and all truth become irrevocably lost.

Such, as I understand it, is the real message in the writings of Father Sylvan. It is certainly the logic behind his several citations of the mentioned key passage from St. Simeon the New Theologian, as I shall now indicate.

On the first occasion, Father Sylvan has just described his experiences among a group of Westerners practicing the Vipassana form of Buddhist meditation. He writes:

> This practice of mindfulness, this practice of self-observation, this practice of attention to oneself in every movement, thought and reaction, has crept out of the jungles of Southeast Asia and has arrived in the modern world all scrubbed and clean. Its purity has not come with it. Its purity depended on its setting in ancient times: its power comes from the powers of death and physical suffering, where all of human life is in question and the gods are strong enough to demand affirmation or denial. God in all His power and immense Selfhood looms immediately in the background of the great methods of the Buddha; God as felt deep, deep within the recesses of the heart, where no word can go, no concept can penetrate. Therefore, deny, separate, observe and accept without passion at once whatever is in front of one—yet with the deep, deep yearning after God, the nameless, the Void in one's heart and inner axis. The self-observers now have no gods, no ideas to reveal to them the weakness of their attention, to call them—without nervousness yet with imperious urgency—toward the renewal of their search. The ego is not rooted in the place where they are working; the ego

they transcend is not the ego, it is the ego's ego, the concept I have of ego, the thought of thoughts, the concept of concepts. May a Master come to them who will throw them again into the great universe of birth and death. All self-observation, which is the necessary first step of transformation, must be connected to self-inquiry, in turn connected to the confrontation with pain and sorrow. You cannot take sorrow away; this is a despicable perversion of monasticism which we have tried too much in the West. You must bring sorrow into clearer focus; the monastery should be a school of sorrow, the sorrow of life without the inner Kingdom. A method is also a monastery of the mind. A method can be a cloister. Or it can be a sword. Attention to myself is a sword, but here it is a saffron robe. It is all too placid. Being placid, it requires too much time.

The next entry in which Father Sylvan cites St. Simeon occurs in a somewhat vaguer context. It was certainly written in America and it is also about Buddhism, but it is unclear which form of Buddhist practice or which group he is referring to:

True: all dualism must be destroyed. But these people are taking it too literally. I see their faces and it is encouraging how different they all are. This could be a good sign. Their postures are all different; this could be a good sign too. It could mean they are experimenting within a great form, under the judgement of a standard which comes from deep within the heart and which does not pass through the head producing rigid postures. It could mean they are searching. But I am not sure. It is the searching that destroys dualism and division, nothing else. Spiritually speaking, to destroy means to reconcile. No one has ever entered nirvana in the literal sense, nor ever will. The Bodhisattva experiences the contradictions of life and returns to them again and again; his face is always pointed in two directions—toward Unity and Multiplicity simultaneously.

To destroy dualism means to have an attention that is

on the border between presence and absence, between good and evil, between A and not-A. Attention directed solely to Presence, to the higher, is the inner equivalent of blind devotion to an external God. For the Higher or the Innermost is actually external to myself here and now. Those who say they are not seeking the external God of the West, but the Innermost self are in danger of a subtle deception. It is still in essence attachment to the world of holy words, images, visualizations. Attention directed solely to the lower is the inner equivalent of atheism and leads to "suicide"—cynicism and loneliness.

The third entry occurs with only a single sentence following it:

This attention of the heart, this quietness within movement is actually another, intimate movement that spontaneously arises in the moment between life and death, when the ego is wounded and God is still distant; this attention *is* prayer in the *sense* of the Psalmist who asks, and asks and asks; it is that which watches and waits in the night.

Chapter Eight

The Soul: Intermediate Being

Six Points About the Soul

How, then, is this attention of the heart to be understood in
our own experience? As I have suggested, the answer lies hidden
within the Christian doctrine of the soul as the intermediate
principle in man and in the cosmos. But we are going to have to
set aside all our usual preconceptions about the idea of the soul
to discover the extraordinary relevance this idea can have, yield-
ing a quite new way of ordering the priorities of the material in
our everyday experience. If Father Sylvan is correct, and I believe he is, it will appear that this "attention of the heart," this
single channel to the development of man's deepest possibilities,
is actually not far removed at all from our lives. It is there, right
in front of us. Yet it is invisible at the same time, because no
one has told us its proper name or its proper value, and therefore
we no longer recognize it or cultivate it. And unless it is understood and cultivated with great care and diligence, it leads us
nowhere.

Throughout the journals of Father Sylvan there are numerous
and varied references to the Christian doctrine of the soul. To
put all of these references together would make a book in itself,
and so here I will limit myself to summarizing his principal ideas
and then proceed to show the light they throw both on our common experience and on the teachings of the historical tradition:

(1) The soul is the intermediate principle in human nature,
occupying the place between the Spirit and the body. The former
term, "Spirit," Father Sylvan defines variously as "the movement

toward Godhead," "the Uncreated," "Absolute Origin," and "Eternal Mind." The term "body" is also defined in a variety of ways, including but not limited to the physical body. Father Sylvan considers "thoughts" as part of the physical body.

(2) The power or function of the soul is *attention;* the development of attention is therefore approximately equivalent to the development and growth of the soul. But the soul also has several components, each with its own power of attention. All components must participate in the perfection of the soul. The principal power of the soul, which defines its real nature, is a gathered attention that is directed simultaneously toward the Spirit and the body. This is "attention of the heart." And this is the principal mediating, harmonizing power of the soul.

(3) The mediating attention of the heart is spontaneously activated in man in the state of profound self-questioning, a state that is almost always inaccurately recognized and wrongly valued in everyday experience. "God can only speak to the soul," Father Sylvan writes, "and only when the soul exists." He goes on: "But the soul of man only exists for a moment, as long as it takes for the Question to appear and then to disappear, as, for example, in the encounter with death between grief and sadness, between shock and fear; or in the encounter with supersatisfaction, between emptiness and boredom; or in the encounter with life's revolutionary disappointments, before free fall turns to self-pity."

(4) The practice of Christianity begins with the repeated efforts to recognize what takes place in oneself in the state of self-questioning. This implies a struggle against attempts to cover over the Question by means of explanations, emotional reactions or physical action. Father Sylvan collectively calls these three impulses "the first dispersal of the soul." Through this term, he points to the fact that the force of attention is wasted and degraded through absorption by one or another part of the psychophysical organism. "Certain Oriental teachers," he writes, "warn us against giving too much attention to the things of the world. Certain of our Christian teachers also say this. But here error creeps in. One may give all one's outer attention to the world without harming oneself in any way. To tell the truth, we are called by the Creator to spend this kind of attention. The struggle of the Christian is to contain the energy of the Question within oneself, not allowing this deeper attention to be mixed with the

attention of the psychophysical organism." This "first dispersal of the soul" is termed elsewhere by Father Sylvan "attachment," and in more traditional Christian language, "worldly cares."

(5) Through containing this special psychic energy that is activated in the experience of deep self-questioning, "the soul comes into existence and begins to gather itself into an independent entity." According to Father Sylvan, this process can never be carried out without proper guidance and is, in the strictest sense, the task of "authentic esoteric Christianity," which he characterizes as "the esotericism of energy, rather than words or ideas." Elsewhere he states: "The commandments of our Teacher, Moses, are, at one level, exercises for the making of the soul." His point, I believe, is that only when this process is underway does an individual come under the obligations and demands of religious morality in its real meaning. This clearly corresponds to the discussion noted above dealing with the definition of "mortal sin." For, once this process is underway, only then can a man gain or lose forever his real inner possibility. Father Sylvan calls this loss "the second dispersal of the soul."

(6) Finally, a truly Christian life is possible only for an individual in whom the process of "soul-making" has gone past a certain point. Such individuals are rare, but only they are capable of altruism in the strictly spiritual sense. In Father Sylvan's language, "the soul begins to radiate." "The task of self-purification becomes fused with the act of helping my neighbor." "The first aim of human life is to pass from dispersal to radiation."

Father Sylvan speaks of other stages as well, but frequently in extremely veiled language. He seems sometimes to reserve the term "mysticism" for these higher stages, but, as I have indicated before, his use of this word is somewhat inconsistent. At one point, he appears to sum up these higher levels of Christian practice by speaking of "the passage from Intermediate Man to Spiritual Man." However, in the same place, he writes, "God created Adam as the Intermediate. The Intermediate is the Beginning. But for me the Beginning is the Goal."

I wish now to expand and clarify Father Sylvan's six points about the soul, especially (3) and (4). I consider these two tenets of surpassing importance, as I believe Father Sylvan himself does. Here lies his central and—actually—revolutionary contribution to modern man's search both for lost Christianity and, which comes to the same thing, for himself.

Gurdjieff

There is another, correlative reason for emphasizing these two tenets. This concerns the relationship between Father Sylvan's formulations and the teachings of G. I. Gurdjieff. I have already cited (p. 122–23) part of a passage in which Gurdjieff vividly characterizes what Father Sylvan calls "the Intermediate Christian." The passage occurs at the end of a talk given in 1923 by Gurdjieff to pupils at his Institute for the Harmonious Development of Man, in France. Here is the passage in full:

> The program of the Institute, the power of the Institute, the aim of the Institute, the possibilities of the Institute can be expressed in few words: the Institute can help one to be able to be a Christian. Simple! That is all! It can do so only if a man has this desire, and a man will have this desire only if he has a place where constant desire is present. Before being able, one must wish.
>
> Thus there are three periods: to wish, to be able, and to be.
>
> The Institute is the means. Outside the Institute it is possible to wish and to be; but here, to be able.
>
> The majority of those present here call themselves Christians. Practically all are Christians in quotation marks. Let us examine this question like grown-up men.
>
> —Dr. X., are you a Christian? What do you think, should one love one's neighbor or hate him? Who can love like a Christian? It follows that to be a Christian is impossible. Christianity includes many things; we have taken only one of them, to serve as an example. Can you love or hate someone to order?
>
> Yet Christianity says precisely this, to love all men. But this is impossible. At the same time it is quite true that it is necessary to love. First one must be able, only then can one love. Unfortunately, with time, modern Christians have adopted the second half, to love, and lost view of the first, the religion which should have preceded it.
>
> It would be very silly for God to demand from man what he cannot give.

Half of the world is Christian, the other half has other religions. For me, a sensible man, this makes no difference; they are the same as the Christians. Therefore it is possible to say that the whole world is Christian, the difference is only in name. And it has been Christian not only for one year but for thousands of years. There were Christians long before the advent of Christianity. So common sense says to me: "For so many years men have been Christians—how can they be so foolish as to demand the impossible?"

But it is not like that. Things have not always been as they are now. Only recently have people forgotten the first half, and because of that have lost the capacity for being able. And so it became indeed impossible.

Let every one ask himself, simply and openly, whether he can love all men. If he has had a cup of coffee, he loves; if not, he does not love. How can that be called Christianity?

In the past not all men were called Christians. Some members of the same family were called Christians, others pre-Christians, still others were called non-Christians. So in one and the same family there could be the first, the second and the third. But now all call themselves Christians. It is naive, dishonest, unwise and despicable to wear this name without justification.

A Christian is a man who is able to fulfill the Commandments.

A man who is able to do all that is demanded of a Christian, both with his mind and his essence, is called a Christian without quotation marks. A man who, in his mind, wishes to do all that is demanded of a Christian, but can do so only with his mind and not with his essence, is called pre-Christian. And a man who can do nothing, even with his mind, is called a non-Christian.

Try to understand what I wish to convey by all this. Let your understanding be deeper and broader.*

Referring to this passage, Father Sylvan writes:

* Gurdjieff, op. cit., pp. 152–54.

The Question appears when I am born and is gradually covered over by the world. But it continues to sound under the surface, as layer upon layer of self-definition is formed around it. In a shattering moment, the Question surfaces and its energy transforms me. In that moment out of time, *to be* and *to be able* exists, speaking now in the sacred language of Gurdjieff.

Father Sylvan proceeds to describe this experience in terms of the parable of the Prodigal Son. "In this moment, the soul begins its return from exile, 'having wasted his substance,' his inner attention, on sensations and thoughts, which is the definition of emotion. But never, almost never, does the soul come the whole way; never, almost never, does he see that the Spirit, the father, is running forward to meet him and to transform him." The Question disappears; "life goes on once again as usual."

But perhaps all is not quite the same as before. The Question leaves a trace in the mind, even in the ego. The mind begins to search—for what? Begins to wish—for what? The Teaching is with me now to guide me—but to what goal? Life goes on as usual. But inside me a new aim exists. The Teaching names it, but does not explain it. The Teaching directs this holy desire, *eros*, toward myself, inquiring, questioning, studying. And I see that the act of self-inquiry is itself a new energy, something young, bearing in itself the marks of future majesty. Gurdjieff has truly named me: *pre-Christian.*

Search as the Transforming Force

Yet another, and very telling, reference to Gurdjieff occurs in this context where Father Sylvan discusses the relationship between self-questioning and sexual morality. Before quoting this passage, however, I need first to point out one particular characteristic of Father Sylvan's manuscript.

Interleaved throughout the manuscript one finds pages written in a completely different hand. Also, the tone and style are often different. The reasons for this soon became clear to me. These pages are excerpts from letters that Father Sylvan wrote, presumably to pupils. I suspect that after his death, these pupils sent copies of his letters to those who had taken on the responsibility of collecting Father Sylvan's writings. Whoever it was that prepared this manuscript copied out portions of these letters and inserted them where it seemed most appropriate.

The present excerpt is apparently written in response to a question about sexual morality, and the collator of the manuscript saw fit to insert it just at the point where Father Sylvan is writing about "the long stretches of time that pass between moments when the Question breaks through in all its force and authority." Such moments, Father Sylvan says, "teach by themselves. There is nothing for us to try when they occur. Our practice consists in remembering to seek the Question when life is not so vivid."

At this point the present excerpt appears:

> All that you tell me about your "sins" calls to mind my own experiences when I was younger. Part of us recognizes that some form of purity is necessary in regard to sex. But we forget that the principal form of purity for us is the love of truth. Remember that, remember that! Don't you understand that the Fathers whose lives inspire you were themselves always close to self-observation and self-questioning? Don't try to imitate, outwardly, the stories told about them. Do you know what preceded their retreat into the desert? Do you know what experiences they had in that civilization which even more than our own, was permeated with sexual excess? Don't you remember what we have said about others who went to the desert to imitate them? How so many came to nothing even with the help of the great masters?
>
> Always seek the Question, even in Hell. Let that search become your permanent center of gravity.†
>
> Concerning our other ancient Teachers and Fathers who did not retreat to the desert, you must stop feeding your imagination by believing everything essential is

† A Gurdjieff term. See P. D. Ouspensky, *In Search of the Miraculous* (New York: Harcourt, Brace, 1949), p. 259.

known about their lives. I tell you now that only very few of those whose attainments we recognize found it necessary to live entirely without normal sexuality, no matter what you read about them. When you have understood more about the laws of the inner life, you will know why this cannot be doubted.

I, too, did not understand this at the beginning. There was a time, in my own life, when this problem brought me to such despair that I was on the brink of abandoning the teachings of Christianity. I could not fathom what was going on. I thought to myself: "This teaching is certainly the word of God. It brings the whole of life together, with everything in its rightful place. Then why do the holy Fathers seem to refuse this part of life? Why has so much suffering, without light at the end, been brought to people because of this?"

I could not bear this contradiction. I felt that if only this contradiction could be resolved I could give my whole heart to Christianity. Something was wrong. Something was twisted or left out somewhere, by someone. But it was incredible. Wherever I turned I met a wall. All roads seemed to lead to the same contradiction. The unanimity of textual writings and statements by respected people was astonishing and depressing. There were beautiful theories and mystical symbols about love and union, but I saw that they still led others and myself to hypocrisy or sadness. I was not seeking a life of indulgence—far from it; I had been through all that many times over. I did not want the "new morality." But I did not and could not want the "old morality" either.

Not out of any conscious decision, but solely because it seemed that all other avenues were closed, I began to investigate and explore this question experimentally, for myself. Can you imagine how clumsy and painful this was without anyone to guide me? I do not recommend it. But I had no other choice at the time.

Two unexpected discoveries resulted from these investigations. In the first place, I saw unmistakably that my feelings of guilt and shame were made of exactly the same cloth as my fantasies and desires. I have spoken about this many times in our gatherings. The guilt and desires originate in the same part of the mind. The first problem of our lives is that this part of the mind captures all our attention and all our soul's energy. It is all, equally, "thoughts." I realized that although what I called "desire" was equivalent to what the holy Fathers designated by that word, this was not the case with what I called "guilt" and "shame." Christian guilt in its real meaning applies only to people in whom there has fully begun the reversal of the first dispersal of the soul. By indulging in these mechanical feelings of guilt I was not at all imitating the holy Teachers. I was only indulging in thoughts, feeding a small part of the mind with a precious force that belonged to the whole self, the inner God. I realized that the holy Fathers were men who had already begun the process of the in-gathered light of attention and that therefore they could speak of shame, the shame of wasting the energy that belongs to the whole. I understood that this waste is the true corruption of the sin of lust, and applies to the system of guilt *and* desire.

This discovery nourished for years my research into all of the factors that contributed to the negative historical alterations in the teachings of Christ. My second discovery pointed me toward the actual beginning of the way.

As my investigations proceeded, I dimly began to realize something which, when it became more distinct, struck me like a lightning bolt. To make a long story short, I saw that the process of inquiry itself was a normalizing influence on my outer life. I saw this in fine and in large.

But, as you know, this inquiry has to be especially intense and long-lasting. I am speaking of the Question. For us fallen creatures the Question is the Son of the Son of God. Or, as we have sometimes expressed it, the Question is the Angel of Man. It is through the medium of total self-inquiry that the forces of good and evil can meet and be reconciled within us.

For the external world, what is called civilization,

the historical events of the life of Our Lord Jesus Christ are the Question and, in its degree, this has been until recent years the reconciling factor in history. But this is a pattern of forces acting on a cosmic scale within which all the war and violence that we see is roughly balanced with goodness according to a mathematics that we do not understand. However, this cannot directly concern you or me. It will all be meaningless and irrelevant if we do not internalize the Question in our own individual cosmos.

When I finally found my teacher, I said to him, "Am I mad? Has what I discovered never been known before?" He answered in a paradoxical way. He said that what I had discovered was completely new, but that everyone who had reached the threshold over the centuries had also discovered it. He said that I must reach this threshold a thousand times before I enter the way.

The Appearance and Disappearance of the Soul

In short, the soul is not a fixed entity. According to Father Sylvan, it is a movement that begins whenever man experiences the psychological pain of contradiction.

It is an actual energy, but one that is only at some beginning stage of its development and action. Every day, every more or less average human individual experiences the appearance of this energy in its most embryonic stage. Whenever there is pain or contradiction, this energy of the soul is released or "activated."

But almost always, almost without any exceptions whatsoever, this new energy is immediately dispersed and comes to nothing. A hundred, a thousand times a day, perhaps, "the soul is aborted." An individual is completely unaware of this loss and remains so throughout his whole life. Without the necessary help and guidance, he never reaches the orientation necessary for enabling these everyday experiences to accumulate.

For Father Sylvan, most of our ordinary emotional reactions—both pleasant and unpleasant—only serve to cover over these experiences of contradiction. And the behavior and actions that result from these emotions thicken the covering and lead to further emotional reactions. Man becomes trapped in "the automatism of non-redemptive experience," a phrase that Father Sylvan juxtaposes with St. Paul's "body of death."

"Lost Christianity" is the lost or forgotten power of man to extract the pure energy of the soul from the experiences that make up his life. This possibility is distinct only in the most vivid or painful moments of our ordinary lives, but it can be discovered in all experiences if one knows how to seek it. Certain powerful experiences—such as the encounter with death or deep disappointment—are accompanied by the sensation of *presence;* an attention appears that is simultaneously open to a higher, freer mind ("Spirit") and to all the perceptions, sensations and emotions that constitute our ordinary self. One feels both separate and engaged in a new and entirely extraordinary way. One experiences "I Am." This is the soul (in inception).

It was a disaster for Christianity, according to Father Sylvan, when it adopted the notion that the soul of man already exists in finished form within human nature. This assumption about the given existence of the soul led to our identification of ordinary kinds of thoughts, emotions and sensations with the soul, the higher part of ourselves, and hence to the futile and mistaken effort to perfect our being by perfecting our thoughts, emotions or sensations, i.e. the futile effort of thought to alter emotion or vice versa. The Christian teaching, as Father Sylvan presents it, says on the contrary that these psychological functions are incapable of altering each other. Change, transformation, can come only through the action of an objectively higher force: the Spirit. And this Spirit cannot find channels of action unless there exists something in man that can receive it and pass it on to all the parts of himself.

The immensity and revolutionary nature of this idea can be seen when it is applied to the efforts of mankind, everywhere, to find "happiness." The quest for happiness, which in one form or another is the main impetus of the whole mass of human life and moral idealism, is from this point of view little more than the vain effort by the mind to alter the emotions, or vice versa.

But the power to alter the structure of human life, inwardly as well as outwardly, does not reside in a partial function of the psyche. Only that function which can be in actual relationship, actual contact, with all the parts of the self has the possibility of altering the self, or of serving as the channel for the force that can alter the whole of the self. That function Father Sylvan identifies as the power of gathered attention, the power of the soul.

When man is in question, he is actually in between the higher and the lower in himself. This state of in-betweenness is unaccustomed to the mind and the emotions, and is always experienced at first as painful or unpleasant. In this connection, however, Father Sylvan several times cites a saying that is actually of Sufi origin:

> When the heart weeps for what it has lost,
> The Spirit laughs for what it has found.

Thus the revolutionary nature of this teaching has a positive as well as a negative side. The hope it offers is as extraordinary as the just-mentioned indictment of the whole movement of human history in relation to the search for "happiness." In brief, and to put the matter in as simple a form as possible, the whole of the Christian tradition, according to Father Sylvan, needs "only one or two adjustments." He writes:

> Let everything go on exactly as it now goes on. May no one in the name of God begin to reform anything. Let even one or two people begin by recognizing in their hearts that Truth is the sustained consciousness of Error. In this way, the Holy Ghost appears within the individual. May even one or two people understand what takes place within a man in the state of Questioning himself. Let them seek help on that basis. For there exists a method and a way to deepen and perpetuate the state of Questioning. There is knowledge and force to support this aim. This knowledge and force is Christianity of another level. Seek for what is possible within yourselves and what is not possible will be added to you.

Chapter Nine

The Soul in the Two Histories

Two Histories; Two Doctrines

In order to demonstrate the value of Father Sylvan's teaching, it is necessary to place his view of the soul in a rather wide context. Its practical implications will then become apparent.

We may begin by stepping outside the specifically Christian formulations and looking at the question of the human soul as it is treated in other of the great teachings. There, too, we will see that on this issue a division appears. Every tradition has two histories according to its teaching about the soul, two histories according to what it tells us about man's nature and his possible transformation, two histories corresponding to the efforts that are required of man and made possible for him.

Standing in one historical stream, all that is demanded of man is that he believe with his mind and conform his outer behavior to the rules and rituals laid down for him. He is not required to be inwardly active; he is not required to surrender his dreams more than once or twice in his life, if at all. Here it is necessary for man to be good, but it is not necessary for him to develop.

This historical stream has many currents and many depths. Where it is most shallow, or even stagnant, it is little more than a superficial consolation about immortality coupled with an authoritarian code of external conduct. Where it is deeper and stronger, it may lead to what is commonly known as "mysticism," or to powerful moral philosophies that can shape entire civilizations. But, even here, inner development of the individual is never more than a secondary and limited aim. The principal aim remains the governance of the lives of the whole of a community or people with respect to the great forces and integrity of nature. It is always "ethical"—sometimes veering off into mere ethical fantasy, where it may result in violence or sentimentality; sometimes reaching great heights of moral idealism, but without exact knowledge of how actually to transform human nature.

The Intermediate in Hinduism

What must be worked for in the second historical stream is already assumed to exist in the first. Thus, in the Oriental traditions, one encounters a great mass of material indicating, as in Hinduism, that man is God (Brahman), or, as in Buddhism, that the ego is illusory. The "first history" of Hinduism offers the belief that the self (or the soul) is one with the Absolute. The multiform rules of living, in all their extraordinary richness, are based on this belief held by millions of Hindus throughout the ages. Yet, in the midst of all these beliefs, rituals and religious practices, there is a distinct current of instruction indicating the need for inner effort before such ideas can be concretely realized in an individual. At its highest, the first Hinduism offers man experiences of union with eternity and liberation from time; the second Hinduism offers man the possibility of creating within himself something that can stand in relationship to both time and eternity. The first focuses man's intention on the Highest; the second directs him, in addition, to develop himself to intermediate levels of being and consciousness that can permanently relate and harmonize all parts of the human structure.

The Brhadaranyaka Upanishad, among the most ancient of India's sacred texts, makes this clear. The text begins with a description of "the horse sacrifice," the term "horse" meaning the whole of the created universe both within and outside of man. It then indicates that in the beginning, at the root of all that exists inwardly and outwardly, there is an absence, a lack, a hunger, which is given the name "death." But what is the primary goal of this yearning? It is not the blending into the Absolute;

that comes "later." No, the goal, the need, is for a real, individual soul or self:

> (There) was nothing whatever here at first.
>
> Death was what covered all, or (rather) Hunger, since
> Death is Hunger.
> Then he resolved, heart and mind:
> "Would that I had a self (of my own)".*

As in Christianity, there is a "lost" or "hidden" Hinduism (lost or hidden to the West, in any case) that guides the formation within the individual of a real self or soul. Only when such a formation exists can there be a striving for direct contact (or "merging") with the Highest.

There is the cosmic and microcosmic Movement outward from the Absolute, and there is the Movement of return—the "breathing" of Brahman. The formed soul is that which stands at the midpoint between these two great Movements of fundamental energy.

Speaking "diagramatically," one may say that the method of living designed to bring man into contact with the Highest can be pursued only after one has acquired a soul, not before. If it is pursued prematurely, it leads nowhere; it becomes at best merely philosophical or theoretical, merely "ethical" in an external sense, with respect to God or humanity. In this case, "mystical" experiences pass through man without integration into a process of personal transformation. As one contemporary Western scholar, herself a longtime practitioner of the Vedanta, described it to me, "The West has known only the top half of Hinduism. It needs the bottom half."

One often hears it said that what distinguishes Eastern from Western religion, at least in the modern era, is that the East has preserved its practical and experiential methods along with its philosophy and metaphysics. This is of course true, but it is irrelevant to the present issue.

Methods or no methods, experience or no experience, here the point is whether or not the teaching guides the formation within

---

* Brhadaranyaka Upanishad, I.2.1, Tilden-Mills-Jackman translation (in preparation).

human nature of true individual being, the creation of *intermediate man*, who alone in the cosmic scheme can care for, or harmonize or relate all the forces of creation. The core of a great teaching can become as obscured by "experience" as by "doctrine."

For the sake of completeness, it must be added that the converse situation, namely the existence of the "bottom half" of tradition without the "top half" leads to what is called "psychologism," the explanation and employment of spiritual methods solely for psychotherapeutic ends. This is the problem facing a growing number of contemporary Western psychiatrists seeking to make use of the practical teachings of the East or the mystical writings of the West. I have dealt at length with this issue elsewhere.†

Micro-monotheism

Before turning to the issue of the "two histories" as it can be seen in the Buddhist tradition, we should emphasize that the notion of the intermediate by no means implies a fundamentally dualistic view of reality. On the contrary, the meaning of unity and oneness actually lies hidden in this hidden teaching. When we speak of the soul as the intermediate, we are speaking of a bridge, a relationship that binds together. The "first history" of Hinduism, and of other traditions as well, often speaks of Oneness as an undifferentiated unity—the God above nature, the pure Void, the ultimate Being. This tendency of the "first history" fully corresponds with its property of emphasizing the "top half" of the teaching, the highest elements, the ultimates, which, as has been said, it is able to do at the price of being largely theoretical or—even when experiential—outwardly geared primarily to the general needs of the human species. In the "second history," we find far more in the way of hierarchical relativism; Oneness is understood in terms of organic unity, harmonization and interaction of forces. This tendency corresponds to its property of guiding the individual to the formation within himself of his own unified self or soul. Many teachings labeled "heresy" or

† See Needleman, Jacob, *A Sense of the Cosmos* (Garden City, N.Y.: Doubleday, 1975), pp. 107–34, and *On the Way to Self Knowledge* (New York: Alfred A. Knopf, 1976).

"unorthodox," due to apparent dualistic or pluralistic systems of ontology or theology, are actually the expression of guidance in the struggle for "a Self of one's own." Often, though of course not always, it is the second history showing itself. In the West this issue manifests around the concept of "monotheism." In Judaism, Christianity and Islam, one must distinguish between the exclusive *macro-monotheism* of the first history and the added *micro-monotheism* of the second history, which, in effect, demands that man have "One God" within himself before he can serve the One God of the Whole of the Creation.

The following excerpt from a conversation with the contemporary Hindu master Sri Nisargadatta Maharaj illustrates how the practical idea of intermediate being can appear within a tradition that is commonly believed to reject everything that is not the Highest, Absolute Being:

> *Maharaj:* Again the personal point of view! Why do you insist on polluting the impersonal with your ideas of sin and virtue? It just does not apply. The impersonal cannot be described in terms of good and bad. It is Being—Wisdom—Love—all absolute. Where is the scope for sin there? And virtue is only the opposite of sin.
>
> *Question:* We talk of divine virtue.
>
> *Maharaj:* True virtue is divine nature (*swarupa*). What you are really is your virtue. But the opposite of sin which you call virtue is only obedience born out of fear.
>
> *Question:* Then why all effort at being good?
>
> *Maharaj:* It keeps you on the move. You wander till you find God. Then God takes you into Himself—and makes you as He is.

So far, there is nothing to surprise the Westerner familiar with conventional expositions of Hindu doctrine: the master is calling the questioner's attention to the Divine nature in man, the Spirit, Brahman, which exists as the fundamental reality in all being. He is countering the subjective, egoistic concept of sin and virtue. But now the conversation takes a different turn:

Question: The same action is considered natural at one point and a sin at another. What makes it sinful?

Maharaj: Whatever you do against your better knowledge is a sin.

Question: Knowledge depends on memory.

Maharaj: Remembering yourself is virtue, forgetting yourself is sin. It all boils down to the mental or psychological link between spirit and matter. We may call the link psyche (*antahkarana*). When the psyche is raw, undeveloped, quite primitive, it is subject to gross illusions. As it grows in breadth and sensitivity, it becomes a perfect link between pure matter and pure spirit and gives meaning to matter and expression to spirit.

There is the material world (*mahadakash*) and the spiritual (*paramakash*). Between lies the universal mind (*chidakash*) which is also the universal heart (*premakash*). It is wise love that makes the two one.

Question: Some people are stupid, some are intelligent. The difference is in their psyche. The ripe ones had more experience behind them. Just as a child grows by eating and drinking, sleeping and playing, so is man's psyche shaped by all he thinks and feels and does until it is perfect enough to serve as a bridge between the spirit and the body. Like a bridge permits the traffic between the banks, so does the psyche bring together the source and its expression.

Maharaj: Call it love. The bridge is love.‡

The Intermediate in Buddhism

Concerning Buddhism, the highest reality and the ultimate goal of human life is generally presented negatively. In psychological terms, this tradition speaks of the destruction of all illusion as the aim of human life; and what falls under the heading

‡ Sri Nisargadatta Maharaj, *I Am That*, trans. by Maurice Frydman (Bombay: Chetana, 1973), Part I, pp. 83–84.

of illusion is a shockingly vast realm of entities—far more than what Western philosophy and psychology generally include under this term. Buddhism presents itself as an unremitting pressure against the error of treating as real anything that is dependent, contingent or relative in any respect whatsoever, particularly in oneself. Metaphysically, Buddhism speaks of the Void, or Emptiness, as the sole reality.

In Buddhism, therefore, the "first history" takes the form of an assumption of the given existence within man of the Buddha-nature, innate freedom from all forms of bondage and illusion. From the point of view of the "second history" of Buddhism, this assumption refers only to a theoretical possibility for any given human being. Before the complete destruction of illusion can take place and before man can realize the Void (which is, in the highest sense, a positive, not a negative, state of being), something has to "come together" or be "formed" in him as a preparatory or intermediate stage.

Of course, one must resist the temptation to imagine this "formation" as literally some *thing*. It manifests itself, so we are told, as a force, or energy; as a *question*, a *search*. But it is equally wrong to imagine it as merely an attitude or feeling or set of convictions in the sense we usually give to these terms. In other words, if matter is real, if the body is material, then it is a "higher body," a "finer matter." If consciousness is real, then it is a "higher state of consciousness." If energy is real, it is a "new energy." But, in all cases, it is intermediate, *central*, relational in the sense of bridging levels within man and the universe.

The first time I personally caught a glimpse of this aspect of the Buddhist tradition in a way that helped me sense its weight came as I was talking with a Tibetan, a friend who used to visit me on numerous occasions. We were walking along a crowded street in downtown San Francisco. I had asked him about the meaning of the notion found in the Mahayana teachings that even the gods are caught in the wheel of birth and death, and that in order to be liberated they, too, like every other being in the chain of creation, must be born in human form. I asked him: "Do you really believe there are such beings as gods 'out there' who must literally be reborn as men?"

He did not directly answer my question, but instead advised me as a start to think of the gods as symbolizing higher, mystical experiences along with the blissful pleasure that often results from these experiences. And he advised me to think of the beings who occupy the lower realms as symbolizing the animal desires and sufferings of human nature. In order to be free, he said, man must be in contact with all of this, the higher and the lower, simultaneously. "That is why we say that man occupies the central place in the scheme of creation." He went on to explain that in the Buddhist teaching it is as much a form of bondage to be identified with the higher as it is to be identified with the lower.

Without really digesting his reply, I then asked him another question: about the idea of the rarity of being born in the human condition. I had always been intrigued by the way the Buddhist scriptures express this. Imagine, the Buddha says, that in the vastness of the great ocean there is a single ox yoke floating free. Imagine also that in this vast ocean a great tortoise swims, surfacing once every hundred years. How rare it would be that when the tortoise surfaces, his head would pass through this ox yoke floating free. Even rarer is it to be born a human being.

I waved my hand questioningly at the hundreds of people passing us in the street, and my Tibetan friend stopped, obviously noticing that I had not grasped what he had just said about the meaning of being a man. I stopped too and waited for his answer. His face, usually full of good humor, was now almost grave. "How many human beings do you see?" he said. I understood.

Buddhism, too, thus contains the "hidden" teaching that something needs to be "formed" in man through inner work. In the Introduction to Lobsang Lhalungpa's translation of *The Life of Milarepa* we find the following:

> Meditation, considered as the foundational act of spiritual effort in the Vajrayana tradition as transmitted by Milarepa, may also be considered in terms of the possible development within man of the link between the Buddha-nature and the ordinary deluded mind. The great idea behind this notion of a relationship between the highest and the lowest in human nature, which (we are told) only the greatest masters have realized, is often expressed in the Vajrayana as the essential iden-

tity of nirvana and samsara: nirvana is the understanding of samsara!

Concerning the role of the human body in the establishment of this link, there are sufficient hints in the text to let the reader know that he must leave behind all conventional notions about the "evils of the flesh" as well as modern fantasies about the sacralization of sensuous indulgence. Emerging from his first intensive period of solitary meditation, Milarepa relates to Marpa, "I have understood that this material body, made of flesh and blood along with mental consciousness, is gathered together by the twelve chains of cause and effect—one of which is volition—originating from ignorance. This body is the blessed vessel for those fortunate beings who wish for freedom, but it also leads sinners into the lower realms. I understand that in this body lies the vital choice between enormous profit and loss, relating to eternal happiness or misery on the border between good and evil. . . ."

It is obvious that, as Milarepa pursues his spiritual search, some transformation is taking place in his body of a nature that is at the same time miraculous and in accordance with law. Yet at no point is the reader ever led to think of this material transformation as anything but a result of the work of meditation. It is never presented as anything to be striven after directly, even though it seems that what we are dealing with here is the creation within the human organism of a spiritualized body that provides extraordinary energy and support to the basic work of meditation. In other words, the link between the sacred and profane natures of man is established within the body itself, which then, in a great Bodhisattva, becomes the stepping-stone to further levels of consciousness and compassion.*

Note that "mental consciousness" is included in the body as characterized by Milarepa. In Far Eastern traditions generally, this is the case. What we ordinarily refer to as mind (thought,

* Lobsang Lhalungpa, op. cit., p. xvii.

emotion, perception, etc.) is referred to as one of the *senses*, along with sight, touch, hearing, taste and smell. This corresponds fully to Father Sylvan's definition of "body" in its ordinary state. The implications here are enormous, as we shall soon see. "We have falsely given the name 'soul' to that in ourselves which functions on the same level—actually even on a lower level in most of us—as our material bodily functions" (Father Sylvan).

We turn now to the Christian tradition, limitations of space preventing our examining the other expressions of this notion of the soul as the intermediate formation in human nature.

The Language of the Second History

First, however, further comment may be needed about the language of "the second history," in order to forestall unnecessary difficulties for some readers. This language is always and everywhere symbolic, whether in written or verbal form, or in pictorial form or in architectural form or in the medium of ritual drama, dance or even in certain scientific forms such as within the disciplines of medicine and mathematics. At the same time, one always encounters indications of what is called "the oral tradition." It is said, and modern scholarship is just now beginning to sense the significance of this, that the real meanings and the complete content of this "second history," or "esoteric tradition," are transmitted directly from teacher to pupil—"orally." "The symbol," writes Father Sylvan, "speaks to the spirit and the body simultaneously, creating struggle, activating and deepening the Question."

The point, I believe, is that symbols and concepts are "planted" in a man within the context of experiences created through the "oral" tradition, which means the day-to-day context of living the conditions of the spiritual community or school. The symbol exists as a mental formulation or image in the surface mind; but it can also sound as the voice of one's own, intimate truth. In that experience, the distinction between external and inner teacher disappears. The symbol has been given from the outside, but it has been given to the part of ourselves that naturally speaks that language. When contact is made with that deeper part of ourselves, the symbol is understood and "remembered" at the same time. What has been given has come from outside, but the part to which it has been given is deep inside oneself. The symbol therefore becomes my own in an extraordinary sense, even though it is not my invention or creation. *What* I remember is not my own (in the sense of the surface personality), but the part of myself that remembers (and is remembered) is deeply my own.

When a symbol or idea is remembered or experienced in this way, it then, for a while, serves to guide all my perceptions. "The symbol guides the search." This form of knowing imparts a degree of certainty and boldness that may seem unwarranted to the conventional student of religious tradition, especially if he is intellectually learned or expert. Certain interpretations of Scripture by individuals with significant inner experience can be maddening to the conventional scholar, because such interpretations are based on a transformed quality of attention, rather than on an intellectual hypothesis subject solely to standards of external evidence and the coherence criteria of conventional logic. The same is true of certain interpretations of a whole body of writings, art, ritual, and moral teachings of a tradition. In fact, the same is true of certain interpretations of the whole of life and nature.

The real problem arises when the individual with such inner experience passes out of his state of transformed attention and begins to operate only on the memory in thought of what was seen in that state. Subtly, and perhaps without his even noticing it, what had been remembered as a deep part of himself and as a guide to his search becomes mixed with ordinary, surface thought and turns into what is only a "brilliant" or "novel" hypothesis. It is this, I believe, that causes unnecessary difficulties for the conventional scholar or scientist. The "mystic" (using this term now simply as a shorthand reference to the individual who has been through experience of the symbol) *knew*, but does not now know in the same way. Where, before, the vibration of his transformed state of attention lent authority and discrimination to his utterances and therefore transcended the need for conventional outside proofs or arguments, now, on the other hand, he is in the same world as the rest of us and is obliged to offer some degree of ordinary justification, some degree of ordinary logic or poetic persuasion. He is obliged to himself to do this, not only to his audience. Otherwise, he may go on imagining he knows, when in fact it is only the registration in ordinary memory (and often a rather poor registration) of what he knew in the past, transformed state of attention. Would that we had more "mystics" offering the results of their experiential understanding, but would that all of them were more aware of when they are speaking from their new state and when they are only speaking from memory of that state. With the difficulties the scholar or scientist faces when confronted with the former, I have no sympathy; "let them suffer!" But I have great sympathy with the difficulties engendered by the latter case; "let the 'mystic' play according to the rules—some of them, in any case!" But would, also, that I, as a scholar or scientist, have the sense of discrimination myself to recognize who is speaking and from where he is speaking, so that my own difficulties will not be of the unnecessary kind.

The *soul* is part of the language of symbol. Therefore, in seeking to discern the "second history" of the great traditions, we must proceed, as it were, hat in hand, not expecting or imagining that the familiar channels of information and philosophy, the familiar scholarly commentaries, the familiar traditional expositions will simply drop the insights we need right into our laps. We are not seeking new theories about Christianity or the other traditions. We are not seeking new theological, philosophical or historical concepts. We are seeking—in any case, I am seeking— the clue to something lost in ourselves. *That means we are seeking to bring back the symbolic power of the idea of the soul,* to recover it as a guide to the search for ourselves, our lost selves. If the search for lost Christianity has any meaning at all, it surely must be this: to bring back Christianity as a guide to the search for ourselves.

But, one may ask, are we not in danger of distorting the tradition if we go at it in this way? I do not think so—or, rather, the danger is far less with this approach than with the usual method of relying solely on the external tools of scholarship and the external functions of the mind. Tradition is either a guide to the search for myself or it isn't. If it isn't, we might as well discover this fact as soon as we can, and then go on to something else— perhaps taking care of our health. If, on the other hand, tradition is such a guide, then this may be the only way to examine it. To put the matter in a few words, let us try to look at the tradition from the point of view of the need for being, rather than the desire for explanations. Will what we know of tradition, the information and expertise that we have acquired through ordinary channels, guide us further in this need, or will we be thrown back once again to the old, sterile alternative or "belief or disbelief"?

The Soul Is Not the "Inner Being"

Having stated the above by way of advance justification—or, it may be, self-protection—I herewith announce the intention to base my further examination of the Christian idea of the soul upon the following statements on the subject by Father Sylvan:

> Man must reverse the first dispersal of the soul by drawing unto himself the attention which he unnecessarily gives to his thoughts, emotional reactions and sensations, and which results in the deformation and distortion of the entire human organism, to the extent that he has fallen to the level of a sick animal. This work is the basis of religious asceticism and is the authentic meaning of religious morality. All civilized men are called to asceticism of this kind; monastic asceticism is only the most extreme and intensive version of it, subject, as history proves, to almost as many misinterpretations and misapplications as the Judaeo-Christian morality of the mass of mankind with its wars and other indulgences. All general morality is asceticism, obviously.
>
> This asceticism can lead to the natural development within man of an inner being, which is his birthright. But this inner being is not the soul. The soul is something higher and of a completely different quality. But the soul cannot come into existence without this inner being.
>
> Holy scripture speaks of the God of this inner being. Mystics and saints can experience this God and give him voice in their teachings and actions. Through their

teachings, man may be delivered from his basic sickness and be *saved*. This God is like the sun radiating its light and warmth over the whole of mankind.

All extrapolations and subjective interpretations about the nature of this inner being are dangerous. It is the function of orthodoxy to hold a firm line about it and orient mankind in its direction. Orthodoxy fails in its function when it either (a) adjusts itself too much to the passing subjectivity of a given era or individual, or (b) rigidifies its forms and teachings to such an extent that the direction toward the formation of the soul is incapable of being sensed.

The movement toward the development of the soul can never begin without the development of the inner being and the contact between the inner being and the body with all its appetites, sensations and thoughts. The movement toward the development of the soul can never begin from the functions of the body alone.

Therefore, it is necessary to withdraw from the body that which does not properly belong to it—a certain initiative energy which, when it blends unnaturally with the impulses of the body becomes what is called passion or emotion. This passion becomes rooted in human nature through the system of egoism. Ego is the systematic affirmation of emotional reaction. This system is fueled by the energy of attention. Therefore as long as a man has no control over his attention his possibilities remain imprisoned in the ego no matter what ideals he espouses and no matter what efforts he expends.

Our holy teachers have handed down clear formulae about the levels of development possible for man. But these levels are portrayed in a simple manner in order to communicate one essential idea. The actual progression from one level to another is much more dynamic and organic than the formulae indicate. For example, the movement from the creation of the inner being to the formation of the soul involves an affirmative impulse of the inner being together with a counter-affirmative movement of the body. In between these two movements there exists the path of the soul. Yet many of the formulae handed down to us concern the development of levels of the inner being alone—this is mysticism as such. But for every level of mystical development there exists the possible struggle with the counter-affirmative movement within the structure of human reality (the "body").

It is an organic process. But religion in general demands simplicity of statement in order to awaken and support the holy desire. The symbol says a thousand things at once, but man can absorb only one of these truths at a time—until the moment arrives when the heart is awakened. The heart understands everything at once.

No one proceeds toward salvation without at the same time developing the soul to some extent. But the two directions are not the same. Full development of the soul is the kingdom of heaven. Salvation is not the same. In the way of salvation a man's interest and understanding are not drawn toward the soul formation within him, even though the soul must inevitably form to some extent. I speak here of great religious leaders and those who advance along the way of salvation through commitment to the commandments of orthodoxy. I am not speaking of empty religion.

When I meet a great religious leader I see his soul, to the extent that I can see. But his mysticism and his Christian morality may be greater than his soul; that is his direction. It is not my direction. That is his aim. It is not my aim. He does not seek to become a soul; he seeks only to serve God and man. For that, he is great, greater by far than the rest of us. He does not know and does not wish to know how it happened that he has become able to serve God. It is because of the formation of the soul in him. He does not know the laws of the progression into God and into the growth of moral power in him. He has arrived somewhere, but he does not know how he arrived. Therefore he does not tend the balance between the inner being and the body and therefore he will never consciously serve the God beyond God. Only the fully formed soul is able to serve the God beyond God.

Because he does not know the process by which he has moved toward salvation he cannot intentionally lead another toward God.

This great religious leader is also the Church, the Holy Church. He offers the path of salvation, but he does not guide the formation of the soul. Many will enter this path of salvation, and many will begin the formation of the soul, but it will not go far. Exclusive concern with the inner being will bring that process to a halt.

And here lies danger, the danger of the second dispersal of the soul. Having drawn the energy of attention away from the body, and having gathered the beginning of the soul within themselves, these men of salvation walk the earth like explosive devices ready to be set off at random. Their energy can combine with impulses in human nature, and in themselves, which they have not seen and understood or which, at the time of their activation, they are not concerned to see and accept. They have become accustomed to the experience and the laws of the inner being deep inside themselves, and have relatively little in themselves to reconcile the inner being with the body. This is mysticism without a soul, roughly speaking. They have known God, but there is nothing, or relatively little, in themselves that can transmit God to their own body.

The Origin of "Heresy"

At this point, Father Sylvan offers a lengthy commentary about the origin of various sects within Christendom and within all religions. A certain inner force is gathered through ascetic morality or through commitment and personal sacrifice to a noble ideal or individual. But, in the absence of the intermediate principle in man, this force eventually "combines" with elements of the "body": emotional reactions, sensations, thought patterns. The result is a *religious leader* or a *charismatic figure*. Through such leaders, religious and moral ideals are spread throughout a group or even a whole culture. Religious fervor, "the caricature of love," may ensue and with it fear, hatred and violence. Father Sylvan observes this dialectic at work not only in what is officially recognized as "religion," but, at a different level, in other realms as well, especially in the sphere of philosophical and political ideologies. "The most dangerous people," he writes, "are those who have achieved inner being without the corresponding development of the soul." And he writes: "The service of orthodoxy is to stabilize the life of mankind as a whole through a morality that not only gives some kind of meaning to the millions, but which resists or absorbs the initiatives of 'great men.'"

Proceeding with the discussion of the soul, he then writes of the centuries immediately following the death of Christ:

> A great division appeared. The sayings of Christ were gathered into a system of moral idealism and belief, attracting more and more followers from the decaying civilization of the Roman Empire. Apart from this form of Christianity, however, there persisted another version of the teaching. It found various expressions. It made innovative use of the scientific language of the period, the language of Greek science and philosophy. It employed mythic symbols in forms carefully altered to convey truth without supporting the formation of belief and opinion.
>
> This version contained and emphasized the theory and practice of the formation of the intermediate principle in man.
>
> Only broken fragments of these expressions have survived the passage of centuries. The force and life of these expressions was great. Those who cherished this teaching never sought to convert people to it. But soon students of the teaching who did not value it or understand it well enough, and others who were only superficially acquainted with it from the outside, transmuted it into a religious movement. Religious leaders began using these fragments of the Christian truth. In this way, the "heresies" appeared. The Church was generally right in opposing them. What they were offer-

ing were indigestible fragments or imitations of the
Christian gnosis.

But many of the Church fathers did not and could
not know that these heresies were distortions not of the
official Church doctrine, but of another doctrine which,
far from contradicting the teaching of Christ, in fact
confirmed the teaching of Christ in a way that even
they might not have dreamt of.

Scholars have lumped all these heresies under the
name "Gnosticism." This is an accurate name. "Gnosticism" is a good word for describing what the
insufficiently developed mind does to *gnosis*. The mind
sees the surface of a great teaching, steals from it what
it likes, and invents a religion around it. "Gnosticism" is
not a heresy of the Church, but a "heresy" of gnosis.

Gnosis Is Not Gnosticism

Father Sylvan now proceeds to an extensive series of references to the doctrines of those teachings that modern scholarship
has groupd under such headings as Gnosticism, Hermeticism
and Neoplatonism. In a future publication, I will reproduce
these lengthy references in full, as in these pages Father Sylvan
atypically makes use of the scholarly apparatus: cross-references,
textual analysis and extensive documentation. Nowhere else in
his journals does he openly reveal such familiarity with academic
conventions and research—in this case the work of such investi-
gators as Jonas, Grant, Smith, Doresse and Robinson, including
the material collected by the latter in the recently published *The
Nag Hammadi Library.*†

Father Sylvan is aware that many contemporary people, including a number of scholars and theologians, look upon the
Gnostic texts as a key to "esoteric Christianity," Christianity's
"answer" to the "new religions" of the East. (The dust jacket of
the American edition of *The Nag Hammadi Library* refers to
Gnosticism as "the Zen of the Western world"). Concerning such
claims, however, Father Sylvan writes, "Anyone who is really
able to interpret these ancient fragments and who is able to sepa-

† James M. Robinson, general ed., *The Nag Hammadi Library* (New York:
Harper & Row, 1978).

rate the few that are spiritually authentic from the rest has already reached a relatively high level of inner work and does not need these fragments for guidance. For anyone else, it would probably have been better if these manuscripts had remained buried in the desert. Their only value is to make people recognize how poorly we understand the teachings of Christ."

Nevertheless, as though going against his own warning, he freely discusses the following Gnostic tenets in the light of his teachings about the "intermediate":

The doctrine of the alien God. In many Gnostic texts, one finds a sharp distinction made between the God of the Old Testament and the Redeemer God, usually identified as Jesus Christ. The most extreme form of this doctrine occurs in the teaching of Marcion, which holds that man is "legally" bound to Jehovah, the Creator of the cosmos and of man himself. Jehovah is the God of justice, against whom man has sinned, and man, by law and kinship, is obliged to pay for his sin. But the good and merciful alien God sends his son, Jesus Christ, to redeem the soul of man.

Other, more common versions of this theme speak of a God beyond the cosmos and a lesser, creator God, the *Demiurge,* who has fashioned this world and who rules over it. The highest God, the supreme reality, is variously characterized as the "Fore-Beginning," the "Inconceivable," the "Immeasurable," the "Beyond-Being," etc. The Demiurge, on the other hand, is a "working principle" (the name literally means "craftsman for the people"), who builds the world we live in out of matter and according to laws that are not of his creating.

There are many, many expressions of this theme in the writings of antiquity. Its best-known formulation is to be found in the *Timaeus,* of Plato, from which it is assumed to have exercised profound influence through the development of Neoplatonism. The idea of the Demiurge is a key element in Hermetic thought as well.

Historical discussion aside, Father Sylvan's point is that this notion is basically and originally an expression of the distinction between salvation and the Kingdom of Heaven. The "God beyond God" is the God of the developed soul, whereas the lesser God is the god of morality and religious sanctity. According to Father Sylvan, many were the Gnostic sects that twisted this idea so far around that it began to look like a challenge to the unicity and harmonious structure (goodness) of the universe itself. And in this form the Church was bound to denounce it.

In fact, says Father Sylvan, the doctrine of the Demiurge is a key element of a world view emphasizing levels of being in man and the universe. Psychologically speaking, the Demiurge represents true and good concepts about creation and life, but which, as concepts, can stand as a screen between the soul and the direct experience of its supreme possibility. On this subject, he cites the following sequence of passages from the sermons of the great medieval Dominican Meister Eckhart. The first citation links the God-beyond-god to the attainment of "immortality," i.e. the real *I* that is independent and active in relation to all other entities or beings both "inner" and "outer," "eternal" and "temporal":

> Therefore I pray God that he may quit me of god, for his unconditioned being is above god and all distinctions. It was here (in unconditioned being) that I was myself, wanted myself, and knew myself to be this person (here before you), and therefore, I am my own first cause, both of my eternal being and of my temporal being. To this end I was born, and by virtue of my birth being eternal, I shall never die. . . . If I had not been there would have been no god. . . . When I flowed forth from God, creatures said: "He is a god!" This, however, did not make me blessed, for it indicates that I, too, am a creature. In bursting forth, however, when I shall be free within God's will and free, therefore, of the will of god, and all his works, and even of god himself, then I shall rise above all creature kind, and shall be neither god nor creature, but I shall be what I was once, now, and forevermore. I shall thus receive an impulse which shall raise me above the angels.‡

After reiterating that in this passage Eckhart is speaking of the awakening within man of the *I AM* and once again equating

‡ Raymond Bernard Blakney, *Meister Eckhart, A Modern Translation* (New York: Harper Torchbooks, 1941), pp. 231-32.

the I AM with the *intermediate*—now in the sense of that which bridges and encompasses all the forces of creation—Father Sylvan cites the following passage from Eckhart:

> The just person serves neither God nor creatures. . . .
> Created things are not free. . . .
> I have been thinking for some time that the fact that *I am a person* is something others hold in common with myself . . . but the fact that *I am* pertains only to me and not to other men or angels, nor even to God, except as I am one with him. . . . Now Plato, that great priest who occupied himself so much with such lofty matters and spoke of them so much, refers to this. He speaks of a purity that is not of this world, which is neither in the world nor out of it, neither in time nor in eternity, which has neither outside nor inside. Out of this purity, God the Father eternal derives the fullness and emptiness of his Godhead and gives birth to his only begotten Son, so that we are at once his Son. His birth is his indwelling and his indwelling is his epiphany. It (the pure abyss of God) remains forever unique, uniform, and self-generating. *Ego*, the word "I," is proper to no one but God alone in his uniqueness. *Vos* means "you" to the extent that all of you have achieved unity in (God's) uniqueness. . . .
> That we may be unique and that our uniqueness may remain, may God help us all! Amen. [pp. 189–91]

And then the following passages are presented without comment:

> Aware of it or not, people have wanted to have the "great" experiences; they want it in this form, or they want that good thing; and this is nothing but self-will. . . . There are thousands who have died and gone to heaven who never really gave up their own wills. [p. 16]

> See! You must observe two things about yourself that our Lord also had to deal with. He, too, had higher and

lower powers, each having its own function. By his higher powers, he possessed and enjoyed the bliss of eternity while, at the same time, by his lower powers, he went through much suffering and struggle here on earth, and still this did not inhibit the function of the higher powers. So should it be with you. [p. 29]

Not that one should give up, neglect or forget his inner life for a moment, but he must learn to work in it, with it and out of it, so that the unity of his soul may break out into his activities and his activities shall lead him back to that unity. In this way one is taught to work as a free man should (dispassionately). Keep your eye on the functioning of your inner life and start from there—to read, or pray, or to do any needed outward deed. If, however, the outward life interferes with the inner, then follow the inner; but if the two can go on together, that is best of all and then man is working together with God. [p. 37]

One should be, as our Lord said, "Like people always on the watch, expecting their Lord." Expectant people are watchful, always looking for him they expect, always ready to find him in whatever comes along. . . . This is what awareness of the Lord is to be like and it requires diligence that taxes a man's senses and powers to the utmost. . . . The man to whom God is ever present, and who controls and uses his mind to the highest degree—that man alone knows what peace is and he has the Kingdom of Heaven within him. [pp. 10–11]

Now you say: "I am afraid I do not devote enough attention to such matters or bother as much as I might. . . ." Let that be a sorrow to you and bear it as patiently as you may; take even this as discipline. . . . [p. 40]

And finally:

We ought not to have or let ourselves be satisfied with the God we have thought of, for when the thought slips the mind, that god slips with it. [p. 9]

Cosmic dualism. Another tenet of the Gnostic heresies that Father Sylvan discusses is the notion of two fundamental forces in the universe, variously called "light and darkness," "spirit and matter," "Good and Evil." From the point of view of the Church, the offending element here is the idea that there exists a principle of Evil that is as real as the principle of Good. The most well-known expression of this idea occurs, of course, in the Manichaean heresy, which St. Augustine was so concerned to refute. Taken at face value, the idea of cosmic dualism places unacceptable limits either on God's power or on His goodness. If Evil is real, then either there is something God did not create (in which case he is not omnipotent), or else there exists an evil that he chooses to allow (in which case he is not all-benevolent). Obviously, the whole logical problem of good and evil, as it has echoed through the centuries to modern times, is contained in this "dilemma." Furthermore, cosmic dualism in general obviously stands against the notion of the unity of God's creation and against the usual interpretation of "monotheism," etc., as we have discussed it above.*

Here, too, Father Sylvan sides with the early Fathers against the Gnostics, but for reasons that are clearly different from those of the Church:

"Here," he writes, "the problem is how to help man to know, feel and sense with the whole of himself how far he is from the development of his divine possibilities. That is the only problem. The Great Knowledge, in whatever cultural dress it appears, also speaks in order to guide us into that experience."

According to Father Sylvan, there are teachings that offer man direct experience of the Higher—this is *mysticism* in its familiar sense. "But it is necessary to have a corresponding experience of the forces of dispersal as well. These forces, too, are part of God's Holy Creation and, in the sense that God is the Whole, they are also part of God."

To experience and understand the movement of descent and dispersal is, he writes, an equally "mystical" or higher experience as the experience of the movement toward ultimate unity. "The soul of man is destined for *two mysticisms.*"

At the hands of Gnosticism, a fateful confusion was bred in which the cosmic movement away from unity was equated with

* P. 181–82.

the illusions, self-deceptions and egoism that distract man from the work of self-perfection, which involves the balancing within himself of these two fundamental forces of Creation and Return.

"For him who seeks the perfection of the soul only that can be called evil which prevents the direct inner experience of Creation and Return. The soul of man is grown through the struggle and harmonization of these two energies of God."

Father Sylvan then proceeds with a striking restatement of Gnostic symbology. Readers unfamiliar with these symbols used by the heresies of the early Church should know that, as presented in historical and scholarly studies, they portray a universe of evil and darkness. The world man lives in, the world into which he was thrown, is a cave, a prison, ruled by "principalities and powers" opposed entirely to the light and goodness of God. Our world is a house of ignorance and illusion, where spirit is captured by the coarseness and density of matter. In that world, man is drugged and intoxicated, forgetful of his real origin and asleep to his higher destiny. Either through some great cosmic error and fall, or through the independent rapaciousness of a separate principle of Evil, this life, this world and everything that is in it, is pervaded by ultimate corruption. And it is peopled by human beings totally in the thrall of this corruption, human beings in appearance only. A few men and women, however, have the spark of God within them, and the sole aim of these special individuals must be to sever their bondage to the world and its people, to remember their real origins and escape from the death-dealing pleasures and pains of the created universe in which they find themselves.

Father Sylvan writes, internalizing this whole symbology:

Father, Lord, grant me to hate this world, without emotion,
In Myself.

May I be deaf to the noise of the world, that I may listen,
In Myself.

May I forget the world and my neighbor, that I may remember,
In Myself.

May I perceive the nightmare in the patterns of this
world that I may awaken,
In Myself.

May I despise the mixing of the world, that I may
separate,
In Myself.

Father Sylvan goes on at length in this vein employing the
Gnostic symbols as metaphors of the human mind, which in his
terms implies treating them principally as guides to self-observation. He concludes:

May I hear Your words in myself,
And Myself in Your words,
That I may be Two, as You are Two,
And One as You are One,
In the Glory of Your Trinity.

Evil is that which obstructs the simultaneous awareness in
oneself of the two principal forces of creation; and at another
stage evil is that which obstructs or diverts the soul's struggle to
grow as the Intermediate or Third Principle that harmonizes
these two great universal movements of Creation and Return.
Return is "heaven," the movement toward the Creator. *Creation*
is "earth," the movement toward manifestation and the multiplicity of beings and elements in the universe. That which holds
these two movements together in their reciprocity is the Lord,
God Beyond God, Cause of all Causes, "Creator of Heaven and
Earth," universal Spirit and individual Soul.

"The Gnosis becomes mere Gnosticism when the language of
silence is used to persuade, provoke or explain." By the term
"language of silence," Father Sylvan means "symbols and formulae" that "support the movement toward individual remorse
based on objective perceptions in the contemplative state of
mental quiet."

Father Sylvan concludes his extended discussion of the problem of Good and Evil by citing, with approval, a text from the
recently translated *The Nag Hammadi Library* called "The Gospel of Philip":

[Most things] in the world, as long as their [inner parts] are hidden, stand upright and live. [If they are revealed] they die, as is illustrated by the visible man: [as long as] the intestines of the man are hidden, the man is alive; when his intestines are exposed and come out of him, the man will die. So also with the tree: while its root is hidden it sprouts and grows. If its root is exposed, the tree dries up. So it is with every birth that is in the world, not only with the revealed but with the hidden. For so long as the root of wickedness is hidden, it is strong. But when it is recognized it is dissolved. When it is revealed it perishes. That is why the word says, "Already the ax is laid at the root of the trees" (Matthew 3:10). It will not merely cut—what is cut sprouts up again—but the ax penetrates deeply until it brings up the root. Jesus pulled out the root of the whole place, while others did it only partially. As for ourselves, let each one of us dig down after the root of evil which is within one, and let one pluck it out of one's heart from the root. It will be plucked out if we recognize it. But if we are ignorant of it, it takes root in us and produces its fruit in our heart. It masters us. We are its slaves. It takes us captive, to make us do what we do not want; and what we do want we do not do.†
It is powerful because we have not recognized it.‡

The two races of men. Although I cannot summarize all of Father Sylvan's "commentaries on the heresies," the theme of "the two races of men" demands our attention due to its relevance to the doctrine of the soul. The Gnostic imagery that has survived seems to communicate a radical doctrine of the elect. Some men are of God, others are of the evil cosmos; some are sourced above, others below; some destined for salvation, others for destruction—and due, moreover, to some element in their own internal makeup. There are two species of human beings, one at home in this darkened, deceptive and evil world; the other an "alien race" thrown into this world, etc.

This, says Father Sylvan, is certainly the language of gnosis,

† Compare Rom. 7.
‡ *The Nag Hammadi Library, supra*, pp. 149–50.

but in the form of *Gnosticism* it becomes twisted into a doctrine of literal exclusivism and provokes opposition by the early Fathers of Church, who insist on an equally literal doctrine of catholicism: "In fact, this distinction applies to every individual."

> Certainly, there are different levels of being that distinguish one man from another. But how to express this in a way that calls *all* men? Few will respond, but all must be called. The difference between men lies in their response to the call of the Way. And the difference between men on the Way also lies in their readiness to respond to the call of the next level of being. Catholicism is the call to all men; the gnosis, however, shows us our failure to respond. In between these two truths, *I*, the soul-in-birth, can appear as I attend to the call of Spirit and see at the same time that I am non-Christian. Seeing that, accepting that, the holy desire arises and the bridge between my two natures forms, immediately to disappear again and again. Only he who has experienced this process in himself a thousand times, a hundred thousand times, and only he who understands this process at its root, has the right to speak of the two races of man. For these two races are in himself. Only he who can call to the multitude in himself can call to the multitude outside himself. And only he can recognize in which man the holy desire lies hidden, and in which man it is dead.

Father Sylvan does then assert that "there are men with souls and there are men without souls," but that this division is not foreordained or fundamental. "The basic distinction between men lies in the ordinary mind, in the ego! In the ordinary mind of man there exists the shadow of the holy desire. It is within every man's power to cultivate this 'shadow,' as was said by Gurdjieff: to wish with the mind. This is the real locus of free-will." And later he writes: "The completion or non-completion of the soul is a distant result of wishing or not wishing with the mind." Only such a man can receive the helping powers outside and inside of himself. "Only such a man can make contact with the holy desire hidden within him, and which alone pulls man upward toward completion." "The shadow of the holy desire is brighter than any other idea or impulse in the mind or body of the ego."

"Sometimes," he continues, "it is necessary to speak in a way that stresses the differences between men. Sometimes it is necessary to speak the opposite way. Sometimes one must talk of stars and planets and the overwhelming influences against which man must struggle. Sometimes one must emphasize the unconquerable force of the holy desire. Language must change in response to the changing furniture of the mind of the ego. But always one must speak to the shadow of the holy desire, the mental wish, which is the choice that divides human beings into men and beasts. Whatever assists and confirms this continuous free choice I call Christianity."

In his discussion of the metaphor of the two races of man, Father Sylvan approvingly makes several passing references to the body of writings known as the *Corpus Hermeticum,* which, he says, has been erroneously classified by some historians as comparable to a Gnostic document. No specific passages from these mysterious writings of the early Christian era are quoted, but the following seems to me so pertinent that I feel sure it must have been what Father Sylvan had in mind. The first passage is from the chapter in the *Hermetica,* entitled "The Basin." In the following passages, translated by Walter Scott in 1924, I have placed in parentheses several translations or paraphrasings that I believe Father Sylvan would have favored over those of Scott. Like all the books of the *Hermetica,* and in fact like most ancient texts dealing with this sort of material, the literary form places essential ideas in the mouth of what we would nowadays call "fictional" personages. In this case, it is Hermes speaking to his "son," Tat (Thoth):

> *Tat:* Tell me then, father, why did not God impart mind (consciousness) to all men?

> *Hermes:* It was his will, my son, that mind should be placed in the midst as a prize that human souls may win.

> *Tat:* And where did he place it?

Hermes: He filled a great basin with mind, and sent it down to earth; and he appointed a herald, and bade him make proclamation to the hearts of men: "Hearken, each human heart; dip yourself in this basin, if you can, recognizing for what purpose you have been made, and believing that you shall ascend to Him who sent the basin down." Now those who gave heed to the proclamation, and dipped themselves in the bath of mind, these men got a share of *gnosis;* and they received mind, and so (ultimately) became complete men. But those who failed to heed the proclamation, these are they who possess speech indeed, but have not received mind also. And these, inasmuch as they know not for what purpose they have been made, are held under constraint (enslaved) by anger and incontinence; they admire (value) the things that are not worth looking at; they give heed only to (all their attention is dispersed in) their bodily pleasures and desires, and believe that man has been made for such things as these. But as many as have partaken of the gift which God has sent, these, my son, in comparison with the others, are as immortal gods to mortal men. . . .

Tat: I too, father, would fain be dipped in that basin.

Hermes: If you do not first hate (struggle against) your body, my son, you cannot love (be drawn toward) yourself; but if you love yourself, you have mind; and having mind, you will partake of knowledge also.

Tat: What mean you, father?

Hermes: It is not possible, my son, to attach yourself both to things mortal and to things divine (It is not possible to become both mortal and divine). . . . (He) who wills to make his choice is left free to choose the one or the other.*

Concerning the nature of this choice—that it is an inner choice, rather than solely an outer renunciation—the following passage from the *Hermetica* is instructive:

* W. Scott and A. S. Ferguson, eds. and transl., *Hermetica* (New York: Oxford, 1924), Vol. I, p. 171.

Hence those who have not that knowledge, and have not travelled on the road of piety (reverence), are not afraid to call a man "beautiful and good"; and that, though the man has never even in dream seen anything that is good, but is encompassed by every kind of evil, and has come to believe that the evil is good, and in this belief is insatiable in his dealings with evil, and fears to be deprived of it, and strives with all his might not only to keep it, but to increase it. Such, Asclepius, are the things which men deem good and beautiful. And we cannot shun these things nor hate them; for the hardest thing of all is this, that we have need of them, and cannot live without them.†

"Practical Instructions"

Father Sylvan concludes his treatment of Gnosticism by naming, without discussion, several of the early Church Fathers who in his judgment understood and transmitted a more nearly complete teaching about the nature of the soul. At this point in the manuscript, in a series of marginal notes, the compiler has inserted some further excerpts from one of Father Sylvan's letters that he, the compiler, terms "practical instructions." As these insertions occur at a point near the end of Father Sylvan's manuscript, it first seemed to me that the only logic behind their placement was the compiler's fear that the reader of the manuscript would not be left with a clear enough idea of the first practical step to be taken toward the attainment of "intermediate Christianity." But, after reading further, I realized that something quite different was involved, having to do with Father Sylvan's views on the relationship between ideas and practice. Throughout the manuscript, he warns of the danger of blind faith, blind practice without a certain level of intellectual understanding. "The intellect cannot be abandoned," he writes, "until it knows why it must be abandoned and can theoretically agree to it. For this, a certain attitude must be developed in the mind through the pure reception, over a long period of time, of the necessary ideas. Then, and only then, another stage of practice can be attempted. But the ego must first become in-

† Ibid.

terested in its own "destruction." Without this interest and attitude, a man will never be able to bear the emotional upheaval
that is necessary for a relationship to the ego and will instead retreat into repetition of old efforts, imagination or even violence
of various kinds. In any case, progress will come to a halt."

The first name that appears in connection with this so-called
"practical instruction" is that of St. Irenaeus, Bishop of Lyons
(second century), whose great work, *Against the Heresies*, provided much of the material for the Church's attacks against the
Gnostics, as well as much of the information upon which modern
scholars have based their own views of Gnosticism. The compiler
writes several phrases in the margin which are from the writings
of Irenaeus: *"subjection to God is incorruptibility; continuance
in incorruptibility is the glory of eternity"*; *"Man has to come
into manhood and having reached manhood to increase, and
thus increasing to persevere, and by persevering to be glorified,
and thus see his Lord"*; *"the vision of God is the acquisition of
immortality."*

The first insertion contains the following:

My dear friend . . . in order to attain the intermediate
you must begin by setting aside the language of the
Christian religion. Many experiences are withheld from
you because you cling to a language unsuited to your
subjectivity. Do not speak to me or to any one of us of
incorruptibility and corruption. Speak instead of perma-
nence of aim and the impermanence of our countless
"selves." Do not speak of the immortality of the soul
until you have experienced a wish that is a material
force in your inner life. Do not speak of the flesh; speak
of resistance to awakening: self-deception, imagination,
dispersal of the energy of attention. Do not speak of
God; speak instead of the next step of understanding
and presence; for you that is "God." Do not speak of
mercy and forgiveness of sins; speak instead of an attitude of interest in yourself as you are. Do not speak of
guilt. Do not frighten yourself and do not make love to
yourself.

We have often discussed the place of language in the regeneration of Christianity in today's civilization. Everything we have said about the Church applies to you and to all of us, down to the letter. The language of religion touches your emotions, but not your heart, which is veiled by the emotions. This is true for many serious people today. The language of our teaching is for the heart and the mind simultaneously. It is not for the emotions. Our language supports our attitude. It is more than mere words. It governs the destiny of our efforts and our attention.

What follows is a repeated emphasis that a new language is the first step modern people can take toward the "intermediate." Although references are made to psychological exercises, meditation practices, breathing, posture, etc., nothing concrete or specific is offered in this regard. The impression is that such instructions have been intentionally left out either by the compiler or by Father Sylvan himself. It is also stressed that this new language cannot be invented by oneself.

"Our language supports our attitude": what is meant here? and why is it given such importance, to the extent of being called the first "practical step" toward the "intermediate"? How is this more practical than, say, the need for a spiritual guide or inner exercises? The answer lies in a statement of Father Sylvan that occurs in quite another context. Speaking about the dogma and the ritual forms of Western religions and contrasting them with the psychological exercises of the newly arrived Eastern religions, he writes:

The mercy or compassion of a teaching consists not only in the contents it brings, but in the conditions under which it brings them. Everything must correspond to the real structure of man. At the beginning, no less than at the end, the Unknown in ourselves must occupy the same place as the Unknown in the universe. No emotion or thought can approach the unknown, the higher level. It is only reached through the destruction of everything at my level of consciousness. If I am a thinker, my thought must be destroyed; then my emotions must be destroyed. What can carry me through these destructions? What can open me to the higher level? Only the authentic attitude of learning. The conditions must shock me to awaken me to the perils of my situation at the same time that they reach the unknown levels in myself. For this, they must be consciously and subtly designed. The conditions of a teaching begin with its language. Religious language can no longer have this effect on most of us. It does not now correspond to the wish to understand, to learn, which is the only attitude that can open us from the very beginning of our search. On the other hand, without this attitude, no conditions, no forms, no techniques will help us. They will only lead us to new forms of dependence. Without this attitude, I will never recognize the spiritual guide, not even if he is standing in front of me. Attitude cannot be given to a man; he either has it or he doesn't. But it can be supported.

The next name mentioned here by Father Sylvan is Gregory of Nyssa (fourth century). Alongside this name the compiler has written the Greek words *morphothenai ton psyche* (formation of the soul) and has cited Romans 12:2: "be ye transformed by the renewing [metamorphosis, transformation] of the mind [*nous*]." The compiler also refers the reader to Gregory's treatise *On Virginity*.

The following excerpt from Father Sylvan's letters, apparently a continuation of the previous one, is inserted:

    . . . and when you speak of transformation, remember that you are speaking of a process that obeys the same laws as the growth of the physical body. "Virginity" is a state of openness, an attention sensitized to both the higher and the lower in oneself, a link [marginal note: *syndesmos*]. Do not speak of purity as a condition of the body. Your physical body is not meant to be pure, except during certain periods. Purity is a condition of the attention whereby we can receive the food of truth through sensations in the body. The body is a "sink" not of iniquity, but of all the substances in the universe. Through the link of a sensitized attention the body will gladly obey the heart and you will become moral without violence. This is a sign of the process of transformation. Meanwhile, ponder, without clinging, those fleeting moments when the body obeys the heart without the passage of time, without the inner violence of ordinary morality. Do not make a religion of your better moments. That way lies the corruption of our teaching. This corruption is inevitable in the nature of things, but you do not wish to be its agent. The offense must come, but woe to him through whom it comes.

An extensive series of marginal notes and excerpts from Father Sylvan's letters occurs with reference to the third name mentioned, the great master of Byzantine spirituality Maximus the Confessor (seventh century). Again the context is the need for a new language as the first practical step toward intermediate Christianity, and along with that the development of a new attitude toward oneself, the attitude of study. I will limit myself here to juxtaposing a few of the compiler's references to the terminology of Maximus with representative selections of statements from the letters of Father Sylvan that the compiler has chosen to insert into the manuscript. This procedure will suffice to show how the compiler has understood Father Sylvan's offering of "an exact language that points simultaneously to the unity of Man and the fragmentation of oneself."

> *Compiler:* See Maximus on *mesiteuo* [Gr.: to mediate]. Man as mediator of matter and Spirit. Free to break his dependence on matter.

> *Father Sylvan:* Your only freedom consists in where to place your attention, how much of it to give in the moment to the outer world and how much, in the same moment, to the inner world. Remember: the outer world is more than external objects. It is also your reactions of like and dislike, and your thoughts, and those of your sensations, such as pain and tension, which channel energy outward.

Compiler: Maximus on the cosmic movements of *systole* and *diastole*. Man contracts and expands. The two natures of Christ are two movements. See Maximus against Monothelitism and Monoenergism [doctrines stressing the singleness of Christ's nature—an issue that was the source of controversy and fractioning in the seventh century and that has had considerable historical repercussions].

Father Sylvan: . . . and why do you cringe before the theories of science? Why are you so pleased when some astronomer or physicist gets interested in mysticism? It is not a good sign of your degree of understanding. At the same time, if you will observe your subjective reactions to science you will see something important about our teaching and the manner in which it has been given. We are not out to destroy myth and symbol; far from it. But in our hearts we are scientific. For us, science is for the heart; science is in the heart. The myths and symbols of the past only evoke our emotions. And not until you reach the heart should you permit yourself to speak the ancient language. Until then, even Christ must be chased out of your mind. You have made Him into a monster through your emotions and conditioning. It was the same with me, I can assure you. I have suffered because of my clinging to the old language. But one day I began to see that the seed of love is the desire to know, to understand. Our world is sick because that seed has not been tended.

How will you cultivate this fragile desire? How will you seek Christianity? How will you seek consciousness and being? How will you seek immortality? love of neighbor? the kingdom of heaven? How will you seek service to God and his creation? How will you seek what has been lost?

The answer is simple, but the work is difficult. You must learn *how* to seek. The whole of our teaching is in that: the knowledge of how to search—for ourselves first and then for our God.

Christianity is lost. How to search for it? When you have lost something, you must look for it exactly where you have lost it. Study, observe, watch: where, exactly, do you lose being and consciousness? In what do you lose yourself? You will not discover this by speaking the old language or by cultivating the old attitudes of religious piety or "morality." You will not find Christ by going to "Christ," but only through seeing, clearly and with precision, how you crucify Him. Only then will *you* appear. May your love of truth give you the strength and the understanding to bear the energy of this suffering and the light that follows it according to law.

A Fateful Ambiguity

Other Christian writers whom Father Sylvan mentions in the context of his distinction between gnosis and Gnosticism, and who he claims taught what I have called "the second doctrine of the soul," include many whom we have already cited: Gregory Palamas, Meister Eckhart, Evagrius, Clement of Alexandria—as well as numerous others whom we have not cited (the Cappodocian Fathers figure prominently in his list). Conspicuously absent, however, are the names of Augustine, Aquinas, Bernard of Clairvaux and others who are commonly recognized as the central shapers of Christian theology. My examination of primary and secondary texts associated with all these authors sometimes left me puzzled about Father Sylvan's choices. It is rare that any Christian writer ever explicitly states that man has a soul only in potential. But Father Sylvan does make it clear that the term "soul" is sometimes used to refer to "natural," "given" psychological functions with which all men are born and sometimes to the potentially fully developed soul. This ambiguity, he says, starts early in the history of Christian doctrine, becomes dominant and even uncontrolled in Augustine and eventually haunts the whole development of Western thought.

Conclusion

The Lost Religion of Love

Where does the search for lost Christianity fit in when meas-
ured against the massive, external crises of our culture: the
threat of nuclear war, ecological catastrophe, famine, economic
collapse, the injustices of class, race and caste? There may be
those who even feel ashamed to speak of it in the same breath
with these crises, as though the quest for contemplative Christianity were a self-indulgence, a refusal to face the real problems
of the world. And because the Christian Church in the Western
world has felt itself obliged to wrestle with such problems on
their own terms, many Christians often regard the whole idea of
interior spirituality with contempt or suspicion. However, such
an attitude rests on a profound misunderstanding both of the nature of these massive problems and the nature of the inner
search.

There is crisis in every field of human endeavor, everywhere a
shaking of the foundations of knowledge and expression. Everywhere, there is increasing fragmentation together with reactive
and ineffectual efforts at unification. In religion, there are countless sects, cults, new religions, "orthodoxies," "heterodoxies," "lib-
eralisms," "traditionalisms"—together with almost as many "ecumenical" programs that break down at the first real test into yet
more sects, countermovements and splinter groups. In the natural sciences, there is the constantly accelerating proliferation of
information, factual discovery and theoretical speculation and,
with almost comical regularity, the appearance of "break-
throughs" demanding "total revision" of fundamental scientific

assumptions and leading to yet more accumulation of information, factual discovery and theoretical speculation—so much so that the whole idea of a single scientific concept of nature begins to seem like an anachronism, and the whole aim of reaching a unified world view, which is so essential to normal human feeling, begins to seem like an unrealistic ideal. In psychiatry and psychology it is the same: hundreds of thrusts and counterthrusts among clinicians and researchers alongside as many "holistic" and even, as it were, "ecumenical" theories of psychotherapy, brain function, neurophysiology, etc. Examples such as these could be multiplied indefinitely for every pocket of modern culture. Fragmentation is the fact; "communication," "ecumenism," "planetization," "synthesis," is the illusion and the dream.

At the personal level, the influence of technological innovation is dissolving the patterns of individual and collective behavior that have guided human life for millennia: the brain manipulated by drugs to produce sensations of happiness and mastery; the genetic code rearranged; biological and economic techniques undermining the meaning of personal identity, work and the family unit. Everywhere, the pressure to learn and use these new inventions in defiance of traditional forms is breeding confusion. People are taking sides for and against technology and find no way to consult their own overall feelings about anything, not even by escaping to the wilderness. The moral education of the human being, his ability to turn to himself at times of difficulty, is so neglected that, in this sphere also, hundreds of superficial techniques are now offered, mass methods of meditation to withstand stress, and so on.

When placed against the background of these external problems and internal questions of our contemporary culture, the word "Christianity" carries no clear sense of hope. On the contrary, it appears as one of many fragments, a glorious fragment perhaps, in a world suffering from unfathomable division.

At the same time, the fragmentation of our culture is mirrored, almost to the letter, in the fragmentation within the Church itself. The conflict between political ideologies corresponds to similar divisions of left and right among Christians; there are Christian relativism and absolutism, Christian secularism and transcendentalism, Christian personalism and objectivism, and so on and so forth.

At its root, Christianity once taught that the world of human society will always be an incurable, open wound; that it is impossible to solve the "problem of the world." It seems equally impossible now to solve the "problem of the Church." Like all the great spiritual teachings of mankind, Christianity taught that the world we live in, the world of human society, is the way it is because men are the way they are. Rearranging the externals of human life can in no way alter the fundamental corruption of human nature and the suffering it produces. Similarly, the institutions of Christianity become what they become because men are what they are.

In the history of the religious traditions, renewal is often preceded by a perception that man has gone too far into the "world," into the externals of life, and has lost access to the higher forces within himself. "Mysticism" in its known forms often appears as a reaction against the excessive turning outward of the human mind and heart. A similar perception lies behind the contemporary search for the Christian mystical tradition. There is a widespread sense that the Church has "gone out" too far: too much emphasis on social action, too little emphasis on the inner life; too much acquiescence to the terms in which society sees its own difficulties and promises, too little emphasis on the understanding of human nature that is offered in the language and philosophy of the tradition itself.

This perception of the unbalanced outward thrust of human life has come to the surface in many areas of our culture. In a way, this perception lies behind the birth of modern psychology itself. But when the religious and philosophical teachings of the East began to take root in our culture, a decade ago, it became clear that the deeper meaning of "inner life" had not yet been understood in the modern world, not even by psychology. An even deeper interiority was sought.

But the rediscovery of the inner world cannot itself be the answer to problems of living. Take, for example, the massive problem of social injustice, which absorbs the energies of many of our best minds, both within and outside of the Church. No one doubts that the oppression of peoples is caused by the internal flaws of greed and egoistic fear. And no one who looks can doubt that the craving for power over others is also, like greed and paranoia, one of the consequences of egoism. But very few concerned people can listen with patience to traditionalist spiritual philosophies that explain and condemn these passions solely in terms of excessive desire for externals such as possessions, wealth, status, etc. ("Yes, yes, it is true, it is true. But don't ask me to wait until rulers become saints. And don't ask the victims of oppression to become 'spiritual' so that the oppressors may have a free hand without fear of rebellion. Marx exposed that strategy a century ago, when he called religion the opiate of the masses.")

When the issue reads out in these terms—spirituality vs. moral commitment, inner vs. outer—something fundamental has been distorted in the understanding of both inner development and moral action. The inner and the outer world have been misunderstood, and this misunderstanding has had disastrous consequences both for Christianity and modern culture. The outer world is not the world of things "out there" in space. The inner world is not the world of thoughts and emotions "inside" the psyche. On the contrary, it is the world of "thoughts and emotions" that is the outer world. Yet these same "thoughts and emotions" have been given a name that was meant to designate what is highest and most inner in man: the *soul*.

The fact of man's injustice to man can be explained in many ways; it may be struggled against in many ways. Yet, from the point of view of lost Christianity, the fundamental problem is completely different from the manner in which we present it to ourselves through our sense of moral outrage. Rather, the question is, how do I sense the suffering of others? from what in myself do I perceive it? how deeply do I feel it? how exactly do I understand it? and from what source in myself will I meet it? Is agitation of the mind and emotions in any sense at all the agent of love or moral action?

The perception of the suffering inherent in the human condition, the perception of man's inhumanity to man: this moment of awareness has been spoken of in all traditions as a tremendous moment in the consciousness of man, or in the consciousness of the founder of a tradition, or in the consciousness of its greatest saints. Think only of the young prince Gautama (Buddha) seeing old age, sickness and death for the first time. The greatness of this moment, however, is not only in the depth and content of the perception, but in the fact that the founder, or the saint, has within him the force to transmit that perception to the whole of himself: to all his faculties of thinking, feeling and will. The compassionate or merciful founder has within him a channel between compassionate awareness and all the functions of the normal human psychophysical body. In short, the founder represents the fullness of what we have termed "the possession of a soul": the power or entity that relates the two fundamental movements within human nature, in this case the *gnosis*, the higher consciousness of the truth of suffering, on the one hand, and the impulses, functions, thoughts and behaviors that originate in the elements of the body of man.

The real perception of suffering or injustice is an aspect of higher knowing. As such it must be distinguished from mere emotional reaction to the suffering of others. If one wishes to speak of the "horror" of man's inhumanity to man, one is then forced to distinguish, as it were, a higher awareness of this horror, free of the emotionalism and inner violence which are attributes of egoism. Egoism, too, can in its way "see" the suffering of man, but it is a "seeing" mixed with illusions and fear, leading to impatience, faulty action and, finally, infliction of yet more suffering upon others, even in the name of love. One is obliged to doubt the value of one's caring actions when they spring only from emotion or moralism.

Certainly there are moments in almost every individual's life when he perceives and feels something of the real suffering of the human race, or of this or that portion of the human race. There are moments of "moral mysticism," comparable in essential aspects to moments of "cosmic mysticism," the felt perception of a greater order and purpose in the universe. But, in both experiences, what is hardest to understand, and what is most easily lost, is the truth that the act of real seeing—what one may call the experience of the Question—is itself the seed, the embryo of that very force within human nature which has the power to respond to the Question and eventually even act upon it and realize the answer. The appearance in oneself of the Question is already the appearance of the soul, my real Self. But as this fact is not understood, the state of Questioning is not cultivated by ourselves or by our educators. Consequently, the force or spirit that has begun to break through is unconsciously dissipated. One longs, as is said, for God, or for Meaning, or for Understanding, or for Justice, and does not see that the longing itself is the beginning of the answer one is seeking. The state of wonder, for example, is itself a higher form of knowing than the explanations one subsequently seeks in the absence of that state. Similarly, the embryonic breakthrough of conscience in the form of perceiving the pain of human life is itself a closer approach to moral power than the reactions and commitments which take place after this fragile and fleeting awareness has given way to the (in ordinary men) more durable aspects of egoism, such as moral outrage. The real moral vision of the human condition is dissipated by emotionalism just as the authentic intuitive understanding of nature is dissipated by intellectualism.

Throughout the writing of this book, one phrase has been in the front of my mind: the definition of Christianity as *the religion of love*. Several key aspects of this definition have already appeared—in particular, the understanding of love as the mediating ontological force in both the individual and the cosmos, the force of reconciling, bridging. But here our question is one of understanding the nature of love with respect to moral action and human suffering. The question is: what is the expression of Christian love toward my neighbor?

Or, simply: what does it mean to help another human being? No sooner is the question put that way, however, than one is assaulted by clichés: feed the hungry, shelter the poor. But surely such actions can only be praised as "virtue" for abnormally egoistic human beings. Is it really an act of transcendent love to throw a rope to a drowning man? Has our understanding of the aims of social order become so distorted that we regard a natural human response to the other's suffering as a noble act of sacrifice? Surely the answer is yes, with the consequence that the Christian commandment to love has been reduced to demands relating only to one aspect of the whole of human nature in ourselves and in others: the aspect we may term "the body," always remembering that under this term are also included the thoughts and emotions mistakenly identified as "the soul."

From all that has been discussed in this book, it is clear that the essential expression of Christian love is, in its roots, *the commandment to transmit the teaching*.

To love my neighbor is to assist the arising and the unfolding in him of that which can harmonize the real elements of his nature. Such exalted love, of course, has many aspects corresponding to the level of being of the individual on each side of the relationship. But clearly the manifestation of Christian love, so defined, is possible only to the degree that a man has transmitted the truth to the whole of himself—the degree, that is, to which he has realized in himself what was once called "self-mastery," the activation of the ruling principle, or soul, within oneself.

The significance of this definition of Christian love is apparent when one realizes all that is involved in the practice of transmitting the teaching to another human being. It involves far more than words or the expression of concepts, or intellectual explanations. This latter kind of "education," whose moral powerlessness has become evident in the modern era, affects only the thinking faculty of human nature; its effects on the emotional and physical elements of man are at best unforeseen. At worst, it leads to the false assumption of superiority, based on the notion that the highest element of human nature is the discursive intellect.

Nor is transmission of truth to be understood solely as persuasion based on fear or camouflaged eroticism or fantastic promises —or as based on any other of the weaknesses in human nature so mercilessly exposed by the great modern critics of "religion": Kierkegaard, Nietzsche and Freud. If this intellectual Christianity is morally powerless, this emotional Christianity is, even at its best, morally blind. Passions are generated and supported whose contagion may bind communities or whole peoples together—but toward what end? History shows that such passion is the fertile soil of war, exploitation and cruelty.

To transmit the truth is, on the contrary, to nurture the growth, in my neighbor, of the soul. To this end, all the elements of human nature must be cared for in such a way that they can, as it were, "accept" the arising in oneself of this new "sun," this new ruling principle or energy. This means caring for the parts in such a way that the movement toward wholeness is also strengthened. From this point of view, it must be said that almost everything we ordinarily regard as moral concern or the expression of love is unchristian in that it strengthens one aspect of human nature to the detriment of another.

But the *soul* is the name for that force or principle within human nature that can bind together all the intellectual, emotional and instinctual aspects of the human being through a mediating relationship to the highest principles of order and mind in the universe. Therefore, as it is said, "love nourishes the soul."

We must distinguish, therefore, three kinds of love: psychological love, mystical love and ontological love. The first represents the ideal of love as it is usually presented: a caring for the outward-directed, or external, aspect of human nature, including the emotions as we ordinarily experience them. When this aspect of human nature is exclusively attended to, the result is progressive fragmentation, because there is no effective ruling principle in such an individual. The physical or psychological desires are cared for. But, in the absence of a ruling principle within oneself, the inevitable conflicts of body, mind and emotion can only be falsely integrated within the structure of egoism—that is, false ideas about oneself more or less successfully screening from view the contradictory impulses within myself.

Mystical love, or religious love, may be defined as the caring for the inward-directed, or internal, aspect of human nature. But such love often ignores or denies the physical and emotional desires of the other and therefore communicates an ideal of inner perfection with no practical means of leading the other to the attainment of that ideal. The result is a form of communication that encourages religious fantasies which, when combined with the volatile and repressed energies of sexuality and emotion and with the automatisms of the isolated intellect, may lead to social and personal disintegration. It is essentially mystical love, so understood, which for these reasons was held in suspicion by the Church from the late Middle Ages up until the modern era and which was strongly condemned by modern psychology.

Finally, ontological love may be defined as the transmission to another of conditions of living, thinking and experiencing that foster the growth of the intermediate principle in human nature: the soul. A great spiritual tradition must surely be understood as an expression, in the life of man, of ontological love. But as the forms of the tradition inevitably break down or are only partially

understood, one or another element of the tradition is emphasized. Basically, a tradition breaks down or descends to a lower
level by becoming primarily mystical, psychological or social.
Within the integrity of the primordial tradition, each of these aspects has its proper place. But when the center dissolves, the aspects misleadingly take on the appearance of the whole. Without
the way leading to the development of the soul, neither mystical
love nor psychological love can lead human beings to the
fulfillment of their real possibilities.

What has been lost everywhere in the life of man is the confrontation within oneself of the two fundamental forces of the
cosmic order: the movement of creation and the movement of return, the outer and the inner. The whole of what is known as
"progress" in the modern world may be broadly characterized as
an imbalanced attention to the outward-directed force of life,
combined with a false identification of the "inner" as the realm
of thought and emotion. The thoughts and emotions that are
given the name of "inwardness" actually serve, as has been
shown, the movement outward and degradation of psychic energy. In Christian terms, this is "flesh." Thoughts and emotions
are not the soul.

Mysticism and spirituality by themselves are not enough. Social action and therapeutic caring by themselves are not enough.
Nor is it enough merely to reach for both at the same time. The
lost element in our lives is the force within myself that can attend to both movements of human nature within my own being
and can then guide the arising of this force within my neighbor
in a manner suited to his understanding. To communicate that
idea has been the single aim of this book.

Index

Absolute Force, 101

Acornology, 59

Adam, 88, 97, 122, 126, 168

Affective prayer, 130

Agape, 137

Albigensian Crusade, 83

Allah, 61

Angelology, 128

Antahkarana, 183

Anthony, Metropolitan, *see* Bloom, Metropolitan Anthony

Apatheia (freedom from emotion), 136–39

Aperçus sur L'Ésotérisme Chrétien (Guénon), 70, 128

Aquinas, Thomas, 39, 107, 213

Arianism, 65

Aristotle, 107

Asceticism, 25, 26, 63, 94, 131, 190

Asian Journal of Thomas Merton, The, 116

Athens, 28–30

Attention: to the body, 83; of the heart, 155–62; mediating, 167; prayer and, 156–57, 162–65; soul as, 167; and virtue, 151–55

Augustine, St., 107, 200, 213

Awareness, 27, 52, 53, 90, 99; attention to the body, 83; Orthodox tradition and, 31

Bamberger, John Eudes, 136

Bar Mitzvah, 45, 46

Belief, 35–36, 46; distinction between reason and, 40, 42

Bernard of Clairvaux, 83–84, 107, 213

Bhakti yoga, 23

Bible, 2, 48, 58, 92, 126, 127

Blakney, Raymond Bernard, 197

Bloom, Metropolitan Anthony, lost Christianity and, 15–43, 52, 105, 106, 136, 139; contact of forces, 33–34; credentials, 15–17, 41; elements people are seeking, 42–43; emotion of Christian mystery, 21–23; feelings of demand being made, 25–28; new emotion and new thought, 41–43; "occult" Christianity, 21–23; origin of spiritual exercises, 35–37; Parthenon (in Athens), 28–30; questions without answers, 19–21; seeing and gnosis ("faith vs. reason"), 37–40; two histories of Christianity, 17–19; vulnerability, 30–33

Body, defined, 167, 187

Boullaye, Henri Pinard de la, 149

Brahman-Atman doctrine, 96–97

Brhadaranyaka Upanishad, 179–80

Buddha, 63–64, 86, 110, 111, 163, 217

Buddhism, 3, 4, 49, 53, 61, 63–64,
   79, 92, 93, 95, 96, 115, 164, 181;
   Ch'an, 4; Christianity and,
   107–13; Hinayana, 95, 96;
   intermediate in, 183–87;
   Mahayana, 53, 61, 95, 96, 110,
   111; Theravada, 53, 86, 111–12;
   Vajrayana, 61

Calvin, John, 89
Celibacy, 74
Chakras, 16
Ch'an Buddhism, 4
Chidakash, 183
Christianity: Buddhism and,
   107–13; distinction between
   Christendom and, 89; Eastern
   meditation and, 107–23;
   Hellenistic, 107–8; language of
   the Second History, 187–90
Christian love, defined, 220
Christian spirituality, foundational
   act of, 124–26
Christian Zen (Johnston), 108–9
Clement of Alexandria, 136, 142,
   213
Cloud of Unknowing, The (trans.
   Johnston), 100–1, 133, 141,
   142–43
Collective egoism, 88
Confucius, 50
Conscience and obedience, 159
Conscious Christianity, 145–65;
   attention of the heart, 155–62;
   attention and virtue, 151–55;
   Jesuit spirituality, 145–51; prayer
   and attention, 162–65
Consciousness, 27, 38, 42, 88, 90,
   97, 111, 128, 133, 143, 155, 157,
   179–80, 184
Constantine, Emperor, 18
Contemplative Christianity, An
   Approach to the Realities of
   Religion (Graham), 111
Contemplative metaphysics, 39–40
Contemplative prayer, fragmentation
   of, 130–31
Corpus Hermeticum, 205–7

Cosmic dualism, 200–3
Council of Trent, 108
Cousins, Dr. Ewart, 126, 132
Cox, Harvey, 112–13, 117
Creator-God, doctrine of, 50–51

Da'ath, 127
Daniélou, Cardinal Jean, 50–51, 52
Demiurge, doctrine of, 196–97
Demons, 92, 137
Desire-nature, 52
Discipline, religious, 94, 137, 155
Discursive meditation, 130
Divini Praecones (encyclical), 51
Dogma, idea of, 42–43
Dolan, Father "Ted," 44, 47
Dualism, 86, 164–65; cosmic, 200–3

Early Fathers from the Philokalia
   (Kadloubovsky and Palmer), 82
Eastern meditation, Christianity and,
   107–23; Buddhism, 107–13;
   intermediate encounters, 117–23;
   Thomas Merton, 113–17
Eckhart, Meister, 4, 197–99, 213
Emotion of a Christian, mystery of,
   23–25
Energy force, 92–94, 96, 138, 175,
   184; development and
   degradation of, 87
Enlightenment, 40, 149
Erigena, John Scotus, 39
Esoteric tradition, defined, 4. See
   also Mysticism
Evagrius Ponticus, 136–39, 213

Faith vs. reason (seeing and
   gnosis), 37–40
Ferguson, A. S., 205–6
Forgiveness, purpose of, 91
Fox, George, 89
Freedom: emotional, 136–39;
   location of, 139–40
French Revolution, 131
Freud, Sigmund, 54, 55, 59, 65, 66,
   220; and human possibility, 60–62
Frydman, Maurice, 183

Gnosis, 33, 42, 85, 115, 127; approach to, 38; and gnosticism, 195–213; seeing and ("faith vs. reason"), 37–40

Gnosticism, 10, 85, 86, 87, 136; distinction between gnosis and, 195–213

Good and evil force (in the universe), idea of, 86–87

Good Friday, 28

Gospel of Philip, 202, 203

Gothic cathedrals, 33–34

Grace of God, 49, 53, 79, 94, 115, 125, 131; opposition between effort and, 54

Graham, Dom Aelred, 108, 109–11, 117, 124

Greek philosophy, Christianity and, 39

Gregory I, Pope, 107

Gregory of Nyssa, 210

Guénon, René, 69, 70, 128

Gurdjieff, G. I., 69, 122; teachings of, 169–71

Hellenistic Christianity, 107–8

Heraclitus, 26

Heresy, origin of, 193–95

Hermetica (eds. Scott and Ferguson), 205–6

Hermeticism, 137, 195, 205–6

Hinayana Buddhism, 95, 96

Hinduism, 3, 16, 49, 96–97, 113, 121, 142, 182–83; intermediate in, 179–81

History, understanding, 87

Holy Spirit, 53, 90

Homer, 107

Human possibility, Freudianism and, 60–62

Humility, 100

I Am That (trans. Frydman), 183

Ignatius the Theologian (Rahner), 149

Inner Being, soul and, 190–93

Innocent XII, Pope, 131

In Search of the Miraculous

(Ouspensky), 172

Institute for the Harmonious Development of Man, 169–71

Intellectualism, 134

Intermediate Being, soul and, 166–77

Intermediate Christianity, 117–23, 152–53; appearance and disappearance, 175–77; Gurdjieff teachings, 169–71; need for, 119; search as transforming force, 171–75; summary of principal idea, 166–68; Zen Buddhism and, 117, 120–21

Introduction to the Great Religions (Daniélou), 51

Irenaeus, St., 208

Isaiah (prophet), 95

Islam, 3, 99, 182

Jansen, Bishop Cornelis, 131

Jansenism, 131

Jesuit House of Prayer (Tokyo), 111

Jesus Christ, 10, 22, 23, 31, 44, 51, 53, 77, 88, 110, 111, 155, 175, 196; idea of incarnation of God in, 64–65

Jesus the Magician (Smith), 22

John, Father, 48, 49, 58, 66, 67

John of the Cross, 141

Johnston, Father William, 100–1, 107, 108–9, 111, 117, 124

Judaism, 1, 2, 3, 4, 60, 107, 118–19, 182

Kabbalah, 3, 4, 127

Kadloubovsky, E., 82, 154

Keating, Father Thomas, 126, 127, 128, 129–30, 131, 132, 133, 139–40, 141, 148

Khrishnamurti, 54–55

Kierkegaard, Sören, 21, 89, 220

Knowledge, 214; contemplation as, 126–27; love and, 129–30; in meditation, 114–15

Koran, 61

Lectio divina, 129
Lhalungpa, Lobsang P., 63–64, 185–86
Liberation, 96
Life of Milarepa, The (trans. Lhalungpa), 63–64, 185–86
Logic, 98, 189
Lost Christianity, question of: Father Vincent and, 44–78, 105, 106, 122; introduction to, 1–11; journal of Father Sylvan, 79–101; Metropolitan Anthony and, 15–43, 52, 105, 106, 136, 139. *See also* Soul, lost doctrine of the
Love, 95, 96, 127–28, 183; knowledge and, 129–30; lost religion of, 214–22
Loyola, Ignatius, 130, 145–48, 149, 150–51, 152
Lubavicher Hasidic community, 3
Luther, Martin, 89, 149

McLuhan, Marshall, 134
Magic, 91, 93, 94, 96, 119
Mahadakash, 183
Maharishi Mahesh Yogi, 135
Mahayana Buddhism, 53, 61, 95, 96, 110, 111
Mani, 86
Manichaean heresy, 200
Marcion, 196
Marxism, 50
Masumi, Toshimitsu, 121
Maximus the Confessor, 211–13
Meditation, 3; discursive, 130; Eastern teachings and, 108–13; knowledge in, 114–15; primal function of, 97–98. *See also* Zen Buddhism
Meister Eckhart, A Modern Translation (Blakney), 197
Meninger, Father William, 140–41
Merton, Thomas, 108, 113–17, 119, 120, 121–22, 124, 148, 162; background of, 113
Metaphysics, 91, 128, 180; contemplative, 39–40
Micro-monotheism, 181–83

Middle Ages, 41, 107, 129
Monasticism, 18, 114
Monotheism, 182
Moses, 101, 168
Mystical contemplation, 130
Mystical love, defined, 221
Mysticism, 6, 80, 84, 118, 131, 168, 178, 190–91, 192, 200, 216, 218; *da'ath* in, 127
Mystics, 101, 113, 189

Nag Hammadi Library, The (ed. Robinson), 195, 202, 203
Neoplatonism, 136, 195
"New Consciousness, The" (Merton), 114
Nietzsche, Friedrich, 220
Nisargadatta Maharaj, Sri, 182, 183
Nobili, Robert de, 108

"Occult" Christianity, 21–23
O'Hanlon, Father Daniel J., 145–51
O Holy Mountain! (Pennington), 132
Old religions, 1–2
On the Way to Self Knowledge (Needleman), 181
On Virginity (Gregory of Nyssa), 210
Origen, 136
Orthodox churches, architecture of, 15
Ouspensky, P. D., 172

Palamas, St. Gregory, 81–82, 213
Palmer, G. E. H., 82, 154
Paramakash, 183
Parthenon, 28–29
Paul, St., 154, 176
Pelagianism, 65, 149
Pennington, Father M. Basil, 132, 134, 135–36, 141
Philokalia, 143
Pius XII, Pope, 51
Planetary consciousness, 88
Plato, 26, 28, 39, 95, 107, 196
Praktikos, The—Chapters on Prayer (Evagrius Ponticus), 136–38

Prayer, 37, 47, 95, 99, 156–57;
  attention and, 156–57, 162–65;
  centering, 132–36; contemplative,
  fragmentation of, 130–31; state
  of, 42; vulnerability, 25
Premakash, 183
Priest, meaning of, 44–49
Prodigal Son, parable of, 171
Protestantism, 108, 131, 149; origin
  of, 89
Psychic energy, 92–93, 168. *See also*
  Energy force
Psychologism (or egoism), 49–50
Psychology, scale of one's search
  and, 52–53
Purity of intention, 98
Pythagoras, 22, 39

Quietism, 131, 149

Rahner, Hugo, 149
Reformation, 41, 108
Religious love, defined, 221
Ricci, Mateo, 108
Rimpoche, Lama, 63–64
Rinzai school of Zen, 148
Robinson, James M., 195
Roman Catholic Church, 3, 131;
  distrust of "mystics," 80
Roman Empire, 18, 194

Saccas, Ammonius, 136–37
Sacred Tradition and Present Need
  (eds. Needleman and Lewis), 16
Sainthood, notion of, 63
St. Joseph's Abbey, 124–44
Salvation, 83, 97, 114–15, 192
Salvational knowledge, *see* Gnosis
Samsara, 92
Sarouk, King of Persia, 26
Scott, W., 205–6
Search, the theory and practice of,
  54–55
Secret Gospel, The (Smith), 22
Self-denial, 25
Self-indulgence, 94
Self-justification, 96

Self-knowledge, 92; psychology of,
  61
Self-observation, 42
Sense of the Cosmos, A
  (Needleman), 181
Sermon on the Mount, 153
Seven Storey Mountain, The
  (Merton), 113, 115
Sexual impulse, sublimation of,
  65–66
Simeon the New Theologian, St.,
  153–54, 156–57, 158, 159, 160,
  161–62, 163, 164
Sloth, sin of, 88–89
Smith, Morton, 22, 195
Socrates, 26, 28, 39, 95
Soto school of Zen, 148
Soul, 151, 155–56; appearance and
  disappearance of, 175–77
Soul, lost doctrine of the, 105–22;
  Christianity and Eastern
  meditation, 107–23; intermediate
  being and, 166–77; lost religion of
  love, 214–22; St. Joseph Abbey
  and, 124–44; search for conscious
  Christianity, 145–65; in two
  histories, 178–213
Soul-making, process of, 168
Spirit, defined, 166–67
Spiritual discipline, 16
Spiritual egoism, 89
Spiritual energy, 93, 94
Spiritual exercises, origin of, 35–37
Spiritual Exercises (Loyola), 130,
  145–48, 149, 150–51
Spirituality, Jesuit, 145–51
Spiritual psychology, 49–52; aim of,
  52
Spiritual psychosis, 41
Spiritual retreats, 37
Stavronikita Monastery, 28, 32, 35
Sufism, 177
Suzuki, D. T., 120
Suzuki, Shunryu, 148–49
Sylvan, Father, 34, 41, 78, 105, 106,
  122, 134, 143, 151, 152, 153, 154,
  156, 158, 161, 163–64, 166–68,
  169, 171, 172, 175, 176, 177, 187,

190–93, 194; on gnosis and
gnosticism, 195–213; manuscript
and journals, 7–11, 79–101,
118–19

Symbolism, 84–85, 189; gnostic,
201–2

Taizé community (France), 3
Tantra, 86
Taoists, 4
Television industry, 134–35
Teresa of Ávila, St., 76, 77, 141
Theravada Buddhism, 53, 86,
111–12
Tibetan Buddhism, 63–64
Timaeus (Plato), 196
Torah, 3, 89
Tradition, 85, 90, 105, 114, 154,
168; hiddenness of, 99–100
Transcendental Meditation (TM)
movement, 135, 143
Transforming force, search as,
171–75
Triads (St. Gregory Palamas),
81–82
Trungpa, Chogyam, 112
Truth, natural attraction to, 62–66
Tulku, Tarthang, 112
Turning East (Cox), 112–13
Two races of men, theme of, 203–7

Vajrayana Buddhism, 61
Vasileios, Father, 28, 35, 36
Vatican II, 108
Views from the Real World
(Gurdjieff), 102
Vincent, Father, Lost Christianity
and, 44–78, 105, 106, 122;

acornology, 59; conversation in
two worlds, 66–70; Freudianism
and human possibility, 60–62;
gin-rummy game, 55–58;
impression (of Father Vincent),
58–59; life and search, 70–78;
meaning of a priest, 44–49;
natural attraction to truth, 62–66;
psychology and scale of one's
search, 52–53; spiritual
psychology, 49–52; theory and
practice of the search, 54–55
Vipassana meditation, 111–12,
163–64
Virgil, 107
Void, notion of the, 53
Vulnerability, 30–33; prayer, 25

Way of a Pilgrim, The, 16
Weil, Simone, 51
Wesley, John, 89
Writings from the Philokalia on
Prayer of the Heart, 154

Yoga, 23

Zazen meditation, 108, 111
Zen and the Birds of Appetite
(Merton), 114, 116, 120, 121
Zen Buddhism, 2, 60, 69, 108–13,
114, 116, 142, 146, 148;
intermediate Christianity and,
117, 120–21; Rinzai school of,
148; Soto school of, 148
Zen Catholicism (Graham), 109–10
Zen in Japanese Art (Masumi), 121
Zen Mind, Beginner's Mind
(Suzuki), 148–49